T0339134

LEADERSHIP
Lessons from the Ancient World

LEADERSHIP
Lessons from the Ancient World

How Learning from the Past Can Win You the Future

Arthur Cotterell
Roger Lowe
Ian Shaw

John Wiley & Sons, Ltd

Published by   John Wiley & Sons Ltd, The Atrium, Southern Gate, Chichester,
West Sussex PO19 8SQ, England

Telephone (+44) 1243 779777

Email (for orders and customer service enquiries): cs-books@wiley.co.uk
Visit our Home Page on www.wiley.com

Designations used by companies to distinguish their products are often claimed
as trademarks. All brand names and product names used in this book are trade
names, service marks, trademarks or registered trademarks of their respective
owners. The Publisher is not associated with any product or vendor mentioned
in this book.

This publication is designed to provide accurate and authoritative information
in regard to the subject matter covered. It is sold on the understanding that the
Publisher is not engaged in rendering professional services. If professional
advice or other expert assistance is required, the services of a competent
professional should be sought.

Other Wiley Editorial Offices

Wiley have other editorial offices in the USA, Germany, Australia, Singapore
and Canada.

Wiley also publishes its books in a variety of electronic formats. Some content
that appears in print may not be available in electronic books.

Library of Congress Cataloging-in-Publication Data

Cotterell, Arthur.
  Leadership–lessons from the ancient world / Arthur Cotterell, Roger Lowe,
Ian Shaw.
    p. cm.
  Includes bibliographical references and index.
  ISBN-13: 978-0-470-02709-7 (cloth : alk. paper)
  ISBN-10: 0-470-02709-6 (cloth : alk. paper)
  1. Leadership. 2. Leadership—History. I. Lowe, Roger, 1954- II. Shaw,
Ian, 1944- III. Title.
HD57.7.C675 2006
658.4'092—dc22

                                                              2006011217

British Library Cataloguing in Publication Data

A catalogue record for this book is available from the British Library

ISBN 13 978-0-470-02709-7 (PB)
ISBN 10 0-470-02709-6 (PB)

Typeset in 10/12pt Trump Medieval by SNP Best-set Typesetter Ltd, Hong Kong
Printed and bound in Great Britain by TJ International Ltd, Padstow, Cornwall,
UK

This book is printed on acid-free paper responsibly manufactured from sustainable forestry in which at least two trees are planted for each one used for paper
production.

Contents

Preface

This book is different. Instead of approaching the question of leadership through analogies drawn from literature, sport or exploration, it offers an entirely new perspective by looking at the actions of ancient leaders; and, in making a selection of leaders right across the Old World, from Rome to China, the book is able to provide trainers and trainees, and managers in general, with leadership examples about which they are unlikely to have preconceived ideas.

The study of ancient events from a management point of view is a unique way of observing how leadership actually works in practice. While it can be argued that in the historical record we are often uncertain that we possess an all-round picture, the unusual perspective gained by looking at remote times more than makes up for any possible shortcomings. For the leaders presented, and discussed here, are significant figures in their own right. Although many of the gambles they took were brilliantly successful, the consequences of their failures were just as spectacular. But all of these leaders decided on a course of action within the context of their own times, being aware of the range of possibilities then open to them. Again, this historical background allows us to note how they responded to very different situations, and how temperament, intelligence, experience, daring and advice came into play as they dealt with really pressing problems. The methods they used to implement their ancient decisions are equally instructive, since they illustrate the advantages and disadvantages that inevitably confront managers as leaders.

The book has 19 chapters, the last of which aims to draw conclusions from the individual accounts and reflect on the direction that leadership development ought to take over the next decade in order to cope with the challenges of globalization, innovation and technological advance. This is why its title is 'Winning as a leader'. Each of the first eighteen chapters addresses a key leadership theme in a structured way. Every chapter introduces a leader from the ancient world in terms of historical setting, personal behaviour and relationships. Then the outcomes of whatever action was taken are outlined. Afterwards there is an examination of recent thinking on the leadership topic under review, with reference to the decisions taken by the ancient leader. Within this section, attention is drawn to possible further sources of study and signposts to key thinkers and writers are also provided. Finally, every chapter presents a 'contemporary leadership challenge' through one or more case studies or development activities based on the authors' own personal experience. They are drawn from a range of organisational settings in both the public and the private sectors. Each chapter is complemented by an illustration, based on contemporary sources, by Dr Ray Dunning.

The authors, an ancient historian, a chartered manager and a trainer in a multinational company, hope that the scope of their interests will be such that they can bring leadership into sharper focus. That there is a crying need for a more accessible approach to the subject they are in no doubt at all. For in this book they have endeavoured to show how ancient leaders can illuminate the complex problems facing those who run, or aspire to run, present-day organisations.

Introduction

L eadership has been a pivotal issue for mankind since the beginning of organised society. In the ancient world, no less than today, the qualities to be found in the good leader as well as the bad leader have caused intense debate. Even more, the effectiveness of leaders always remains a matter of acute interest, and especially during times of crisis, when risks are taken and gambles are bound to occur. Contemporary concern about change, as well as its increasing pace, only serves to focus the spotlight once again on the nature of effective leadership, as organisations both in the private and public sectors try to deal with the challenge of new circumstances. In this book parallels, and indeed stark contrasts, between the situations of leaders, ancient and modern, are used to throw new light on the perennial problems involved. That leadership is now the subject of an immense body of theory, a seemingly endless literature, has persuaded the authors of the value of a fresh look, a new perspective, on leadership which combines, for the benefit of the busy reader, ancient dilemmas along with accessible theory and present-day problems. Each chapter, except for the final one, tackles separately a key leadership concept.

One thing the reader will notice in the selection of ancient leaders is an absence of women. This is not a result of any lack of interest on the part of the authors in female achievement. Rather it is a function of the fact that, with very few exceptions, women did not become significant leaders in the ancient world. Except for Boudicca and Cleopatra in Roman times, there were virtually no women who made strategic decisions at the highest level in the West. Only Hatshepsut, the stepmother of Thutmose III, succeeded in occupying centre stage in Egypt during his minority. As she then seized power for a number of years, it inevitably meant that Thutmose, on becoming pharaoh at long last, in 1428 BC, demolished her monuments and in the process obliterated the record of her reign. A similar situation occurred in China, where from AD 690 till 705 Empress Wu became the only woman to sit upon the dragon throne. She pushed aside two of her sons in order to achieve supremacy. Gifted though she undoubtedly was, this determined woman had a streak of cruelty in her character which created a reign of terror, although she was careful not to alienate her senior officials. Again it ensured that we lack any sympathetic record of her brief period of rule.

Courage is the aspect of leadership investigated in Chapter 1, which begins with the tremendous crisis faced by Ramesses II at Kadesh in 1274 BC. Then the young pharaoh was surprised by 3500 chariots in a trap carefully laid by the Hittite king Muwatalli II. Only a series of desperate counter-attacks, led by Ramesses in his own golden chariot, prevented an utter rout. The supreme courage that Ramesses demonstrated in the battle saved his army from destruction. Although all military leaders make mistakes, only successful ones like Ramesses are capable of recovering from potential calamity. The relevance of courage to leadership, therefore, is explored with particular reference to the idea that only a talented individual can rise to the challenge of the unexpected. It suggests that bravery remains a key element in the make-up of an effective leader, and not just in adverse circumstances. The practical problem accompanying this chapter focuses particularly on the changing attitude to leadership, the dramatic shift from command and control to cooperation and joint effort. So the case study considers the need for courage when there is a need to regenerate a business hopelessly stuck in a non-competitive mode.

Chapter 2 looks at risk taking. Starting with Pharaoh Thutmose III's astute handling of his forces at Megiddo in 1460 BC, it shows how risk taking powerfully points up the difference between management and leadership. At the battle of Megiddo, Thutmose risked a very dangerous advance: his army's subsequent attack from an entirely unexpected direction ended in a total victory over his Canaanite opponents. This overwhelming success reveals how leaders can effectively act on the basis of their own intuition rather than relying on detailed research, often ignoring in their actions the considered advice of colleagues when taking calculated risks. Modern managers may seek to control risk, but it is the leaders who have to risk a gamble, because there is no such thing as guaranteed profit. Also discussed is the nature of the self-confidence required in the successful risk taker. In the case of Thutmose, this comprised being certain that he could anticipate the disposition of the Canaanite army. This intuitive sensitivity to other people's thinking remains an important feature of an effective leader, particularly when it is combined with a systematic approach to decision analysis, as is featured in a case study addressing the challenges that face a young manager coping with cultural change in a business.

In Chapter 3 the role of motivation in leadership is considered. The remarkable military revolution inaugurated by the Chinese ruler Wuling is the ancient example of the ability to motivate others. He overcame stubborn opposition, and took no notice of the derision of fellow princes, when in 307 BC he adopted nomad cavalry tactics. Strengthened by this reform and the conquest of new territory, Wuling's small state enjoyed a century of peace and prosperity. Because there are obviously huge advantages for a leader like Wuling, who can identify and act on what motivates people in his or her team or organisation to deliver a high-quality performance, the search for the secrets of motivation has become a preoccupation for management thinkers. Admitted now is the importance of the organisational context in creating a motivational climate, something Wuling recognised as he carefully explained his purpose to key people, his ministers, in order to get them on side and ensure that they then spread the message more widely. As Professor Fred Herzburg succinctly put it: only when an individual no longer runs on a recharged battery but possesses 'his own generator . . . can we talk about motivation. He wants to do it'. Getting people to this stage is far from easy, as the case study illustrates. This analyses the actions of three young managers brought into a failing business. They quickly identify that a lack of motivation is a key factor in its underperformance and then turn the organisation around.

Vision is today very much part of a leader's profile. Often an expression of personality, the organisational vision may be compulsive, passionate and intuitive. Yet there can be no doubt over its growing importance as businesses move from the traditional management model of central control and planning towards 'vision thinking', a beacon which indicates the direction that an organisation should take and illuminates the goals it should be aiming to achieve. Chapter 4 argues that a compelling vision like that of Liu Bang, the peasant who founded the Han dynasty in 202 BC, is a necessary prerequisite for present-day organisational success. Liu Bang's desire for a civil service dedicated to the welfare of his people was the enduring foundation of the Chinese empire, which lasted until the early twentieth century. His vision was so compelling that China could not, until modern times, conceive of any other way to exist. The case study reflects on the value of a CEO having such an outlook, when endeavouring to convince the workforce of a factory that a secure future really is worth fighting for.

Chapter 5 examines how people can be developed to their potential and begins with the approach adopted by the fifth emperor of the Han dynasty, Wu Di. Such were the external and internal problems then threatening China that Wu Di had to introduce major organisational changes and, at the same time, recruit reliable and imaginative administrators to oversee their effective implementation. In the process he pioneered the system of public examinations, still a fundamental part of systematic career development today. What Wu Di struggled to do in the first century BC is no more than CEOs have to tackle now: seeking reliable means of guaranteeing that an initiative or development is actually delivered in the way imagined, given that a leader can only work through his or her own people. As he could not afford to micromanage all his officials, Wu Di had to trust their 'deep learning'. A way in which any perceived shortcomings would be handled now is through coaching, a critical leadership skill. Yet the interest Wu Di took in his top officials' actions could be seen as something akin to coaching, because his serious interventions were restricted to consistent failure. Two individuals in need of coaching are represented in the case study, which draws a telling distinction between 'what' and 'how' in setting developmental objectives. It notes, too, the need for managers to know their employees on a deeper personal level, so as to align their employees' goals and ambitions with those of the organisation.

The Athenian statesman Themistocles provides the starting point for a discussion about focusing on results in Chapter 6. It was his foresight, skill and ingenuity which led directly to the defeat of the Persian navy at the battle of Salamis in 480 BC. His strategic method of saving

Greece from Persian domination is at one with the way in which management thinking is now actually evolving. Not for Themistocles, a target-driven approach to what appeared an impossible problem, the repulse of the overwhelming might of Persia, but rather preparing Greece's defence step by step according to the changing situation. Jack Welch, the former CEO of General Electric, could be describing Themistocles' leadership style when he wrote: 'You pick a general direction and implement like hell'. Just how critical such flexibility can be is obvious in the case study. This focuses on an organisation's use of visual and graphic facilitation techniques, used in an intensive review and development planning session within an advertising agency. Through this exercise, the creative and imaginative use of resources emerges as a critical success factor.

Chapter 7 poses the question of integrity in leadership through an analysis of the reasons for Pericles' long period of political ascendancy in Athens. Pericles alone was elected to an almost continuous period of office from 455 BC onwards. After his death no political leader or party was able to control Athens, as different groups held sway on different occasions. The result was serious inconsistency in the conduct of the war with Sparta which culminated in Athens' surrender in 404 BC. The close scrutiny of leaders in democratic Athens meant that every word and action of Pericles was judged on its merits: no spokesperson could be used to explain away shortcomings. Political, like executive, integrity is indivisible as Pericles well knew and so concerned was he to preserve his reputation that in 431 BC, at the start of the war, he turned over his private property to the state, asking that no suspicion of seeking personal gain should be attached to him. It was an action that would have delighted Norman Schwarzkopf, the US commander in the first Gulf War. He held the view that a leader, in particular during a major conflict, should be absolutely above suspicion. 'Never lie', he said. 'Ever'. Where there is a lapse in ethical leadership, as the case study shows, the results can be catastrophic. The defence of Bernard Ebbers, the boss of WorldCom, at his trial in 2005, was pathetic in that he claimed to be quite unaware of fraud being carried out in his company. Over the next quarter of a century in prison he has the opportunity to reflect on the jury's rejection of this claim. If one assumes responsibility as a leader, then with it comes the duty to see that it is properly carried out. Ethics are not something a CEO can put into the drawer of a desk, and then conveniently forget.

In the same manner a leader has to know when to take decisive action, although it might land him or her in trouble, as happened to the Theban general Epaminondas in 369 BC. Then he was put on trial for extending his generalship beyond its allotted time, although his invasion of the Peloponnese permanently broke Spartan military power. Chapter 8 discusses the skills involved in such decision making. At the most senior level, decisions that are likely to affect the entire future of an organisation can be a daunting task. For, as David Taylor notes in *The Naked Leader*, 'a true decision means quite simply to close off all other options. And it is not an easy thing to do, because to move away from where you are at the moment . . . may mean leaving something behind you'. It is a dilemma faced by any CEO who subscribes to the hard-ball approach to management, as the case study makes abundantly clear. The exploitation of opportunity is the key to commercial success, according to George Stalk and Rob Lacenauer, the advocates of its go-getting manifesto.

A leader's ability to influence people is the subject of Chapter 9. That Alexander the Great, prior to his death in 323 BC, was so influential in establishing a multi-ethnic kingdom provides a fascinating example of the art of persuasion. As the historian Plutarch commented, 'Alexander considered that he had come from the gods to be a governor and reconciler of the world. Using force of arms when he could not bring the men together by reason, he employed everything to the same end, mixing lives, manners, marriages and customs as it were in a loving-cup'. Even though Alexander's kingdom broke up after his death, as his senior commanders fought each other for a share of the vast territory he had conquered, his ideas were not entirely forgotten or abandoned. Where perhaps Alexander scored his greatest success was in making clear for all time how a persuasive leader must have whole-hearted belief in his own ideas, if he or she is to have any chance of influencing people. Cultural sensitivity was absolutely critical to his success in dealing with such a range of different peoples. Experienced leaders today are able to adopt different styles to suit a variety of audiences so that, if not handled with great tact, this can lead to the dangerous perception that they are either inconsistent or cynical, resulting in their employees feeling confused as well as distrustful. Handling teams, an instrument now widely used in large organisations for sharing ideas, overseeing developments and problem solving, demands persuasive powers of the highest order on the part of senior managers. Not even Alexander's god-given authority was adequate in every situation, as the mutiny of his Macedonian troops revealed in India. Yet influencing is now a much sought-after skill in matrixed organisations, a need which is explored in depth by the case study: it details the stages an effective manager has to go through in order to bring about change in the pattern of behaviour at work.

No less challenging for a leader is the timing of stepping down. In Chapter 10 Candragupta's abdication provides the focus for a discussion of this vexed question. The first Indian ruler to found an empire, Candragupta came to the conclusion that he ought to relinquish power and devote himself to a religious life in 297 BC. That he could abdicate in favour of his elder son and leave his imperial legacy intact says a great deal about his competence as a ruler and also something about the quality of the officials who served him as an emperor. To his chief minister he owed much, but there is little doubt that it was the loyalty he inspired in all his subjects, which really permitted Candragupta's successful abdication. Given that for an individual a lifetime career in a single business is no longer the dominant model, moving on has become a much more frequent event. This is why succession planning for change at the top is now such a difficult and time-consuming business. Untypical in this regard is Toyota, the Japanese car manufacturer, which remains wedded to a policy of 'growing your own', for the reason that in this company great emphasis is placed on the maintenance of its own distinct culture. Other large organisations tend to buy in leaders, although increasingly pressurised working environments have made senior executives conscious of the need for a work–life balance. In the case study there is an example of how legacy planning can revitalise a business's performance. A sales force is renewed, in every sense, by a radical career development scheme.

Chapter 11 examines how a business can best be represented in the wider commercial, political and social environment, after looking at both the successes and reverses experienced by Hannibal during his invasion of Italy. From 218 to 202 BC this Carthaginian general managed to harass Rome, literally in its own backyard. Historians, ancient and modern, are amazed at the leadership skills Hannibal demonstrated during this gruelling campaign. Possibly his powerful public persona helped to sustain him for so long in hostile territory: he was completely identified with his own city-state of Carthage in the same way that Bill Gates always now is with Microsoft. As these two leaders have more than a little of the showman about them, they could cope easily with an ambassadorial role on the grand scale. Creating a public image can thus be seen as not just a modern phenomenon. Hannibal's image continued to exert a powerful influence over the Romans long after the Italian invasion ended. Yet this high-profile style of leadership was not enough to secure a Carthaginian victory: supplies and reinforcements were always in short supply, while Rome had the capacity to raise new armies and keep them in the field. Securing adequate resources is, therefore, a key function of a leader and failure to maintain an adequate level of investment means a business, or an invasion, will always fail. The case study develops this idea by looking at the government's leadership programme for failing secondary schools, with its 'superheads' and 'hyperheads'. The pressures on these individuals to succeed are reminiscent of those Hannibal suffered during his Italian campaign.

With the resourcefulness of Zhu Geliang, a famous minister in third-century AD China, the whole issue of managerial creativity is considered in Chapter 12. During the crisis which briefly split the Chinese empire into three warring states, Zhu Geliang's ingenuity alone was enough to ensure the survival of Shu, the weakest of these bitter rivals. Time and again he pitted his wits against Shu's enemies, using psychology to stop apparently irresistible invaders. A modern leadership challenge is discovering similar bright ideas in order to enhance management performance and devise solutions to supposedly intractable problems. Corporate creativity is in fact now an urgent concern for large organisations that have lost the ability of 'thinking outside the box'. That is why so much attention is being given to fostering a creative working environment. If innovation and creativity are so important for organisational renewal, then a situation has to be engineered within an organisation that supports those employees who are capable of imitating Zhu Geliang. How this can be done is indeed the point of the case study. It outlines the innovation process and suggests a way in which teams can advance new ideas through brainstorming and review. Also recommended is the need for senior managers to give timely recognition of creativity.

In Chapter 13 self-managed development receives attention. Leaders often have to learn how to lead, a circumstance clearly highlighted in the advice that Li Shimin, the second Tang emperor of China, required from his minister Wei Zheng. Wei Zheng was keenly aware that during Li Shimin's reign precedents and patterns were being set which would affect the conduct of government for generations to come: hence his willingness to stand up to Li Shimin when he felt a wrong decision was about to be taken. Although the emperor always listened to his chief minister and seriously thought about his comments, no matter how inconvenient they sometimes were, Li Shimin could not but become annoyed on occasions when Wei Zheng seemed to pointlessly resist what he wanted to do. Only after Wei Zheng's death in AD 643 did the emperor really appreciate the full value of the advice he had been given. Emotionally intelligent leaders of course are never unwilling to learn. Self-awareness, self-management, social awareness and relationship management would be impossible for them otherwise. Yet there is still a tendency, which Wei Zheng discovered in Li Shimin, for leaders to become less attuned as they grow in experience and authority. Keeping one's feet on the ground is not so easy as many people think. As the case study indicates in its discussion of the Chartered Manager scheme, there are always good reasons for comparing one's own performance with that of other managers. Benchmarking makes sense only when it is realistic and relevant to what happens in the workplace.

Chapter 14 considers Sulla's constitutional reforms. His attempt at radical change in the late 80s BC failed for a number of reasons, the chief one of which was an inability to gain enough support to take his initiatives permanently forward. He challenged too many deeply rooted traditions, and as a result many people saw his determination as serving his own political ambitions, rather than bringing any significant benefits to the struggling Roman republic. It is easy from our perspective to recognise that

Sulla sought a transformation, not just change. Although today such a fundamental alteration is often seen as imperative in an organisation facing totally new circumstances, it needs to be understood how time consuming this kind of process inevitably is, and how leadership skills of a very high order indeed are required to see it effectively through. Sulla's reliance on force never stood a chance of success. In one sense this Roman dictator was correct, for he grasped that only a supreme leader could ever hope to deal with the immense crisis then undermining the republic. Where he got it wrong was in tackling reform with headlong haste. The case study, however, offers a better way of managing the profound impact of change on people.

Networking is the subject of Chapter 15, which follows the efforts that Cicero made to find political allies 20 years or so after Sulla. In an attempt to control the growing instability caused by army-commanders and their political agents in Rome, he tried to put together an alliance of interest and sentiment which embraced the upper classes and the well-to-do. But excessive self-belief simply let Cicero down, because oratory and intrigue meant nothing against naked swords. He also failed to identify in any detail the common ground that he and his political partners might have or the detailed aim around which they might rally. Cicero obviously missed the first rule of networking, the maintenance of social relationships which include a distinct agenda. For good networking helps leaders to promote their values and interests, and then translate their purposes in action. So vital is networking in the modern business world that companies actively promote its use as a means of harnessing and directing the experience, information and wisdom locked away inside them. Effective networking can be said to reduce the likelihood of inflexible or categorical judgements being taken, while at the same time helping to ensure an organisation develops visions which are both linked and compatible. For this reason the case study focuses on the experience of a senior executive in a multinational pharmaceutical company. She discovers for herself, and for her human resources colleagues worldwide, the real value of regular networking via new technology.

In Chapter 16 the role of a leader in dealing with conflict is examined. Few leaders were ever faced with the legacy of conflict which greeted Vespasian in the year AD 69. He was in fact the fourth Roman emperor that year. On his arrival in Rome he discovered both large-scale burnt out areas as well as the architectural excess of Nero's last years. It was the extravagance of the emperor Nero that had led to the year of civil war which Vespasian's succession ended. A 100-metre-high gilded bronze statue with the face of Nero still overlooked the devastated and bankrupt city. In a quiet and business-like manner, Vespasian reorganised taxation, restored discipline to the army, strengthened frontiers, put down rebellions and began a programme of renewal in Rome itself. One of his projects, completed by his son Titus, was the Colosseum, a truly gigantic amphitheatre designed to seat 50,000 spectators. To return an organisation to a healthy, harmonious and productive condition when it has been torn apart by internal conflict requires a particular set of leadership skills, totally distinct from those needed to keep an already successful business on track, or initiate new projects or products into established routines. Vespasian possessed these skills in abundance, and they are discussed in the context of outsiders being brought in today in order to turn around failing companies, hospitals and schools. Pointed out, too, is the danger involved in seeking consensus at all costs. Since this can lead to mediocre decision making and even stagnation. It is something taken up in the case study, where a manager has the task of reallocating space in a business head office during a system's software upgrade. The purchasing department has to go for six months into temporary accommodation in the car park. All the problems this difficult move entails are discussed and analysed.

The difficulties involved in delegation and empowerment are the subject of Chapter 17, which looks at the Roman emperor Diocletian's radical scheme for imperial administration in the late third century. What he was most anxious to avoid was a repetition of the conflicts that had surrounded the accession of emperors over the previous 50 years. So Diocletian established a collegiate system of government, with two senior rulers and two juniors. It was understood that the juniors would automatically move up to the top positions on the death or abdication of their seniors. This arrangement is now echoed within Philips NV in Holland, for its organisational structure is built on joint responsibility being shared by two top managers, one representing the 'commercial' end of the business and the other the 'technical'. Also discussed in this chapter is the radical empowerment approach used at SEMCO, the Brazilian conglomerate. Over-empowerment is touched upon in the notorious case of Barings, the merchant back brought down by Nick Leeson's uncontrolled gambling on the Tokyo futures market. Two case studies explore further the problems inherent in delegation and empowerment. In one, a newly appointed deputy head teacher struggles to introduce a managerial attitude at the level of subject heads in a secondary school, while in the second a new CEO tries to introduce a more empowering culture into a food factory.

Chapter 18 ponders the need for senior managers to recognise achievement and celebrate success. It starts with an account of the late Roman general Belisarius' career in the sixth century. From Emperor Justinian's point of view, the services this commander famously rendered the throne were a mixed blessing. His resolute action during the dreadful riot in Constantinople, his remarkable victories over the Vandals in northern Africa and the Ostrogoths in Italy, were of course achievements for which Justinian could only be thankful. Yet the possibility that Belisarius harboured imperial ambitions of his own always worried the emperor, despite the fact that the general had publicly turned down the offer of a Gothic throne. For the recognition of achievement always has a political context, a circumstance which Belisarius' enemies were ready to exploit by spreading rumours about his desire for even greater honours. Just as today, a rising star in any organisation can often be seen as a threat by senior management. The converse, as Jack Welch once again points out, is the danger of egotism. 'I've seen talented young people promoted too quickly', he says, 'and their ambitions spin out of control'. Keeping the balance right is thus the secret of successful leadership when it comes to celebrating achievement. The case study explores this idea through an account of a newly introduced recognition scheme at a run-down NHS hospital. That the first winners declared at the annual Quality Improvement Awards ceremony was a team of porters says it all: the scheme had successfully improved everyone at the hospital.

This book ends with an attempt to identify some significant issues in the actions of the 18 ancient leaders. It also considers the future of leadership development. Given globalisation and technological change, Chapter 19 asks where training in leadership should now go. The chapter endeavours to sum up those aspects of leadership that are critical today, and point out ways in which they can be better understood, and applied to a particular set of circumstances so as to increase the chance of developing a winning individual style.

Suggestions for further reading are provided so that readers who wish to do so can pursue matters of special interest. A personal selection of books and articles covers all the leadership topics addressed in this book. Hopefully it will assist those wanting to explore them in greater depth.

1

Courage: The Daring of Ramesses II at Kadesh

What happened?

The leader

In Egyptian tradition Ramesses II (pronounced 'Ram-e-sees') was remembered as a colossus as large as his own monumental statues, the ideal warrior-king whose 67-year reign secured the country's survival as a great power during a period of intense international rivalry. But at the battle of Kadesh in 1274 BC, in the fifth year of his reign, the 29-year-old pharaoh was lucky not to have suffered a disastrous defeat.

The historical setting

Rivalry between the great powers of the ancient eastern Mediterranean was at its greatest in Syria. There, Egypt's sphere of influence stopped at Kadesh, a city built on the banks of the Orontes river. However, there was one great power that always found this frontier difficult to accept. It was Hatti, whose inhabitants are now known as the Hittites, a name derived from the Bible authorised by King James I. The Hittites had expanded their territories beyond Asia Minor to exercise control over what is today eastern Turkey, Armenia and northern Syria. When King Suttarna sent the forces of Kadesh against Hittite troops operating close by, he was soon defeated and led off into captivity, along with his son Aitakkama. Although this put a strain on Hittite–Egyptian relations, there was no immediate reaction from Egypt. However, Aitakkama's return to Kadesh as a Hittite ally was less well received, and so the pharaoh Sety I recaptured this Syrian city. An inscription relates how he 'smote the land of Hatti, causing the cowardly rebels to submit'. The accession of Sety I's son, the young Ramesses II, seems to have been regarded by the Hittite king, Muwatalli II, as a good opportunity for intervention. So it happened that Ramesses found himself suddenly confronted by the Hittite army at Kadesh.

Ramesses' behaviour

News of Kadesh switching its allegiance to Hatti had brought a determined response from Egypt. Riding in his golden chariot at the head of an army of four divisions, named after the gods Amun, Re, Ptah and Seth, Ramesses sped past Gaza along the road next to 'the shore of Amor', as the Egyptians called the Mediterranean. This impetuous advance was very much part of the young pharaoh's character, and it set the scene for the near disaster at Kadesh.

For Ramesses was unaware that the Hittite king had set a trap for his forces there. With an army of 47,000 men, including a complement of 3500 chariots, Muwatalli waited in a concealed position. Against this host Ramesses could not deploy so many soldiers, nor were they all available at the start of the battle: the Amun division was just behind him, the Re division was crossing the ford near Kadesh, while the Ptah and Seth divisions still remained south of the River Orontes. The Hittite

Ramesses II, the victor at Kadesh. The war god Montu, with whom the young pharaoh was identified, was a falcon-headed deity worshipped at Thebes. The personal identification became so strong that a cult statue was venerated in Ramesses' honour during his lifetime.

attack came when the Amun division was establishing a camp chosen by Ramesses near the city itself. 'There His Majesty', we are told, 'sat on a golden throne', presumably to receive ambassadors from an overawed Kadesh. Ramesses received instead a rude shock. Two Hittite scouts sent by Muwatalli to ascertain the exact position of the Egyptian army were captured and, after a beating, revealed the location of the Hittite army. 'The King of Hatti', they admitted, 'together with soldiers from many lands, is armed and ready to fight behind Kadesh'.

Ramesses' senior officers were stunned by the news and abashed at the anger of the pharaoh over their carelessness. After a hasty conference, messengers were dispatched to hurry on the divisions still on the march. By then the Hittite chariotry had 'charged the Re division, and cut through the middle, as it was not drawn up for battle'. This collapse almost engulfed the Egyptian camp when in panic troops from the broken division rushed there in order to escape pursuing Hittite chariots. A total rout seemed inevitable, until Ramesses asserted his leadership. 'Then His Majesty rose like the war god Montu and seized his weapons, putting on his coat of mail'.

As the Hittite chariotry surrounded his camp in an ever-tightening circle, Ramesses launched a desperate counter-attack. First, infantrymen were sent to tackle enemy chariots that came too close to the camp, pulling down charioteers and killing them with short swords and spears. Then, taking advantage of this confusion, Ramesses mounted his own chariot and drove into the Hittites with tremendous force. Even though we know how Menna, his charioteer, 'saw the vast number of hostile chariots hemming the pharaoh in, and went deadly white with terror', the counter-attack gave the surrounded Egyptians a respite, which Ramesses used to rally his troops. He also noticed that the eastern wing of the Hittite chariotry was the weakest part, and next he turned in that direction, a change of tactics that again disconcerted his opponents. If this move, inspired by another of Ramesses' headlong charges, was meant to convince the Egyptians of their ability to hold out until reinforcements arrived, they were right to trust the judgement of their young, inexperienced pharaoh. For the arrival of an allied column from the Mediterranean coast soon relieved the Egyptian camp, leaving Ramesses free to drive the Hittites into the Orontes, where abandoning their chariots 'they plunged likes crocodiles face first into its waters'. Perhaps these timely reinforcements had a similar effect to that on the French of Blücher's Prussians at Waterloo, not least because the distraction may have caused the Hittites to hesitate in driving home their attack on the hard-pressed Amun and Re divisions.

Outcomes

Gathering round the triumphant pharaoh, the Egyptian army 'praised His Majesty, seeing what he had done to the wretched ruler of Hatti', although it was severely scolded by Ramesses for leaving him in such a perilous position at the start of the battle. By this time the Ptah and Seth divisions had arrived and the Hittites were discouraged from further action. Muwatalli's losses were largely confined to his chariotry, but without this striking force he knew his infantry was now vulnerable. So he sent an envoy to propose peace, which Ramesses would only accept as a truce, because he wished to reserve the right to reclaim Kadesh and other cities conquered by his predecessors. That the truce more or less held is an indication of a reluctance on the part of the Egyptians as well as the Hittites over returning to the battlefield.

The Egyptians had taken heavy casualties. Yet Ramesses managed to save his army and his reputation as a commander. 'Braver than hundreds and thousands combined, he went into the multitudes, trusting his strength alone', according to an inscription carved after the battle of Kadesh on an Egyptian temple in Karnak.

Why does it matter?

Facts and myths of courage

At Kadesh the Egyptian army was lured into a trap by local men who had been sent by the Hittite king, 'to speak falsely to His Majesty in order that he might not prepare his troops for battle'. This clever piece of disinformation nearly cost Egypt dear, because it was only the last-minute capture of the two Hittite scouts that revealed the true military situation. That Ramesses saved the day through his undoubted courage there is no question: after the battle he was hailed by his troops as a great war leader. Though he acknowledged their praise and gratitude, the young pharaoh knew he had been very lucky indeed. Had King Muwatalli of Hatti chosen to ride with his chariotry, like the Egyptian pharaoh, instead of waiting with the bulk of his forces behind Kadesh, then Ramesses might have found it harder to rally his own men. As it was, Muwatalli left the chariot battle in the hands of one of his commanders. This tactical mistake determined the outcome of the battle, since the king's presence would have stiffened the resistance of the Hittite charioteers once the Egyptians fought back with such determination, following Ramesses' own courageous example.

All military leaders make errors of judgement, but successful ones like Ramesses are capable of recovering from potential calamity. At a recent leadership training course, delegates were asked in advance to identify one leader for whom they had particular respect and admiration. They identified a range of contemporary and historical figures.

Among the less predictable responses were Bobby Moore, who captained the England soccer team to World Cup victory in 1966, and General Slim, leader of Britain's 'Forgotten Army' in Burma during the Second World War. The most commonly cited names included Abraham Lincoln, Winston Churchill, Horatio Nelson, Margaret Thatcher, Nelson Mandela, Aung San Sui Kyi (the Burmese democracy movement leader) as well as Martin Luther King and Rosa Smith from the civil rights movement. Although a smattering of sports stars appeared in the list, there was scarcely a mention of a leader from the world of business or the public sector. The justifications for these choices varied and many of the characteristics pinpointed will feature in later chapters of this book. However, one aspect of behaviour mentioned over and over again was the fact that their chosen leader had shown exceptional bravery: he or she had demonstrated real courage through relentlessly difficult times and had, in the end, won through against the odds. In discussion it also became clear that what was felt to be admirable about these leaders was not some form of unthinking recklessness, but rather a sort of moral courage which flowed from a powerful sense of purpose and, as frequently, from a desire to improve the lot of other people.

In implementing a significant change in an organisation, or in driving a substantial project, progress rarely runs as smoothly as the carefully wrought plans originally envisioned. The basis of decisions which may well have seemed wholly rational and coherent when first made can quickly come to appear questionable when unforeseen challenges, or changes forced onto the agenda by unanticipated external factors, adversely impact on the pace or direction of the development. Under these circumstances the shared enthusiasm and dedication shown by a project team in the early stages of an initiative can dissipate rapidly, to be replaced by disillusionment, disappointment and, perhaps most damaging, by the search for scapegoats to blame for likely failure. The determination and courage of a leader to steer a contentious change through difficult and complex challenges can be vital in maintaining the commitment of team members to the task. Such courage associates the leader closely with the task itself in the eyes of the organisation and is at its most purposeful when the leader's commitment is based upon a genuine conviction in the underlying aims of the project.

The relevance of courage to leadership

How applicable the personal histories of the sort of exemplary leaders named above are to the everyday world of organisational management might at first appear questionable. Though their stories are clearly inspirational, what manager could feel anything but daunted if measured too rigorously against their achievements? There are echoes here of what is sometimes termed the 'Great Man' (and it almost always was a man!) theory of leadership. Familiar to students of the late nineteenth and early twentieth centuries, this thinking is based around the belief that a few men are gifted with particular innate skills at birth, inexplicable to lesser mortals and certainly impossible to learn, which make them fated to be our leaders, our heroes. But do organisations need heroes any longer? As Peter Senge says in *The Fifth Discipline*,

Our prevailing leadership myths are still captured by the image of the captain of cavalry leading the charge to rescue the settlers from the attacking Indians. So long as such myths prevail, they reinforce a focus on short-term events and charismatic heroes rather than on systematic forces and collective learning.

Charisma certainly was an important feature of Ramesses II's character, judging from his image and reputation, but equally evident in accounts of his actions at Kadesh were the rather less attractive personal characteristics of arrogance and impetuosity! In common with some of the other leaders already mentioned, Ramesses II came perilously close to total disaster at his great testing ground. That he turned what looked like inevitable humiliation and defeat into victory is testimony to his exceptional courage, even if it was undoubtedly born of desperation. If a lesson is to be learnt from this pharaoh it is that a leader cannot shirk the responsibility for his actions, and especially at the point of crisis. There is a time for sitting on the golden throne and a time to get out in front of the troops in a chariot and show them what really has to be done. Literally, to take the lead.

This is why courage remains a key element in the leadership mix, and not just at times of crisis. Because all organisations work in uncertain and turbulent times, they need leaders who are willing to put their own credibility in the balance and dare to volunteer for personally risky missions. Visibility always makes a person vulnerable, yet we all respect and look to leaders who take decisions on their own initiative and then stand up for them. According to one management thinker, D.M. Woolfe, in his *Executive Integrity, the search for high human values in organizational life*,

It takes a special kind of courage to stay in tune with your feelings when those feelings conflict and seem to work against you . . . It takes courage to live by one's beliefs and values, to persist in actions that run the risk of failure or the hostility and rejection from others.

What does it mean for you?

The modern expectation, indeed the imperative for leaders, is that they are fiercely demanding of the organisations they lead, yet at the same time display considerable humility when dealing with the people they lead. They need to be both strong willed and empowering.

This difficult and demanding model of leadership takes a great deal of courage to implement; as in the old model, a strong will invariably meant directive behaviour. In other words 'I tell you what I want and I will tell you what to do', compared to 'I tell you what I believe this organisation can achieve, you tell me how we are going to do it'.

Therefore in today's context courage can be defined as having the confidence in one's own capability and judgement. It means understanding the risks and taking responsibility for the outcomes, however surprising they may be. It also means taking risks, both for the leader and the led, something Ramesses quickly appreciated in the crisis facing the Egyptian army at Kadesh.

Even though in the heat of battle Ramesses did not have the time to do so, it really does help when you are about to make a big bold decision, to capture the facts first on paper. You can quite easily end up with a 10-page analysis which is no use to anyone, so rather aim to get all the key facts on a single sheet of paper, as shown in Figure 1.1.

Project:		
What is the current situation (AS-IS)?	What is the future situation look like (TO-BE)?	What changes do I need to make?
What support will I get?	What barriers will I find?	What actions do I need to take?
What are the risks?	How can I reduce these risks?	How confident am I in achieving my aims? Scale of 1–10 My assessment =

Figure 1.1 Project analysis

Now review the following case study, and see how such a project analysis can be used.

Oshito had jumped at the opportunity to leave his native Japan and take an expatriate job in South Africa. He had previously visited the country with a group of automotive engineers five years after Nelson Mandela had taken over the leadership of the country. These were exciting times and he had fallen into the feeling of hopefulness that embraced the country. Now, five years later, he had been offered a manufacturing director's job, which would mean three to five years in South Africa.

On arriving he set out to spend his first six months gathering information and talking to as many people as he could. He made sure he met a good cross-section, from the shop floor to the senior directors, from the sales office through to the union. There was one item that concerned him greatly, and that was some of the key appointments that had been made over the years. In the rush to embrace affirmative action, too many underqualified local people had been appointed to key jobs. The message he got from the old guard was that there was little that could be done, as these appointments were political in nature, and that changes could not be made without causing trouble.

Oshito knew he had to do something to transform the current situation. The business could no longer endure quality scares, missed targets and generally disappointing results. It needed real leaders in key jobs, developing and motivating their teams for a transformation to take place. So he drew up the project analysis shown in Figure 1.2.

Project: Selecting the best		
What is the current situation (AS-IS)?	**What dose the future situation look like (TO-BE)?**	**What changes do I need to make?**
Business results have declined – a key contributor being the lack of motivation	A meritocracy where the right people are appointed to key jobs and are recognised and rewarded	Assess current strengths and weaknesses
What support will I get?	**What barriers will I find?**	**What actions do I need to take?**
HR director strongly supportive. The business needs to improve results. Potential team leaders who are currently being blocked by the current system	Political fears Managers sitting on the fence	Define team leader competencies Assess all current leaders Demote those who do not make the grade (and red flag their current salary) Accelerate the development of potential team leaders
What are the risks?	**How can I reduce these risks?**	**How confident am I in achieving my aims?**
Strike action More demotivation Industrial sabotage	Early discussions with union reps Give everyone the chance to be developed Communicate what I am going to do in an open and honest way	Scale of 1–10 My assessment = 8

Figure 1.2   Oshito's project analysis

Having reflected on a strategy, Oshito called all the management together, and outlined his plan to take decisive action to ensure that only the very best were promoted to the key jobs in the organisation. He displayed his strong resolve, but he was also humble in his manner and his call for assistance. He explained that all team leaders demoted would not lose their salaries, and would have the opportunity, if they had the potential, to be trained to do the job. When he had completed his presentation, there was a roar from the audience: every manager in the room, regardless of colour and status rose to their feet and clapped and shouted with approval. At last someone had had the courage to do the right thing for the business and for the people of the organisation. For Oshito was prepared to select only the best.

2

Risk Taking: Thutmose III's Handling of His Forces

What happened?

The leader

In 1504 BC Thutmose III (pronounced 'Tut-mose') succeeded his father to the throne of Egypt at the tender age of 10, and his stepmother Hatshepsut ruled in his stead, first as a regent, later as a pharaoh in her own right. Hatshepsut reigned until 1482 BC, when Thutmose finally came to the throne, ostensibly in the 22nd year of his own reign. With over 30 years to rule ahead of him, in which he effectively reasserted Egypt's authority in adjacent areas of West Asia, Thutmose had plenty of time to erase the evidence of Hatshepsut's usurpation by destroying all her monuments.

The historical setting

Egypt had experienced occupation by the Hyksos, West Asian warriors who overran the Nile delta in 1664 BC. Even though the Egyptians were able to expel them by

1555 BC, they remained apprehensive about the Canaanites, who might combine together and assist the launch of yet another West Asian attack on their country. Rather than relying any more on a sphere of influence, reinforced by periodic military activity, the pharaohs' foreign policy became more direct, with close supervision of allies, to the extent of keeping Egyptian officers in loyal courts. Within this buffer zone, local rulers were designated 'His Majesty's tenants', swearing obedience to the will of the pharaoh. Not even the succession problem caused by Hatshepsut seems to have weakened this new approach.

In 1460 BC, therefore, Thutmose was not prepared to ignore the news of a large Canaanite army gathered at Megiddo, a fortified city occupying a commanding position midway between the Mediterranean and the Jordan valley. An Egyptian army of 20,000 men marched quickly to Gaza in nine days. From this forward base Thutmose pushed on to Aruna, a town on the southern slope of the Carmel mountain range. Megiddo was situated on its northern slopes, and could be approached by three routes: however, a direct, narrow pass, modern Wadi Ara, attracted the pharaoh's attention in spite of grave warnings from his senior officers.

Thutmose's behaviour

At a conference called to discuss tactics, the pharaoh was told that it would be risky to take the direct route. As one of his commanders said,

What is it like to march along this narrow road? The enemy is waiting at its end and daily becoming more numerous. Will not horse have to follow horse, and the soldiers likewise? Will not our vanguard be fighting while there are still troops waiting to start out from Aruna? Now there are two other roads – one, to our right, comes out at Taanach, south of Megiddo, the other, to our left, comes out to its north at Djefty. Let our victorious

Thutmose III, the victor at Megiddo. Logistical problems may have persuaded this pharaoh that a quick decision on the battlefield was required. Ancient armies had limited supply trains.

Lord proceed along one of the easier routes rather than the difficult one in front of us.

Thutmose was not convinced and commented on how the rebels would scoff at him if he chose a roundabout route. But it is apparent that the pharaoh was less concerned with his reputation than with tactical surprise. Assuming that the Canaanite leaders would think like his own war council, he gambled on an advance through a pass, which shrinks in places to a width of less than 10 metres. A whole day was needed for the Egyptian army to get through Wadi Ara, whereupon Thutmose pitched his camp. Except for a minor skirmish, the passage was as uneventful as it was unexpected. For Thutmose was proved right. The rebels had not anticipated his daring move, and had concentrated their forces at Taanach and Djefty, with only a small force guarding the narrow pass.

The sudden appearance of the Egyptians near Megiddo demoralised the Canaanites, when at dawn Thutmose launched his attack. 'As soon as the rebels saw His Majesty prevailing over them', we are told, 'they fled away to Megiddo with faces of fear. They abandoned their horses and their chariots of gold and silver, so that they could reach safety. Now the people of Megiddo had shut the city gates, but they let down garments in order to hoist them over the walls'.

Outcomes

So swift was the Egyptian attack that it is possible the Canaanites hardly fought at all. Thutmose had gained a great victory, with the result that, according to an inscription, 'at the mere sight of an Egyptian the kings of Canaan flee'.

At the battle of Megiddo Thutmose used surprise and mobility as his main weapons for overcoming the Canaanites. These and his own bravery in leading the attack contributed to the swiftly won victory. They mark him out as a commander who had the self-belief to take risks, though only after calculating the odds carefully. Thutmose considered that they were in his favour and the gain was so great that he dared to reject the advice of his most trusted advisors. Given that the strength of the armed forces on the two sides was about equal, he knew that the concentration of his own forces close to Megiddo would give him the initial advantage, as the Canaanites had divided their army in order to cover both the northern and southern routes of his advance. And they had largely ignored the narrow pass at Wadi Ara. After the battle, all the rulers of Canaan were obliged 'to kiss the ground to the glory' of Thutmose and 'to beg breath for their nostrils'.

Why does it matter?

Risk and uncertainty

Leadership is concerned with taking difficult decisions, frequently on the basis of incomplete or inadequate information, while being exposed to constantly changing and highly complex external conditions. In these circumstances, risk is quite unavoidable, and the ability to understand risk becomes a critical attribute of an effective leader. Biographies of both contemporary and historical leaders from the worlds of politics, warfare or business tend to emphasise those moments in the subject's career when they heroically took a great risk, and succeeded against overwhelming odds or resolved an impossible position. Frequently, these stories also describe how the individual leader acted on the basis of their own intuition rather than on careful research, often ignoring in their actions the considered advice of their peers and subordinates. The description of Thutmose at Megiddo is very much in this mould. Such extraordinary narratives of decision making in battle can conceal the fact that risk is, in reality, an inescapable and everyday condition of organisational life, and that in situations of risk, the organisational locations of leadership and authority may be significantly different. That is to say that the person taking a 'risky' but necessary decision in response to a crisis facing the business may well not, in fact, be the individual designated as the leader; although, in taking action they are undeniably demonstrating leadership qualities.

In some analyses, leadership is, at its heart, equated very closely with risk taking, and it is certainly true that in taking clear and decisive action leaders run the risk of meeting unforeseen circumstances and failing to meet their goals. We expect leaders to make decisions, and decision making can be a risky business. However, the alternative, to play safe and hope to maintain the status quo, will almost certainly mean missing opportunities for growth and development, and settling for mediocrity. Peter Ellwood from TSB summarises this outlook concisely in a statement quoted in Paul Taffinder's book, *The New Leaders*: 'Senior roles are largely about risk. We must understand risk, not remove it. If we remove risk, we remove profit'.

This is of course something Thutmose fully understood. The military advantage of a surprise attack offered the Egyptian army great profit, and possibly at very little cost. Even now the loot his men carried away seems impressive: it comprised

340 living prisoners and 83 hands (cut from the slain); 2041 horses, 191 foals, 6 stallions; a golden chariot belonging to the enemy; a fine chariot worked in gold belonging to the ruler of Megiddo and 892 chariots of his wretched army; a fine bronze coat of mail belonging to the enemy; a fine bronze coat belonging to the ruler of Megiddo; 200 leather mail coats belonging to his wretched army; 502 bows; and 7 wooden tent poles, worked with silver, belonging to the enemy.

Thus the triumphant pharaoh recorded the extent of his victory at Megiddo on his return to Egypt, by having the details carved on a temple wall.

Managing risk

Risk management as a specialised field is, in itself, a big and growing business, with many specialist consultancies offering expert help to organisations in managing the huge range of potential threats which may confront them in the complex social, environmental and legal environments in which they now have to operate. As Mike Pedler, John Burgoyne and Tom Boydell explain it in *A Manager's Guide to Leadership*,

[Risk management] is key to the managerial control of safety, confidentiality, individual and professional accountability, competence, training, and many other aspects of effective organisation. Making sure that lines of accountability are clear, that safety systems are in place, that people are properly trained . . . are the very essence of good operations management.

Organisations are justifiably concerned to develop a realistic estimation of the risks involved in choosing a particular course of action, and with being able to assess whether the risks attendant upon a given decision are justified in terms of the potential benefits that would accrue to the organisation if the desired results are actually achieved in practice. For some organisations this sort of detailed scrutiny and analysis will routinely precede anything other than the most basic of decisions. The process of rigorously gathering and testing masses of information and data is an attempt to control risk, and a huge range of management tools, procedural techniques and software is available to managers to support this rational and analytical approach, the type of techniques which Thutmose's generals would probably have liked to have seen deployed before committing the Egyptian army to a highly risky advance. There are, however, problems with this rational approach to risk management. Absence of evidence does not actually mean that risk is absent and if risks are, to an extent, unpredictable, then an overly rational approach can lead to a false sense of security.

Thinking of this sort underpins the approach to risk management in a wide variety of organisations, and even the most 'go-getting' and entrepreneurial of leaders take care to calculate risks when they have time. Richard Branson of Virgin, for instance, started his low-cost airline with just one plane, and acknowledged the anxiety he felt when he thought about the risk he was taking when he says that, 'I had an agreement with Boeing to take it back if things didn't work out!' In an article in *The Harvard Business Review on Entrepreneurship*, William A. Sahlman draws attention to the difference in public perception about entrepreneurs and the reality when he writes that,

One of the great myths about entrepreneurs is they are risk seekers. All sane people want to avoid risk. True entrepreneurs want to capture all the reward and give all the risk to others.

Risk taking is one of the areas that powerfully points up the difference between management and leadership. Understandably, managers attempt to control risk, but leaders perceive risk from a different angle; for them the issues and question of risk taking are less well defined. Managers may control risk, but it is the leaders who really take risks. Not that this is necessarily a part of the role that all leaders relish. There are those who actually enjoy risk; those who go to work to enjoy an adrenaline rush, or see the next project as some sort of 'white-knuckle ride'; but running a business is not by any means an extreme sport. Even though it is the leaders who gamble and 'win big' that gain public notoriety, some of the most successful leaders have adopted an approach which is more about taking risks by constantly generating small wins and learning from mistakes.

Self-confidence

For leaders to select a risky course of action and carry their people with them in the decision requires considerable self-confidence, a belief that their 'inner voice' is right.

Leaders with a high degree of self-confidence will draw on their own feelings as strongly as they will on intelligence, information and data; it is part of the decision-making mix. In the case of Thutmose, this involved his being able to imagine, predict and act upon the likely thinking then going on in his adversaries' minds. This intuitive sensitivity to other people is an important feature of an effective leader, but it is also critical that their self-confidence is based on a similarly sensitive and accurate appreciation of their own strengths and weaknesses. As Daniel Goleman puts it an article in the *Harvard Business Review on What Makes a Leader*,

Self-aware people can be recognised by their self-confidence. They have a firm grasp of their capabilities and are less likely to set themselves up to fail by, for example, overstretching on assignments. They know, too, when to ask for help. And the risks they take on the job are calculated.

What does it mean for you?

A smart CEO knows that taking risks is what will give his or her organisation the edge. This is not just the big strategic risks taken at the top, but the risks taken on a daily basis by all levels of the organisation.

What we mean when we say we want people to take risks is that we want them to take calculated risks, and that is very different from just being rash in the way you approach making decisions. There is always a trade-off between the amount of analysis you do and the speed with which you want to make the change required.

As a leader you have to prepare yourself for risk taking and the following inventory will assist you to do this.

- **Personality** – Are you inclined to takes risks based on your own intuition or sixth sense, or do you naturally require sufficient evidence before you will make an important decision?

- **Know yourself** – Do you find ways to balance your natural personality traits? If, for example, you tend to be naturally too intuitive, do you 'force' yourself to get more analysis done?

- **Success rate** – How successful have you been in the past in taking risks?

- **Advisers** – Do you have access to the right quality of information to enable you to make an informed choice? Do you tend to take advice?

- **Vision and values** – Are you clear on what your end goal is, and the values that you will not sacrifice in order to make a decision?

- **The reason why** – Are you clear enough over the real reason for the decision that you are about to make?

- **Have you localised your decision-making process?** – Too often we base our risk taking on previous experience. We need to ask ourselves how relevant it actually is to the circumstances faced today.

- **Contingency plans** – What will you do if things go badly wrong?

Now have a look at a few examples of where international marketing has failed because of a lack of analysis. These are taken from *Brand Failures* by Matt Haig.

Pepsi wanted to keep a single and distinct identity across the world, with one marketing campaign and brand message across every country. Unfortunately, 'Come alive with the Pepsi generation' was translated in Taiwan as 'Pepsi will bring your ancestors back from the dead'. Coors beer had bad luck in Spain with its 'Turn it loose' slogan being translated as 'You will suffer from diarrhoea'. When Clairol launched its 'Mist Stick' curling iron in Germany, the company did not realise that 'mist' was a slang term for manure, and that was why women were not rushing to buy the new product. So when it comes to risk taking, even the big guys can get it badly wrong.

How then does a leader strike the right balance between rushing in where angels fear to tread, and creating the inertia that doing nothing brings to an organisation? Consider Figure 2.1.

In today's world, with extreme change all around us, a leader needs to be able to make rapid but rational decisions, or he or she will be left behind.

The following case study covers a way of getting people to take risks in a rational way.

Risk taking

Figure 2.1   Risk-taking matrix

Brad Visser had seized the opportunity to take a posting in East Asia: his children were still young and his wife very supportive, and an overseas posting was good for his career progression. Although Brad had an academic background, he had always been very commercial in his thinking, and it wasn't surprising when iLearn International headhunted him. Initially he had been taken into account management in the education sector where his contacts opened many doors in government, colleges and universities. In order to widen his knowledge, he had spent the last two years getting to grips with the commercial sector and dealing with the large multinationals. During his short career with iLearn he had sold in the proprietary learning system to many large organisations, and was fast becoming a highly sought-after speaker at 'people development' conferences across the country and across all sectors.

So it was with a great deal of excitement that Brad approached his first day in his new job. The team supporting him were well educated, young and to a large extent in awe of Brad's reputation. After three months, however, the honeymoon was over and Brad happened to be chatting to a friend at the local tennis club that he had joined. He confided 'I don't know if it is my lack of knowledge of Asian cultures, but I find that my team, who are a talented bunch of people, simply avoid taking risks. They want to push all the key decisions on to me!' Brad's friend, a veteran of many different cultures, had the solution. 'I experienced something similar in Africa about 15 years ago. There the culture called for decisions to be made on a collective basis, and from a commercial point of view I found that very restrictive. So I brought in Kepner-Tregoe and we trained everyone to run their processes and it made a huge difference. KT as a business started in California in 1957 and is still going strong today, so

I can introduce you to Nadiah who runs the business here'.

So KT were brought in, completed the training, and coached the group and, most important of all, ensured the results were coming through.

For Brad the rational process that had the biggest impact on the iLearn team was 'Decision Analysis'. The process is divided into the following activities:

- state the decision;

- develop objectives;

- classify objectives into MUSTs and WANTs;

- weight the WANTs;

- generate alternatives;

- screen alternatives through the MUSTs;

- compare alternatives against the WANTs;

- identify adverse consequences;

- make the best balanced choice.

Six months later Brad met up with his friend, who asked him how things were now going. Brad was delighted with the behavioural changes that KT had brought about and wanted to share his experience with his friend. 'It's changed the way we handle our business. One of my guys is trying to get into one of the big corporates. I sit down with him and agree the decision and the key objectives. Together we brainstorm the criteria and then split them into MUSTs and WANTs. For us an example of MUSTs are "It must be compliant with our iLearn Learning Management System", or "It must fit the government classification of training and learning". Now they all know that if a business proposition does not satisfy the MUSTs, they just walk away from it and don't go any deeper. Previously they would waste so much time on analysis, but now they are taking risks at an earlier stage and that has speeded up the process'.

Brad added, 'We then go on and look at the rest of the criteria against which they will measure the final decision, and I agree the framework. Once they have the framework they go away to look for options and then they come back to me and say "this is my decision and the risks are . . ." and as you can imagine this is just music to my ears'.

Brad had in fact implemented a tried and tested methodology that, with management support and role modelling, will transform any business.

To sum up risk taking:

- Know what you want to do.

- Define the criteria by which you will make your decision, before you get confused by the options.

- Lay down the two or three 'must have' criteria and if an option doesn't fit, just walk away!

- Rationally evaluate your remaining options against the criteria.

- Assess the risks of your decision, and think of actions you can take to mitigate the risk of failure.

Take the risk and make the decision.

3

The Ability to Motivate: The Military Revolution of Wuling

What happened?

The leader

Ignoring the ridicule directed by other Chinese rulers at his reform programme, Wuling (pronounced 'Woo-ling') decided that it represented the only hope for his own state of Zhao. Nothing less than a thorough overall of its armed forces would guarantee its security.

The historical setting

Wuling had become the ruler of Zhao at a time of great turmoil. Known as the Warring States period, these years witnessed an unprecedented bout of internecine conflict among the feudal powers, which constituted the Middle Kingdom, as ancient China was then called. Seven major states fought for supremacy and devoted their resources to almost continuous warfare. One of the states least able to defend itself was Zhao, because it had to contend with rival Chinese powers as well as nomad tribesmen along its northern border. Zhao was indeed constantly at war with nomad raiders who swept down on horseback from the steppelands north of what was to become the Great Wall. So difficult did the Zhao army find repelling these intruders that, in 307 BC, Wuling determined to take radical action. Not only was a large corps of cavalry formed, but even more trousers were borrowed from the nomads in order to make it easier for the horsemen to ride and shoot their bows. Trousers were then looked upon by the ancient Chinese as a garment only suited to barbarians.

For centuries the long northern frontier had been a worry for Chinese states. Sudden incursions caused real misery for their inhabitants, especially as the nomad raiders were only intent on looting and destruction. Uninterested in settling there, they regularly set fire to towns and villages once valuable items were removed. Zhao had bitter experience of nomadic violence and tried various means of countering the threat without success. Fortifications, flying columns of infantrymen and frequent counter-attacks, all these were tried prior to the accession of Wuling. But the quickness of the mounted nomad archers always meant that Zhao was on the defensive.

The famous debate of 307 BC in Wuling's court about the adoption of cavalry and mounted archery, inspired by the superior riding abilities of the nomads, was concerned with more than the defence of Zhao's northern frontier, however. The arguments for and against such a change should be seen in the context of the overall weakness of this small state. For Wuling was aware of a general lack of military strength, whether facing nomads or Chinese competitors. He knew that nothing short of a thorough-

A cavalryman leading his horse and wearing 'barbarian trousers'. By the time these life-size terracotta figures were placed, in 221 BC, inside underground chambers at Mount Li, the site of Qin Shi Huangdi's tomb, horsemen dominated the northern frontier of ancient China.

going military revolution would be enough to protect Zhao. There was no room for half measures.

Wuling's behaviour

The ancient Chinese chronicles tell us that Wuling believed he had hit on a solution to this apparently intractable military problem. One day he said:

'The way of rulers is to be mindful of the virtue of their ancestors while they are on the throne; the rule for ministers is to devise ways to enhance rulers' powers. Thus it is that a virtuous ruler, even when totally inactive, can guide his people and conduct his affairs with success; when active he can achieve such fame that it may exceed the past, to say nothing of the present ... Now I intend to extend the inheritance I have received from my forebears and make provinces out of nomad lands; but though I shall spend my entire life in this enterprise, my eyes will never see its completion. I propose to adopt the horseman's clothing of the Hu nomads and teach my people their mounted archery. Just think how the world will laugh! But though all China laughs, I shall acquire the lands of the neighbouring nomads.'

When a distinguished and loyal minister expressed grave reservations about this policy, Wuling frankly told him of the vulnerability of Zhao along its northern border. 'We have river frontiers but command not a single boat upon them. We have land frontiers without a single mounted archer to defend them. Therefore I have collected boats and boatman to guard the first, and deployed mounted archers in suitable clothes to guard the second'. Abashed, the minister apologised for appreciating neither the gravity of the situation nor the ruler's strategy for dealing with it. Instead he had had 'the temerity to mouth platitudes'. A delighted Wuling immediately presented him with a set of horseman's clothes.

Afterwards the balance of forces in the Zhao army tilted towards cavalry. Chariots were abandoned completely and the size of the infantry was cut down in number. And Wuling stood firm against all objections: he was certain that the terrain over which his forces had to operate was best suited to mobile archers. As he pointed out,

'My ancestor built a wall where our lands touch on those of the nomads and named it the Gate of No Horizon. Today armoured foot soldiers cannot safely go beyond this wall. Since benevolence, righteousness and ritual will not subdue the nomads, we must go and defeat them by force of mounted arms.'

So it was that Wuling 'dressed in barbarian garments, led his horsemen against the nomads, leaving the Gate of No Horizon'.

Outcomes

The stunning success of this first campaign opened up to Zhao the possibility of acquiring vast new territories. It also demonstrated the military value of mounted archers. Derision greeted Wuling's innovation throughout China but, in other northern states facing regular nomad incursion, the advantages offered by the new cavalry were not entirely missed by their rulers. They could see how greater mobility was a means to dominate the steppe and the marginal tracts of land adjoining it. Through Wuling's ability to motivate the people of Zhao, from his ministers downwards, mounted archers became the specialised troops of the northern frontier of China, and especially for forays beyond the defences which in 210 BC were incorporated into the Great Wall.

Zhao, strengthened by Wuling's military reforms and the conquest of nomad lands, flourished for a century. Its army got the better of those belonging to other Chinese states, allowing Zhao to acquire extra territory within China itself. Arguably this run of success proved the undoing of Zhao, since its rivals were obliged to copy the military innovation of Wuling in order to survive as well. Gradually their greater resources for war told and Zhao was reduced once again to a position of relative weakness, and finally conquered by Qin in 228 BC. This northwestern state, however, went on to defeat all its rivals and in 221 BC unify China as an empire. It was to be Liu Bang's destiny to overthrow Qin rule and found the Han dynasty a few years afterwards.

Why does it matter?

Early theory

Possibly because ancient China had such a variety of landscape, from the steppe in the north, through the great plain of the Yellow river valley, to the wet rice-growing areas of the south, its armies were bound to develop in several distinct ways. Infantry rose to prominence first in the lower Yangzi valley, where lakes and swamps limited the use of chariots and cavalry. In the far north, where Zhao faced nomad attack, the mobility of the mounted archer was critical for defence as well as attack. Wuling's successful introduction of nomad-style cavalry gave this state a respite, but it succumbed to its Chinese rivals in the end. What Wuling had demonstrated, however, was the value of military innovation when confronted by an unconventional opponent. And it should not be over-looked that his farsightedness was at first misunderstood and opposed by his conservative advisers. Not only did Wuling have to convince them, and then the rest of his subjects, about the correctness of his proposed military revolution, but he also had to face down the jibes thrown at him by rival rulers. As he said, 'Nomad clothing is not thought well of in the world, but it is a necessity for a mounted archer. We shall have to ignore the laughter of those who do not understand this'.

There are obviously huge advantages for a leader, like Wuling, who is able to identify and act on what motivates the people in his or her team or organisation to deliver a high-quality performance. Not surprisingly the search for the secrets of motivation has, therefore, preoccupied management thinkers for many years and research from this branch of psychology is avidly analysed for potential practical applications to the business world. Despite this continuing focus on motivation, it still seems surprisingly difficult to reach definite conclusions and draw readily applicable lessons about the best ways in which a business can organise itself to create a genuinely motivational climate or, more immediately, what sort of behaviour from a leader promotes motivation among his or her staff.

Thinking has moved a long way from the relatively crude principles of what was once termed 'scientific management', with its emphasis on measured efficiency, targets, the assessment of output, and creation of incentives based on individual performance. Scientific management led managers to develop complex financial incentive schemes based on the measurement of work outputs, the assumption being that offering extra pay for each increment of work would maximise output. Though now largely discredited, this approach, with its assumption of man as a rational economic creature whose motivation can be managed, directed and stimulated by a skilled manager through the use of rewards and punishments, still lies only a little way beneath the surface of the sophisticated performance management schemes within which so many of us are obliged to work today. Such structures tend to enshrine stable sets of performance standards and create rigid expectations of what is and is not possible or acceptable in terms of working practices. As Wuling found in ancient China, an overdependence on what was deemed to be the established and appropriate military tactics, not to say equipment, hugely disadvantaged his armies when confronted with a rival force who had developed a radically different method of warfare.

Motivation in the workplace

Many managers must ask themselves on their way to the office on a Monday morning, 'What will motivate my people to do a good job this week?' This question can lead to predictable answers concerned with, for example, the better design of pay and reward schemes on the basis that pay, status and fringe benefits all contribute to increasing the motivation of the workforce. This, in spite of employee surveys which appear to show that workers do not recognise improvements in these areas as genuinely 'motivational', and that subtler, more 'intrinsic' factors related to job satisfaction are more likely to lead to improved motivation.

A more subtle question for a manager to ask, and one whose answer is more likely to address the core of motivation, is perhaps: 'What motivates some people to work harder than they need to?' We have all worked with colleagues who seem willing to 'go the extra mile', maybe to work longer hours than they need to but, more significantly, to put in extra effort, to spot problems before they arrive and take action, and to use their initiative in changing the way things are done. Certainly, in some cases, the high level of motivation demonstrated by such people can arise from a sort of 'delayed gratification', the hope that in the near future they will be rewarded with promotion, pay rises, a named place in the car park or some other external acknowledgement; but for many individuals the source of their obviously powerful motivation lies deeper.

The much-quoted 'Hawthorne studies' from the 1930s started out as an attempt to identify the ideal environment for maximum work performance. In fact, the studies revealed that throughout a whole series of carefully managed and observed changes in working conditions, there were definite improvements in productivity, whether the environment was actually improving or deteriorating, and this led to the recognition that relationships at work could have an overwhelming influence on morale, motivation and productivity. Attention shifted, as a result, from the 'scientific' management of work to the notions of what became known as the 'human relations school', with much increased emphasis on the importance of sensitive supervision and team development.

Human needs and motivation

In the 1950s and 1960s the emphasis was on the satis-faction of human needs as the key to motivation. A social scientist, Abraham Maslow, developed an influential model of a 'hierarchy of needs', usually presented as a pyramid with basic issues such as safety, fair pay and reasonable working conditions at the lower levels, while social, interpersonal and self-expression needs were placed higher and seen as much more motivational in the true sense. Another influential thinker and researcher, Professor Fred Herzberg, who developed a 'two-factor theory', suggested a two-step approach to understanding employee motivation and satisfaction. For Herzberg 'hygiene factors' such as job security, company policy and administration, wages and remuneration, the quality of supervision and interpersonal relations are significant in that a perceived lack of concern by the company for such matters causes dissatisfaction at work, but they are not in themselves motivators. As he wrote in the *Harvard Business Review* (Jan–Feb 1968)

I can change a man's battery, and then recharge it, and recharge it again. But it is only when he has his own generator that we can talk about motivation. He then needs no outside stimula-tion. He wants to do it.

Herzberg's research suggested that less tangible issues such as achievement, recognition, responsibility, per-sonal growth and advancement were the actual source of motivation. A focus on job design, on job enrichment and enhancement, was the outcome of this thinking, so that work itself could become meaningful and, therefore, motivating. This is a continuing thread in contemporary thinking about leadership. As James M. Kouzes and Barry Z. Posner put it in *The Leadership Challenge,*

> If work comes to be seen solely as a source of money and never as a source of fulfilment, organisations will totally ignore other human needs at work – needs involving such intangibles as learning, self-worth, pride, competence, and serving others.

More recent research has only tended to highlight the significance of the different needs and aspirations of individuals as well as the importance of the organisational context in creating a motivational climate. What motivates one individual will not necessarily work with another, just as what works in one organisational setting may not be as effective in a different context. It is highly likely that individual soldiers within Wuling's army were driven by very different motivations. For some, fear of the consequences of further defeats at the hands of the barbarians for themselves, their families and homes would have been a spur to continue the struggle. For others, the hope of material reward would have been an important motivator.

Such reasons could all be placed at the lower end of Maslow's hierarchy of needs in explaining their motivational basis. It is also true that Wuling's army would have been subject to a rigorous regime of discipline and control, which would have been far more unforgiving than anything that the 'scientific managers' of the 1930s would have dreamt of! It is, however, worth noting Wuling's concern over the maintenance of the rule of law and respect for tradition. One of the consistent complaints made by dissatisfied employees in attitude surveys is that their managers are 'unfair' or 'unjust' in distributing rewards and that the criteria for promotion and advancement are left deliberately obscure. A perceived lack of fairness is a great demotivator.

Leadership and motivation

This unpredictable nature of human motivation does not seem to offer much of a clue to a manager seeking some method of boosting motivation. Yet it is undoubtedly true that some leaders seem much more adept at motivating their employees than others. Wuling clearly shows some of the chief characteristics of motivational leaders. For a start, it is transparent that he had a very well-defined and powerful sense of what needed to be done and why, however odd his vision may initially have seemed to the Chinese people. It is also very significant that he took time to carefully explain his purpose to key people, his ministers, in order to get them on side and ensure that they then spread the message more widely. Yet the exceptional achievement of Wuling was his ability to convince his army that they could actually win battles by making radical changes in the way they operated, by acting in ways that had previously been considered completely alien and literally 'barbaric'. Wuling's story also illustrates another key feature of a motivational organisation. Success breeds success and success is a great motivator. As John Kotter of Harvard Business School puts it in an article in the *Harvard Business Review on Leadership*:

Finally, good leaders recognise and reward success, which not only gives people a sense of accomplishment but also makes them feel like they belong to an organisation that cares about them. When all this is done, the work itself becomes intrinsically motivating.

That Wuling's action eventually became respectable in ancient China, as other states copied the changes he made to the Zhao army, is an indicator of his real success as a motivator. In the end, all rulers had to acknowledge both his foresight and his skill in implementing radical reform.

What does it mean for you?

Organisations thrive when their employees are firing on all cylinders; somehow the magic of a highly motivated team translates into results. Then success breeds success and, if this is well managed, the organisation goes on to enjoy a period of sustained achievement.

This is illustrated through a case study of how the management team of an unprofitable division of a major frozen food business turned the business round over a three-year period.

The Ultimate Pea was the name of the business, and it had been going for some 30 years, the last 10 years of which had been as part of a national corporation. Over the last five years, however, losses had been mounting, and the last two general managers had been fired when they failed to turn the business round. In desperation, the CEO decided that, rather than bring in another hotshot GM, he would appoint three young managers with a lot of potential and a great deal to prove. Ingrid was the marketing director, and came with a real success record in the fast-moving consumer foods sector, Max was a rising manufacturing star, and Harvey provided the commercial side, covering finance and logistics.

When the three of them had their first meeting with the management team, they met with a group of highly demotivated people. The team had been together for a long time, had seen the fortunes of their business decline and expected each month a shutdown and the loss of their jobs. Its members had got to the point of doing what they were told, and you could see they could not wait for the day to end, so that they could go home to their families.

Ingrid, Max and Harvey spent the next three months understanding every aspect of the business, and then put together their strategy for rapid turnaround. It was going to take real courage, they explained to the CEO. The business has been pushing for volume over the last five years and what it had ended up with was a low-priced, low-quality product that cost almost as much as a high-quality product to make. To top it all, the business was being run by a management team that had lost the will and the pride to succeed.

The transformational solution was to up the quality, rebrand the product, get out of the high-volume, low-margin business, and shut down surplus capacity. This strategy was personally communicated by Ingrid, Max and Harvey. It was a brave strategy, and would take a lot of managing, but drastic moves were clearly needed.

Unexpectedly, motivation started to rise with the announcement of the strategy. At last someone was doing something to try to save the business. People always know when a business is in terminal decline, and there is nothing more demotivating than seeing something you once felt a great deal of pride for gradually disappearing.

As the surplus capacity was shut down and people lost their jobs, Ingrid, Max and Harvey made sure that every effort was made to ensure that redundant people found jobs elsewhere. There were a few of the management team that also became casualties, but every farewell was turned into an opportunity to celebrate successes and to motivate the people who were staying on.

Throughout the 18 months it took to register the first profit, communication across the business was very open, very honest and, it would be fair to say, that everyone knew what the strategy was, as well as what progress was being made. The management team had all agreed that they would practice what they had preached, and as a result they had got rid of management excesses such as flying business class. Everyone was in this together, and everyone was doing their own bit to bring about success. As the motivation rose, so did pride and the willingness of people to take necessary risks.

The business went on to shut down low-profit canning plants, launch a highly successful super-premium brand, reduce overhead costs and, by the third year, was making regular profit. Within five years it was viewed as a high-performing division of the corporation.

What do you think are the implications of this case study?

If you are looking for the roots of demotivation in organizations, always start with management: what is the strategy it is supposed to be following and how is it being implemented?

Bad times in organisations bring down the motivation but, by devising a route to better things, motivation can be dramatically improved. For instance:

- Acknowledge the extent that things are going wrong.

- Recognise that people have feelings.

- Spend time, interview as many people as you can, but come up with a strategy that will work.

- Communicate what you plan to do, in a simple, honest and open fashion.

- Build trust and you do this by matching your behaviour to the words you use.

- Find ways to reward the right kind of behaviour.

- Let each person know they are appreciated and how you want them to contribute towards the improvement.

- Be consistent in everything you do.

- Stick to the strategy.

- Communicate process, failures and successes.

- Celebrate success whenever possible.

- Walk the talk – never talk cutback while you redecorate your office and purchase comfortable furniture in Italian leather!

Then see what improvements occur.

4

Creating a Compelling Vision: The Commoner Emperor Liu Bang

What happened?

The leader

Liu Bang (pronounced 'Lee-you-bang') was the first peasant to found in China an imperial dynasty, the Han (202 BC–AD 220). Ancient Chinese historians recall the remarkable features of Liu Bang, his prominent nose, 'dragon' forehead and the 72 black moles on his left thigh, just as they list the supernatural events surrounding his conception and early manhood, but they cannot disguise the historical fact of a peasant background, which left this leader almost illiterate.

The historical setting

China was first united under the Qin dynasty in 221 BC. Qin Shi Huangdi, the First Sovereign Qin Emperor, had defeated all rival kings and then ruled by sheer force of arms. Such was the repression of this earliest imperial regime that the ordinary people rose in rebellion and in 206 BC overthrew Qin rule. Three years before this nationwide event took place Liu Bang joined the rebels. Having lost several convicts from a group he was conducting to the capital, he released the others and put himself at their head, because punishment for this failure, like most other offences, was death under the harsh Qin code of law. So it was that Liu Bang soon found himself leading one of the rebel armies battling against the Qin imperial forces.

Even though the soldiers at the disposal of the Qin dynasty were seasoned fighters and put up a very determined resistance, they were scattered in garrisons throughout China and unable to concentrate quickly enough to nip the rebellion in the bud. They won major engagements but the unpopularity of Qin rule meant that there was no shortage of rebels to make up for losses sustained in battle. The chief rebel leader was a nobleman by the name of Hsiang Yu. While Liu Bang's army captured the capital, Hsiang Yu's forces defeated Qin armies still fighting elsewhere.

Liu Bang treated the inhabitants of the surrendered capital with restraint, forbidding his men from plundering its riches or taking captives. Then in 206 BC Hsiang Yu arrived with the rest of the rebel forces and sacked the capital. 'More than a month after Liu Bang captured the capital', a chronicler tells us, 'Hsiang Yu arrived with the main rebel army of 400,000 men. Then all the members of the imperial house were beheaded, and a massacre followed. Palaces and houses were looted and fired. The burning did not cease until the third month. Thus it was that the Qin empire was lost'. This devastation, and the subsequent division of China between the rebel leaders, was beyond Lu Bang's prevention, but in 203 BC he was ready to make a bid for the throne. Within one year he had founded his own dynasty, the Han, and taken as his reign title Gaozu, meaning 'High Ancestor'.

A literary gathering in a garden. The 'ink boy' is making sure that the scholar about to compose verse will not have to pause once he dips his brush. Even though Liu Bang understood his own need for educated administrators, he disliked scholarly pretention, and relieved himself in a scholar's hat.

Liu Bang's behaviour

His mildness was a genuine part of his character, a singular virtue in what was a violent age, and it made his accession a popular event. People felt that this commoner would govern in their interests unlike the absolute Qin emperors. On the throne Liu Bang neither aped aristocratic manners nor slackened his compassion for his poorer subjects, but his habit of squatting down, coupled with an earthy vocabulary, unsettled polite courtiers. Prior to his final victory in 202 BC he had displayed his dislike for the excessive ceremony attached to learning. When some scholars came to him in costume, wearing their elaborate hats, Liu Bang snatched one of these pieces of headgear and urinated in it. Yet the new emperor understood how war-torn China yearned for a sound administration, and so he turned for help to scholars untarnished by service under the Qin dynasty.

This insight had much to do with the influence of Lu Jia (pronounced 'Loo-gee-are'), his court chamberlain. Dismissing as useless quotations from history books, the new emperor once commented on the fact that he had conquered the empire on horseback. Chamberlain Lu Jia replied, 'That is correct, but Your Majesty will not be able to govern the empire on horseback. If the Qin had governed with humanity and righteousness, if it had followed the precepts of the ancient sages, then Han would not have gained the empire'. At this the new emperor blanched and said, 'Explain to me the reasons for the fall of Qin and the rise of Han, as well as that which won and lost in kingdoms of old'. In obedience to this imperial wish, Lu Jia wrote a book about statecraft, in 12 chapters. When Emperor Han Gaozu listened to the chamberlain reading aloud his book, he praised his ideas strongly. And to bring order to the daily life of the palace he asked Lu Jia to work out a new court ceremonial for his boisterous followers. His only instruction was 'Make it easy'.

Outcomes

Liu Bang, unlike the rebel leader Hsiang Yu, deplored acts of unnecessary violence. Whereas Hsiang Yu enjoyed watching his enemies die in cauldrons of boiling oil, Liu Bang was concerned to restore peace above all else. He endeavoured to find a way of putting the troubled years of Qin rule and the bitter civil war, which ended this first imperial dynasty, out of the Chinese people's mind. So he embraced the humane teaching of Confucius, and let officials like Lu Jia form an imperial civil service dedicated to the welfare of the empire. Within a century it was recruited by examination and was over 100,000 strong. It would loyally serve China until 1911, giving this country the most enduring political structure in world history. Compared with the administrative system the Han dynasty founded, other countries were until recently undergoverned. Its vision was so compelling that the Chinese people could not, until modern times, conceive of any other way in which to live.

Another outcome of the first Han emperor's willingness to listen to advice was an acceptance by later rulers of the independence of ministers. The post of Censor became a powerful one at court. That his duty was to pass censure on the actions of the throne, as well as ministers, was unique. Ruler–official relations were of course often turbulent and those who opposed the imperial will sometimes paid for their outspokenness with their lives, although banishment to a remote province was the usual outcome of such disputes. Yet Confucius had pointedly said, 'Do not try to oppose a prince by roundabout means. Always speak openly when the occasion demands'. This open honesty, a fundamental requirement of Confucius' moral philosophy, was balanced by a powerful sense of loyalty to the throne. It was indeed the submissiveness of Confucian scholar-officials that led to one of Liu Bang's successors, the forceful Han Emperor Wu Di, to adopt Confucianism as the state ideology in 136 BC.

Why does it matter?

Vision and leadership

Despite the brief unification imposed by the Qin dynasty, China remained under Liu Bang a confederation of recently independent states with still vigorous regional cultures. Yet Confucian standards and rituals together with inherited Qin administrative practice did eventually bring about cultural unity. The transformation was a slow one because Liu Bang settled for a political compromise after the oppression of Qin. He allowed the restoration of certain feudal houses and granted fiefs to his own close relatives, but these diminished holdings were intertwined with districts controlled by imperial officials. It was Liu Bang's successors who completed the vision of an empire administered for the benefit of all its inhabitants. This ancient idea of a professional civil service, recruited by public examination on the basis of personal merit, came to the West during the nineteenth century through the English East India Company. As Robert Inglis, a British resident in China, remarked in 1835, 'the Company have adopted the principle and the full development in India of this Chinese invention is destined one day, perhaps, like those of gunpowder and printing, to work another great change in the states-system of Europe'.

Liu Bang's realisation of the urgent need for a compelling vision is reflected in the interest today in the decisive role played by a leader. The literature of management and leadership is full of charismatic leaders who have created a business from scratch, or radically redefined an existing organisation, through the force of their personality and the strength of their vision. In many cases the individuals identified appear as a sort of 'hero-leader', holding true to their deeply held inner convictions and to their belief in what their business can become through tough times before finally winning through. Their vision is often an expression of their personality, typically compulsive, passionate and intuitive. The characteristics of this sort of youthful, visionary entrepreneur are well demonstrated in a quote from Neil Hirsch, who founded Tolerate Systems at the age of 21 and later reflected,

I think I was too stupid to know that it was impossible. So I did it.

Vision has become a crucial component of a leader's profile. The ever-growing emphasis on the importance of vision to an organisation's success marks a distinctly different way of thinking about businesses from the traditional management model of central control and planning. Rather than a carefully structured process of strategic planning and review, 'vision thinking' focuses on the need to create a beacon, showing the direction that the organisation should take and illuminating the goals it should be aiming for. (A much-quoted example of this was the way in which President Kennedy used his vision of putting an American on the moon within the next decade to galvanise the country's space programme. His fateful escalation of the conflict in Vietnam was, of course, a quite different matter.) As Michael Bloomberg, CEO of the business information corporation Bloomberg, commented in 1997,

Central planning didn't work for Stalin or Mao, and it won't work for an entrepreneur either.

Obviously this leaves questions as to how an individual actually develops such a strong personal vision and communicates it to others in a large and complex organisation. Notwithstanding his humble background, Liu Bang developed as emperor a radically different notion of what the state could be like from the one his countrymen had experienced, and he was able to carry people with him because of his own conviction and inner strength. It is also clear that his vision was a powerful expression of his own personality and character, the truths of which remained constant and recognisable even when he eventually ruled supreme.

Such a vision often arises from the passion, dedication, drive and initiative of the individual who originally created the organisation in his or her image. It is important to remember that not all such creative visions are actually achievable, or indeed ethical. For each of the famous entrepreneurs whose names regularly feature in the chapters of books on leadership (Jack Welch at General Electric, Richard Branson of Virgin or Anita Roddick of The Body Shop for instance), there are undoubtedly hundreds whose vision never found expression in the creation of a great business. It is also worth bearing in mind that not all the businesses quoted as models in the last five or 10 years have been without their problems more recently.

Sharing the vision

Organisations founded on a cult of personality often fail to outlive the tenure of their creator since megalomania is no substitute for leadership. That is why Liu Bang's readiness to seek help from Confucian scholars, despite an obvious annoyance at their unpeasant-like ways, is so instructive for us. He was self-aware enough to admit his own personal shortcomings as a ruler, as well as his urgent need of advice and guidance. For long-term success requires not just that a vision is effectively articulated, but that it is shared and aspired to by staff throughout the business. It has to belong to everyone. The idea of developing a shared 'corporate' vision within a business has led, in many cases, to the obsessive agonising over 'mission statements' which have been hard to avoid in recent years, and even to the establishment in some companies of 'vision task forces', charged with imagining futures for the business in five or 10 years' time. At their best, they create the overarching themes that can be taken forward to detailed planning stages and which identify the outstanding goals on which resources need to be focused. At their worst, such activities generate little except bland or overcomplex statements of future intent which exert no discernible influence. As John Rock of Oldsmobile once put it,

A bunch of guys take off their ties and coats, go into a motel room for three days, and put a bunch of words on a piece of paper and then go back to business as usual.

Many of these exercises would have benefited from some early guidance in the style of Liu Bang's memorable instruction to his chamberlain Lu Jia – 'Make it easy'!

The need to find ways of embedding a vision in the every-day thought and life of a complex organisation has led, of course, to some fascinating debates. Some writers believe that this is best realised through traditional models of strategic planning at senior and middle management levels, while others seek for ways of releasing the same sort of energy and creativity shown by the leader himself or herself throughout the organisation. As Jack Welch of General Electric said,

Our managers' natural strong suit is the energy and creativity of an irreverent, aggressive, impatient, and curious people. It is ours to win with – if we can shift gears from decades of *controlling* things to a decade of liberating – turning people loose to dream, dare and win.

But there is also an acknowledgement that vision is not always the answer to a business problem, or indeed appropriate to each and every context. As Lou Gerstner famously commented when he took on the CEO position with the troubled IBM in 1993,

There has been a lot of speculation that I'm going to deliver a 'vision' of the future of IBM. The last thing IBM needs right now is a vision. What IBM needs right now is a series of very tough-minded, market-driven and highly effective strategies that deliver performance in the market place and shareholder value.

Perhaps the most powerful message from the story of Liu Bang lies in his acknowledgement that, although it was his determination which had helped to drive a repressive regime from office, his limited experience and expertise in the exercise of power meant that he needed other people with different skills to help him create a dynasty with an enduring vision. As Lu Jia remarked, 'It is easy to start something, not so easy to sustain it'. Perhaps Liu Bang was more than fortunate in ruling a China ready for peace: his subjects responded positively to his vision of a benevolent empire. That his closest associates shared his vision also helped the Han dynasty get off to a good start. They knew that there was no scope for lavish expenditure after the ravages of a terrible civil war.

What does it mean for you?

The case study describes a situation where developing and communicating a vision is critical to future success. Some of the issues that face the manager reflect concerns addressed already in this chapter. So what advice would you give Calum?

Calum had started off his working life as a graduate working in the Glasgow factory of Bravo Jams. He was always destined for better things, and had taken advantage of working for an international business to travel the world. Over the last 15 years he had worked in Thailand, Australia, Peru and he was just coming up to the end of a three-year assignment at the international head office in Paris. During this rich period of working life he had met and married Morag in Sydney, and they had two daughters, Kelly aged 13 and Bronwin aged 10. Calum and Morag both craved to go back to their roots, and especially to allow the girls to complete their education in mother Scotland. Unfortunately there were not many international assignments based in Glasgow.

Even though Calum started off life as a mechanical engineer, he has spent his time well in manufacturing. Industrial engineering, production management, logistics scheduling, capital maintenance and for a spell he even managed the HR function. He had also worked with a wide range of colleagues and has always taken time out to get their buy-in to the changes he has made.

Calum had discussed his dilemma with Serge his boss, the manufacturing director Europe. Serge had a great deal of time for Calum and wanted to keep him in the business. When the factory manager's job at Bravo Jams fell vacant, Serge hatched a plan to get Calum and family back to Scotland. Serge phoned him up and explained the plan ... 'You take the job of factory manager, a job which you can do with your eyes closed, but you also manage the industrial performance of the European Jam category. This way you get back to Scotland, but you don't waste away in a job that you are overqualified to do'. It was too great an opportunity to pass over, and although it meant travelling two to three days a week visiting the 20 factories scattered across Europe, Calum and family returned to Glasgow early in the summer.

Calum knew that his career was safe, but he also wanted his factory's future to become more secure. There was an industrial rationalisation task team looking at performances across all factories in the group, and Glasgow was not looking totally secure. The workforce was highly skilled and tremendously loyal, with generations of families working for the plant. Industrial relations couldn't have been better; the plant itself had been refitted three years earlier; so had state-of-the-art process control, and it enjoyed an enviable quality record. The main problem was the location, Glasgow being seen by many as on the outer rim of Europe, and as most of production went to the large urban areas of Britain, France and Germany, there was always a transport penalty.

Calum decided that what the factory needed was a vision for a more secure future. Flexibility, speed to market, highly skilled workforce and low-cost high-quality manufacture were all attributes that the plant could offer. This needed to be captured into a vision that everyone in the factory felt passionate about. People working in the manufacturing sector of Glasgow tended, after seeing so many factory closures around them, to be fairly pessimistic about the future. As the age profile of the Bravo Jam workforce was early 50s the promise of a redundancy payout appeared more attractive than continuing employment. Yet there was something compelling about Calum as the plant's returning son, now wise with the experience of world-wide manufacturing, returning to save the plant from certain closure. If anyone could convince the workforce that the future was worth fighting for, it had to be Calum.

5

Developing People: The Han Emperor Wu Di's Approach

What happened?

The leader

Han Wu Di (pronounced 'Han-woo-dee') was the fifth emperor of the Han dynasty, which the commoner Liu Bang had founded in 202 BC. Born in 156 BC, this energetic and forceful ruler was only 16 when he began his reign of 54 years, one of the longest in imperial Chinese history. Although much of the initiative for the new policies introduced during his reign can be traced to his ministers, there is little doubt that Wu Di's own determination was the decisive factor behind the sweeping changes he presided over.

The historical setting

In spite of the fact that it was during the reign of Wu Di that Confucianism became recognised as the official ideology, this event was by no means a foregone conclusion.

There were strenuous arguments between officials who preferred rigorous government like that of the oppressive Qin dynasty which the Han replaced, and those who looked further back to the less centralised period of the feudal states which had preceded the Qin unification of China in 221 BC. As one Confucian philosopher put it, 'the heavenly mandate to rule had passed to Han, for the reason that Qin had grown tyrannical. So Han was able to overthrow Qin. The dynasty in possession of Heaven's favour smote the one lacking it'. Thus, it was argued, an emperor's authority was granted and taken away by Heaven, whose agents for affecting change could be humble men like Liu Bang, virtuous individuals supported by the mass of the people.

This ancient theory of Heaven's limitation on imperial power formed the basis of the Chinese constitution until quite recent times. While Wu Di would not accept the belief that Heaven's disapproval was shown in natural phenomena such as floods and drought, he appreciated how delay in mounting adequate relief measures must inevitably encourage rebellion. He also understood that his own policies could never afford to be seen as a major disruption of everyday life. They had to work smoothly in order to meet the difficulties which were then undermining the very foundations of the Chinese empire.

Wu Di's behaviour

The chief problem for China was security. Along the northern frontier, the line of fortifications known as the Great Wall were no longer adequate against nomad attack. The Xiongnu, probably the Huns who later invaded the Roman empire, were such a constant source of anxiety there that Wu Di ordered his troops to go over to the offensive. But the prolonged struggle from 134 to 91 BC proved to be beyond the empire's strength. Losses were high and the nomads seemed forever reviving as a

Wu Di's son, the Han emperor Zhao Di, who confirmed the innovations introduced by his illustrious father. Zhao Di accepted the advice of his ministers over the Chinese empire's need for reform.

potent enemy. As China could not remain forever on a permanent war footing, an uneasy peace returned to the northern frontier, which was only maintained by the payment of substantial subsidies to the Xiongnu. Internally, Wu Di was confronted by serious problems too.

Mounting difficulties in the production and distribution of basic commodities, the worsening condition of the peasantry, the growing wealth of merchants and inflation caused by the private minting of coin, all called for drastic action. To meet immediate financial commitments Wu Di was advised to sell titles and call in privately minted coins by issuing treasury notes made from the skin of a rare white stag. In 119 BC, the same year that merchants were forbidden to own land, a state monopoly was declared over the iron and salt industries, the control of which was given to senior officials, until their incompetence compelled the recruitment of professional salt boilers and iron masters. Such an arrangement henceforth became part of imperial policy, though a monopoly also declared on the production of alcohol was eventually replaced by the payment of tax. To thwart speculation in foodstuffs public granaries were established in 115 BC. Provincial officials were ordered to buy when prices were low and sell in times of shortage. The system was known as 'the price leveller'.

In order to implement these ancient policies of state intervention Wu Di urgently needed reliable and imaginative administrators. From 135 BC onwards would-be civil servants were expected to prove their abilities by answering questions which were set, in theory, by the emperor in person. Thus began the system of imperial examinations, the ultimate origin of present-day public testing. An ideal candidate for the imperial Chinese civil service was said to be distinguished by abundant talents, respect for the family, loyalty to the emperor, moral rectitude and deep learning. Wu Di's interest in examination answers extended to individual grades, so that he would revise the pass list whenever he spotted someone whose ideas he liked. Such a candidate was Hong Gongsun, to whom he entrusted in 125 BC the reorganisation of finance and education.

Wu Di could not agree with the low mark awarded to Hong Gongsun, who was so poor that he supported his family by breeding pigs. The emperor's interest in the recruitment of administrators is hardly surprising in the context of his personal style of government. Critics believed that Wu Di stifled the expression of any views that ran counter to his policies. And it has to be said that he ended the early Han compromise of shared power with the nobility and subjugated the bureaucracy to his own wishes. Doubtless Wu Di would have replied that the times required urgent measures, but he was always prepared to back people with potential, like Hong Gongsun, who proved to be an exceptional minister. That the emperor also was willing to admit his mistake over the running of the salt and iron monopoly shows how he could change course when necessary. And he came to see how war with the Xiongnu could no longer be sustained as well.

Outcomes

Even though he did not direct military campaigns himself, Wu Di was remembered as a fighting emperor. Criticism of his policies, during his reign and afterwards, failed to tarnish his reputation, for as a later historian wrote: 'If Wu Di, with his superior ability and his great plans, had not departed from the modesty and economy of his predecessors, and if, by means of his policies, he helped the common people, in what respects have any of the famous kings of old surpassed him?'

Why does it matter?

Deep learning

A remarkable debate took place in 81 BC, when Emperor Han Zhao Di, Wu Di's son, was attempting to review the policies of his illustrious predecessor. An account of the discussion, entitled *Discourses on Salt and Iron*, records the arguments put forward by reformers and traditionalists within the highest ranks of the imperial bureaucracy. The result was a victory for the reformers, who claimed that state monopolies were needed to achieve the greatest exploitation of the empire's resources and the most efficient distribution of its products. They justified the imposition of controls on the grounds that they ended private profit, stabilised prices and ensured a fair distribution of iron tools to the peasantry. Against the advocates of monopoly, the traditionalists argued that government regulation would be seen as harsh and oppressive, besides pointing out the poor quality of the tools actually produced by the imperial iron agency.

Any major process of organisational change, such as that inspired by Wu Di, will highlight the need to train and develop the people charged with implementing the new ways of working. Wu Di's creation of an educated 'cadre' of able administrators attuned to his plans and with the motivation to deliver his vision, is a model which has parallels in the modern world. That this group had its intellectual capabilities tested and measured against national standards so as to provide some assurance of their future potential has clear resonance, for example, with France's sponsorship in the eighteenth and nineteenth centuries of a national system of 'grandes écoles', designed to identify and train the most able and talented young people in preparation for their future roles as the senior executives of industry and the civil service. The legacy of this system is still evident today in the 'Ecole Nationale d'Administration' (ENA), whose graduates, known as 'énarques', although destined primarily to furnish the state with its echelon of senior civil servants, in fact dominate the senior levels of both the private and public sector organisations throughout the country.

Han Wu Di's project, and indeed the way he chose to develop the people he believed were necessary to see it through, illustrates an important contemporary issue for leaders: finding a reliable means of guaranteeing that an initiative or development is actually delivered in the way imagined, given that the leader can only work through his or her own people. If the solution is to train people to fine and exact functional detail in each facet of the project, then the leader will inevitably end up micro-managing the team and be absorbed with technical intricacies and training specifications. If, on the other hand, a successful outcome is more likely to come from a team that is encouraged to develop its own ways of implementing the leader's plans, and which is actively engaged in providing imaginative solutions to problems in its own ways, then the leader needs to hand over a significant amount of responsibility and accept that in practice things may not develop precisely as he had imagined, or hoped. To do that with confidence requires staff who are not simply trained to follow instructions, but able to draw on their full potential. Han Wu Di's belief in 'deep learning' suggests his response fell into the second category. In an article entitled 'The Work of Leadership', published in the *Harvard Business Review*, Ronald Heifetz and Donald Laurie explore the difficulties many leaders face in actually seeing through major change programmes. They argue that the notion of a leader having a vision and aligning people with it will not, on its own, be successful. Indeed, they point out how,

Adaptive changes are hard to define and resolve precisely because they demand the work and responsibility of managers and people throughout the organisation. They are not amenable to solutions provided by leaders; adaptive solutions require members of the organisation to take responsibility for the problematic situations that face them.

Leadership – the development role

The priority accorded to learning and development has as its rationale the changing needs and structures of organisations. Firstly, in the leaner organisations in which most of us work today, people are expected to take on a broader range of responsibilities and tasks and, consequently, require a wider range of skills. This is particularly true of those with supervisory or managerial roles. Secondly, the increasing importance of 'knowledge workers', and the significance of 'knowledge capital' place a premium on the possession of high-quality skills and expertise and, thirdly, there is a growing acknowledgement of the importance of recruiting, retaining and developing talented people. Howard Schultz, CEO of Starbucks, has an interesting take on this: 'I believe in the adage; hire people smarter than you and get out of the way!'

In this context a leader's responsibility for developing staff takes on real significance, and requires a very different understanding of the role of training and development. Sending an employee on a training course should be seen as a reward for high-quality performance, rather than a short-term solution to underperformance, since training is the only means available for preparing people for the next stage of their development. It is also important that leaders appreciate that a whole range of organisational practices and policies will have an impact on people's skills, knowledge and confidence; not just recognised training activities. A shrewd manager will be aware of the part these factors can play in developing staff and manage them actively. Examples would include the following:

- fair and flexible pay and reward systems;

- clear and unambiguous roles and responsibilities;

- recognition – a sense of being valued by the organisation;

- job security;

- safe and pleasant working conditions;

- opportunities for social interaction with colleagues;

- performance review and management;

- opportunities to work in teams;

- opportunities to work autonomously, showing initiative and enterprise;

- feeling involved in the goals of the business;

- opportunities for promotion and advancement.

Different individuals will, of course, respond differently to components of this list; what motivates and stimulates professional development for one may well have little impact on another. The challenge for a leader is to know enough about the key people in the organisation, as indeed Wu Di clearly did, so that they can deploy the strategies necessary to help each individual move forward.

Coaching

Coaching has now been acknowledged as a critical leadership skill. Essentially, it is about helping team members to assess their own performance, record their strengths, realise their shortcomings and, last but not least, identify their training needs. Typically, the coaching process moves on to the development of a training and learning action plan and the use of review meetings with the coach to monitor progress and reassess individual levels of competence. Becoming an effective coach will inevitably alter the nature of the relationship between the leader and the member of staff, and not all leaders are comfortable with the role. It recognises that the key opportunities for personal and professional development are likely to reside within the working situation itself, rather than flowing from participation in external training programmes, and that the coach is responsible for actively seeking out ways to expose the 'trainee' to new experiences and supporting them as they move into new areas. In *Primal Leadership*, Daniel Goleman emphasises that coaching requires managers to know their employees on a deeper, personal level, in order to make the link between the employee's own goals and ambitions and those of the organisation. He suggests,

Coaches are also good at delegating, giving employees challenging assignments that stretch them, rather than tasks that simply get the job done ... Further, coaches usually tolerate short-term failure, understanding that it can further an employee's dreams.

The tolerance of failure is frequently highlighted in surveys of coaching, not that all leaders find this easy. As Michael Eisner of Disney famously said, 'Failing is good as long as it doesn't become a habit'. It is also clear that if carried out without commitment or competence, coaching can be counter-productive. Goleman reminds us that,

When executed poorly, the coaching approach looks more like micromanaging or excessive control of an employee. This kind of misstep can undermine an employee's self-confidence and ultimately create a downward performance spiral. Unfortunately we've found that many managers are unfamiliar with – or simply inept at – the coaching style, particularly when it comes to giving ongoing performance feedback that builds motivation rather than fear or apathy.

Thus the reign of the Han Emperor Wu Di is here something of a model. The interest he took in his top officials' actions could be seen as akin to coaching, because his serious interventions were restricted to consistent failure. Otherwise, Wu Di let them get on with their jobs, and only commented when he considered that more could be achieved.

What does it mean for you?

Performance matters

In today's world leaders are looking to empower people, who in turn are expected to take on responsibility at a much earlier stage of their careers. It could well be argued that the essential glue that makes all of this hang together is to have competent and committed people working in organisations.

Most modern performance management systems give equal weight to 'what' people achieve and 'how' they do it. Previously a salesman who always exceeded his sales targets but, in the process, upset everyone in the admin department, and was not a team player, may well have succeeded in his career. The chances are he would have been promoted, and continued with his bad behaviour, but now with the addition of power which would have made him even more dangerous to the organisation.

In fact how you develop people to reach their potential depends very much on the 'what' and 'how' of performance.

The 'what' refers to the objectives set at the beginning of the year, and in order for these to be effective they need to be SMART:

- **Specific but Stretching** – this leads to higher performance rather than a vague general goal, so that employees actually understand what is required of them.

- **Measurable** – there should be the ability to quantitatively measure the outcome.

- **Aligned and Achievable** – something agreed between employee and boss that is aligned with organisation's objectives.

- **Realistic** – that performance tasks can be completed in a given time, taking into account both resources and workload.

- **Timebound** – there always needs to be a clear date for completion.

The 'how' is the competencies of the organisation – the skills, abilities and knowledge that matter in the organisation. Competencies are enduring traits or characteristics that help determine job performance.

Let's take two people in an organisation and look to how we would develop them further.

Marty the salesman

Marty is a pretty driven guy, he is determined that by the time he is 30 he will have been promoted to sales controller level, and by 35 have made sales director. He has a good educational background, and is also quick to learn. Every target he has been given he has beaten and he is constantly asking for more. Unfortunately, he achieves his results at the expense of his internal relationships. The customers love him, as he really does treat them as special; however, he applies none of this charm internally. He is seen as having the potential to go far, but needs to do something about his people skills.

Lee the brand manager

Lee has been impressing people every since her graduate interviews. She has great communication skills, somehow making everyone feel a part of what she is doing. She takes time out to understand what people need and finds a way of building their requirements into whatever she is doing. Everyone feels she has the potential to go right to the top, the only drawback is that she has not achieved the results that were expected of her. Her brands have just not achieved budgeted performance, and perhaps she has been too 'nice' and accommodating when she actually needed to be a bit more driving in her demands.

This is a fairly typical dilemma that a leader might have to sort out, for whereas Marty is great at the 'what', and Lee is great at the 'how', between them you have one complete high-performing person.

To make this more easily understood, make use of this 'what'/'how' matrix shown in Figure 5.1.

Marty would fall into the Learning the 'how' box, and as such the leader would have to coach him on his deficient

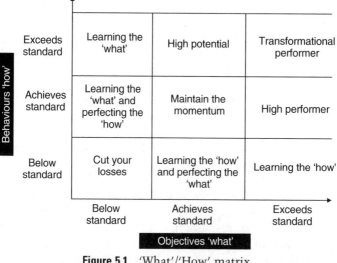

Behaviours 'how'		Objectives 'what'	
	Below standard	**Achieves standard**	**Exceeds standard**
Exceeds standard	Learning the 'what'	High potential	Transformational performer
Achieves standard	Learning the 'what' and perfecting the 'how'	Maintain the momentum	High performer
Below standard	Cut your losses	Learning the 'how' and perfecting the 'what'	Learning the 'how'

Figure 5.1 'What'/'How' matrix

people skills. Lee would need help on her objectives, to understand why she hasn't achieved her budget. She would be in the Learning the 'what' box.

When you look at the matrix, it becomes clear that in any organisation you need a small group of transformational performers who can drive overall performance to new levels, but to do so you also need the majority of people to maintain the momentum – keeping the ship running.

As good leaders identify talented staff and provide them with 'deep learning' so that they can realise their potential, it is no surprise that learning occupies the majority of the boxes on the matrix.

Deep learning

In coaching employees to reach their full potential, it is important to note where people typically learn what they need to know. All too often when people have a gap in their competencies they are simply put on a training course. So, for example, Lee's manager may well feel she lacks assertiveness: so put her on a course and the problem goes away! She does the course, comes back with a few new ideas, but her performance does not improve.

For training at best only provides skills and knowledge. If that is all that is lacking, then the problem will be solved. However, in many cases, people have the skills but for some reason they are unable to use them effectively. So often the most effective way forward is to understand the roots of the person's problem, which can only come by having leaders who show empathy for their staff, and take the time to coach them. Take the case of Lee. Further discussion and understanding of that person would identify that Lee comes from a fairly traditional Chinese family with considerable respect for others and particularly those in authority. Lee does not have an assertiveness problem; she just needs to be coached in how to behave in a western-style organisational context.

Over 80% of all learning that takes place in organisation is informal, so a good leader will ensure a 'deep learning' experience for all staff includes:

- work assignments;

- job rotation;

- career planning;

- coaching and mentoring;

- eLearning;

- projects;

- role modelling;

- feedback.

Summary

Organisations thrive through having committed and competent people doing responsible and rewarding jobs. All it takes to get to this situation is to understand what you want to do – objectives and competencies. Find out where the gaps lie by making use of the performance matrix. Then use empathy, creativity and common sense to develop the best in your people.

6

Focusing on Results: The Strategy of Themistocles

What happened?

The leader

Themistocles (pronounced 'Them-isto-clees') had the foresight to persuade the Athenians that their salvation against the Persians lay in a powerful fleet. On his recommendation in 483 BC the Athenian assembly voted to devote the profits from a newly discovered vein of silver at the state mines to the construction of 200 warships. As the historian Herodotus remarked, this decision 'saved Greece by forcing Athens to become a maritime power'.

The historical setting

The Persian invasions of Greece occurred in 490 BC and 480–479 BC. Their unexpected, apparently miraculous repulse became the 'great event' in Greek history, which portrayed the war as the defeat of an overwhelming barbarian host content to live under a despotic king. Actual events were not quite so simple: many Greeks fought alongside the Persian invaders, while others openly sympathised.

Behind the heroic confrontation lay a desire on the part of King Darius I of Persia to consolidate his frontiers. As in distant India, he wanted in the far west to secure the borders of his enormous realm, which for the first time had brought the whole of West Asia and Egypt under a single ruler's control. It was the Ionian revolt of 499–494 BC that gave Darius reason for concern in the west. The Athenians and the Eretrians had sent naval aid to their cousins, the Greeks living in Ionia, the present-day Aegean coastline of Turkey. After the Ionian revolt was crushed by the Persians, Darius sent an expeditionary force to punish Eretria, a city-state on the island of Euboea, and Athens. Eretria was taken through treachery and its population deported as slaves, but at the battle of Marathon, in 490 BC, the Persians were driven back to their ships by the Athenians. Following this partial success Darius decided a more coordinated attack was required to settle the troublesome European frontier, but he died in 486 BC before preparations were complete. Against this renewed threat Themistocles, the leader of the democratic party at Athens, was the moving spirit behind the build-up of Greek resistance. That the Greeks now faced a determined foe in Darius' son, Xerxes, there could be little doubt, for the forces he personally led into Europe in 480 BC comprised an army of 400,000 men and a navy of 800 ships.

Within months the Persians had overrun northern and central Greece and had reached Athens. On Themistocles' recommendation, the bulk of the Athenian population was evacuated to the nearby island of Salamis. He argued that the advice received from the oracle at Delphi about the Athenians putting their trust in 'a wooden wall' referred to the newly built ships and not the improvised defences of the Acropolis. In early September Xerxes occupied Athens, slaying its stubborn defenders after breaking down the Acropolis' wooden gates. In the sub-

The Athenian statesman Themistocles was the architect of Greek naval supremacy, a critical factor in the defence of Greece against the Persians. Few campaigns have ever depended more upon the intelligence and resolve of a single man like Themistocles.

sequent naval action, however, the Greeks decisively defeated the Persians in the narrow waters of Salamis.

Themistocles' behaviour

According to Thucydides, a later Greek historian than Herodotus, Themistocles 'was a man who displayed an unmistakable natural genius. Without studying a subject in advance, but using simply the intelligence that was his by nature, he had the power to reach the right conclusion in matters that have to be settled on the spur of the moment and do not admit long discussion'. This rare ability allowed him to found the Athenian navy and effectively deploy it against the invading Persians.

Not that events were quite as simple as the Persian defeat seemed to the Greeks at the time. First, Themistocles had to persuade the Athenian assembly that 'a wooden wall' was none other than the ships it had recently built. Then he had to ensure that these vessels were not used by the Athenians to abandon Greece and move somewhere else in the Mediterranean. Having got most of the Athenian population safely to the island of Salamis, Themistocles' next concern was making sure a naval engagement actually took place, since there was a proposal to abandon the Athenians on Salamis and withdraw the combined Greek fleet to the Isthmus, the neck of land which joins the Peloponnese to the rest of Greece.

It was Themistocles who brought on the naval action by sending a message to the Persians, warning them of a possible withdrawal southwards. Their blockade forced the Greeks to fight in the narrow waters around Salamis, where the greater number of Persian ships conferred no advantage. The Persians in fact lost most of their fleet, and an anxious Xerxes returned hastily to West Asia in case news of this naval reverse encouraged rebellion among subject peoples there. Behind in Greece he left his brother-in-law Mardonius with 300,000 men to continue the campaign on land.

Outcomes

The naval victory at Salamis was the beginning of the removal of the threat of Persian domination over Greece. In the summer of 479 BC at the battle of Plataea in central Greece the army left under Mardonius' command was routed and Mardonius killed. Afterwards the Greek fleet sailed to Ionia and inflicted another defeat on the Persians there.

In subsequent campaigns against Persia it was the Athenians who took the lead, with the result that over time the defensive league they led turned into a maritime empire which embraced most of the Aegean islands and its long coastline. Themistocles did not live to see this unsought outcome of his strategy. His own political position had been weakened by the recall of banished opponents on the eve of the Persian invasion. They were soon strong enough to banish him in turn from Athens.

It is somewhat ironic that the single-minded victor of Salamis should have spent his final years living under Persian rule. Forced to flee from Greece, he was well received by King Artaxerxes I of Persia, who gave him 200 talents, that amount being the price set by the Persians on his head. Themistocles died in 462 BC as the governor of a city in Asia Minor – it was rumoured from a draught of poison that he had taken in order to avoid helping the Persians against the Athenians, who were then engaged in expanding their naval league.

Why does it matter?

The culture of targets

'We Athenians have a city so long as we have our ships', Themistocles said prior to the naval engagement at Salamis. For he alone saw that a battle there, in the confined waters around the island, offered the only hope of a Greek victory over the much larger Persian fleet. Numbers would not count in such an engagement. A mixture of foresight and guile, therefore, saw Themistocles through this crisis and broke the Persian king's navy as well as his nerve. Themistocles' strategy had worked.

The target Themistocles set for himself was exceeded beyond all expectations. How many of us in our target-obsessed world can hope to match him? There cannot be many people in the workforce today who do not have their progress and performance measured by how well they have met their individual or collective targets. If we are fortunate, we may have had some input into the discussion that produced these measures for us, although in a depressingly large number of cases they are determined, calculated and imposed from somewhere else. Such target-driven thinking has been a widespread and pervasive part of corporate management for a long time, sometimes hidden beneath the apparent adoption of a more 'participative' or flexible management style, but with a tendency to reinvent itself in different guises and with different labels. In recent years, of course, management in the public sector has adopted the target-setting mentality with the enthusiasm of a new convert: targets to measure waiting times in NHS hospitals, targets for schools to improve their test and examination results year on year, targets for train companies to meet in relation to punctuality. The list goes on.

In many settings performance measurement impacts on individual workers in very concrete ways, through appraisal schemes which may determine salary increments, bonuses or promotions, for example. But does this necessarily help the organisation in the long run. W. Edwards Deming, a 'quality guru' from an earlier era in management thinking, explained perceptively some 50 years ago that, 'People with targets and jobs dependent upon meeting them will probably meet the targets, even if they have to destroy the enterprise to do it'.

We now find commentators expressing grave concern at the unexpected negative effects of target setting on public sector organisations, a feeling that also finds expression in recent press articles about the manipulation of statistics by hospitals and schools to achieve their targets. The annual budget provides, in a wide range of organisations, the most powerful, and easily quantifiable, measure of performance when broken down to efficiency targets at departmental or branch level but, again, there are serious worries about the undesirable effects this can produce, including the games which managers play in response to the process, well summarised in some ironic advice in a recent article, entitled 'Escape from the budget straitjacket' by Simon Caulkiny in *Management Today*.

To make the target easier, underestimate potential sales and overestimate spend.

Use it or lose it – never underspend your budget otherwise it will be reduced next year.

Never give the real picture . . . at some stage you'll need to find excuses for variances, so the less transparency the better.

That applies to other teams too – you're competing for the same resources, so never give away your best tricks.

Perhaps this sounds familiar? The most dangerous result of an internal fixation on targets and results of this type lies in the way that the whole procedure tends to fix people's attention on internal reviews and appraisals, often at the expense of realising the ways in which the external market is changing or how competitors are introducing new products or services.

'If it ain't broke . . .'

The leadership style of Themistocles illustrates a very different way of thinking about results and one that is much more in tune with modern thinking. What organisations seem to be seeking today is an approach which creates a results-orientated business without the rigid adherence to the measurement of performance which can stultify the internal mechanisms of the business and distract people from being outward-looking and inventive. Logic dictates that the model for such organisations to aim for needs to come from its leaders.

Successful leaders are focused on results. They know what they want to achieve and are willing to take calculated risks to get there. They are restless, unwilling to accept the status quo, and are always seeking improvements to the ways things are done. They rely on their intuition and trust their own judgement in finding a route to their targets; a characteristic very well exemplified in Thucydides' evaluation of Themistocles – 'using simply the intelligence that was his by nature, he had the power to reach the right conclusion in matters that have to be settled on the spur of the moment and do not admit long discussion'. His highly imaginative use of resources is a further feature of the successful 'results-orientated' leader.

How might you know if you are working for a leader with a focus on results? When a change in direction or procedure is proposed at a meeting try responding with 'If it ain't broke, don't fix it'. If your career ends soon afterwards there is a strong likelihood that your boss is such a person. (On the other hand if your response is applauded you are quite likely to end up in the same situation anyway as the business decays away.) Leaders with a focus on results will be seeking to position the organisation for the future, not the present, and will be constantly changing the way things are done.

They are also likely to be passionate about the quality of their products, sometimes to the point of obsessiveness. Sochiro Honda, founder of the Japanese Honda corporation, was, for instance, so intolerant of poor quality that he could, on occasions, be physically violent towards underperforming staff. A colleague, Saturo Otsuki, who later became a president of Honda recalled in his memoir *Good Mileage* that:

When he got mad, he blindly reached for anything lying around, and started throwing whatever was in reach randomly at people; it was dangerous! The desks in our office were covered with dents and scratches from the wrenches and hammers that the boss threw around.

Strategy

Thinking about results and targets inevitably brings us to the subject of strategy. Strategic planning is intended to help organisations predict the future, and secure and control their own position within it and, as such, it has become something of a totem for management. In the 1960s it was still a fairly simple process but ever more elaborate models and theories were developed in the 1970s and 1980s. In this period, for instance, corporations began to create separate 'planning departments', staffed by expert management analysts and strategists, the high priests and priestesses of the cult. The publication of Michael Porter's *Competitive Strategy* in 1980 took the science of strategy to even higher levels.

In the 1980s, however, strategic planning received something of a shock when Japanese car companies suddenly made massive inroads into the US markets, competing on cost and quality despite the fact that the American car industry had been strategically planning so assiduously in the years leading up to the emergence of this challenge. What made it harder to explain was the fact that the Japanese made such little use of the elaborate strategic-planning models so beloved of business schools and consultancies! Strategic planning had in actual fact become a numbers game and had effectively replaced strategic thinking. The numbers should have been the outcome of planning, not the plan itself. Jack Welch, then CEO of General Electric, took a lead in dismantling the elaborate architecture of strategic planning in that corporation, and others soon followed suit. More recently, Welch has reflected on the planning process from his experiences at General Electric and elsewhere in his book, *Winning*:

Forget the arduous, intellectualized number crunching and data grinding that gurus say you have to go through to get strategy right. Forget the scenario planning, year-long studies, and hundred plus page reports. In real life, strategy is actually very straightforward. You pick a general direction and implement like hell.

How well Themistocles would have understood this sentiment. For him the preservation of a free Greece, expressed most of all in democratic government, was the only direction worth taking, and he used every means to keep the Athenians on course. And he splendidly achieved this aim.

What does it mean for you?

A focus on producing outstanding results by maximising the impact of the available resources, the notion that 'less is more', lies at the heart of business success. In practical terms thinking in this manner means taking actions that truly make a difference to performance.

The case study relates to a traditional advertising agency, JJB&A, which is struggling to come to terms with today's advertising market. JJB&A's main revenue source had always been advertising, dealing with big companies with big budgets, lavish entertainment accounts and trips to exotic locations in order to shoot emotional hard-sell videos showing beautiful people experiencing life to the full. Then along came the internet, followed by technological advances in the home with downloads on demand, pausing live TV, skipping the ads, and life as JJB&A knew it had really ended.

After revenues dropped by 40% the CEO took the drastic action of getting the top 30 movers and shakers from across the organisation to his English estate, Wilton Grange. He called in two facilitators from G-Force Consultants, a group well known for their ability to focus top teams on the three to five key areas that would make a difference.

Winston Langton, the CEO, stood up in front of the assembled people and said: 'We are a small proud organisation that has succeeded in a highly competitive market for the last 25 years. We are gathered here today to make sure we survive and thrive for another 25 years. We are here to briefly look back on the past, spend quality time looking at the new age we live in, and then we are going to agree on our vision for the future, the three to five things we must get right if we are going to have to win over the next two years. Finally we are going to agree the game plan that we will all follow when we head back after the workshop'.

Winston introduced Laura and Ian, the two facilitators, and then the meeting kicked off with introductions and a sharing of expectations. The room had been stripped down to chairs, beanbags and empty walls.

While Ian covered one of the walls with a 4 by 12 foot drop of white paper, Laura explained that the group were going to write the history of the business in 60 minutes. The history would cover all the main events, including the star products, where revenues had been generated from, where losses had been made, when key people joined and left, and the problems that they had overcome. The challenge was to make the history as colourful as possible and to help this the group was given coloured pens, coloured paper, paper, scissors and shading pastel chalks. They had old magazines that they could cut from and for the rest they could use their own ingenuity and animal cunning.

The history map was soon filled with many proud moments, and, when linked to some of the cock-ups, it started to paint a very realistic picture of where the business came from and how it had ended up in the mess it was now in.

Now the focus turned to the environment in which they operated: what were the factors, trends and forces at work in the market and what was the unique web of relationships?

The library at Wilton Grange was now starting to take on a new vibrancy, with the very colourful flip charts starting to bring its wood-panelled walls to life. The

Figure 6.1 History map

Figure 6.2 Business Environment map

group commented over lunch that they couldn't believe they had covered so much ground in only half a day. They were all bursting with ideas for the future, but the facilitators had done well to keep them focused on the present.

The after-lunch session had to be a lively one, and it was that and more. The facilitators explained that the time was two years into the future and JJB&A had made it to the front cover of *Marketing Week*. What were the major accomplishments that had come to the attention of the journalists of *Marketing Week*? Now the group was broken into three teams of 10, and each given the task of explaining what had happened. The CEO was given another task to prepare his acceptance speech that he would deliver at the annual marketing awards dinner, and as part of his preparation he was to visit each of the teams and check out their thinking.

The teams completed their cover-story vision within the 60 minutes, and were then allowed another 60 minutes to do a real 'ad agency' type presentation to the 'press', where they underwent a typical tabloid grilling.

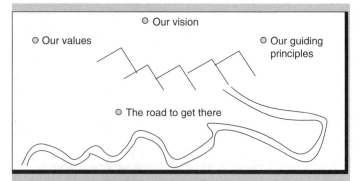

Figure 6.3 The road to the vision

Now it was time to capture the aspirations of the cover stories and turn them into the JJB&R vision for the future.

With so many creative people and word-smiths in the room it did not take long before the vision-wall map was finalised, capturing the visions, values and guiding principles, plus the road that needed to be taken in order to get there.

The day ended on a high note with each team presenting their vision and Winston Langton delivering his acceptance speech. At this stage champagne had found its way into the room, and in an atmosphere redolent of the annual 'Oscars' awards evening the energy and noise levels of the group were raised to an even higher level.

The next day started with validating the vision. It had survived the wine and port of the previous evening and the group was even more fired up to get on with constructing a critical game plan.

The first part of this process was to take the vision and road maps and capture the three key questions that

JJB&R needed to ask itself. To do this each team was given 20 minutes to come up with its three questions, then the facilitators took them through a voting exercise where they all agreed on the three burning questions that needed answering.

As Joel Barker had said, 'Vision without action is a dream. Action without vision is simply passing the time. Action with vision is making a positive difference'. So the last stage of the workshop was to convert the vision via the three questions into a game plan.

The game plan broke down the actions that would need to be taken in order to make the changes necessary to achieve the vision.

What we have described above in the case study is a very interactive and highly visual workshop running over a two- to three-day period.

If the facilitators have done their job well, then there will be great commitment to getting started and turning the dream into a reality. What happens next is critical, as the whole organisation needs to be focused on the same set of results – in other words to buy into the game plan.

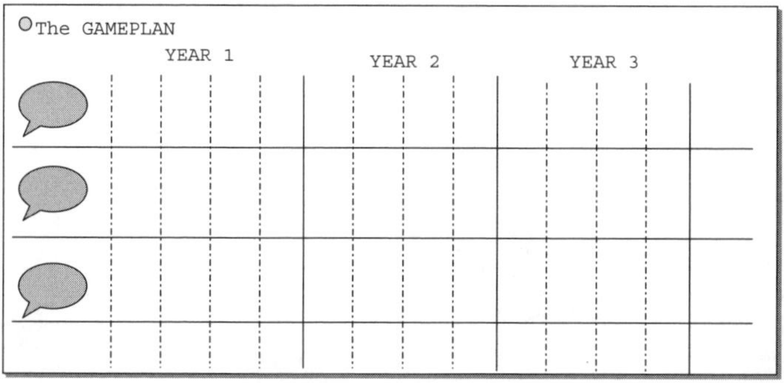

Figure 6.4   Five bold steps

So the first job of the 30 'vision warriors' is to convince the rest of the organisation of the value of their plan for the future.

To sum up, the key learning points from this case study are simple. If you don't want to overburden your organisation with initiative after initiative, you do need to stand back and take stock of where you really are. And avoid the over-engineered, hugely demanding strategic planning process, and find easier ways to focus people on what matters for their organisation. Then to repeat the words of Jack Welch, having found your direction, 'implement like hell'.

7

Integrity: The Political Supremacy of Pericles

What happened?

The leader

In the judgement of the historian Thucydides (pronounced 'Thu-sid-idees'), Athens' greatest leader was Pericles (pronounced 'Perry-clees'). 'During the whole period of peace-time', he wrote, 'when Pericles was the head of affairs the state was wisely and firmly guided, and it was under him that Athens was at her greatest. And when the war against Sparta broke out, he alone estimated what the power of Athens was. He survived the outbreak of hostilities for two years and six months, and after his death his foresight with regard to the war became more evident. For Pericles said that Athens would be victorious if she bided her time and took care of her navy, if she avoided trying to add to her empire, and if she did nothing to risk the safety of the city itself. But his successors did the exact opposite, and in matters which apparently had no connection with the war personal ambition and profit led to policies which were bad for the Athenians and for their allies'.

The historical setting

Outlined by Thucydides here is the classical view of Pericles' effectiveness as a leader, but even the admiring historian admits that because Pericles turned Athens into such a strong imperial power he made conflict with Sparta inevitable. It was the growth of Athenian influence in Greece which 'frightened the Spartans and forced them to war'.

Yet the historical circumstances of Pericles' long political supremacy were more complicated than the quotation from Thucydides suggests. Shortly after the banishment of the aristocratic leader Cimon in 461 BC, Pericles became the leader of the democratic party and asserted the right of the citizen assembly to determine how Athens was run. Soon no question seemed too important and very few too trivial to be exempt from popular decision, either in a council chosen each year by lot, or in the law courts whose juries were again chosen by lot, or in the assembly of citizens itself. Executive power, civil as well as military, had already moved towards a body of 10 generals, who were usually members of leading Athenian families, like Pericles' own. But there was nothing to prevent any citizen becoming a general, for even the most aristocratic politician still had to be elected annually and was rigorously judged on his performance by the people as a whole. Pericles alone was elected to an almost continuous generalship from 455 BC onwards.

During this extended period of office Pericles presided over the conversion into an Athenian empire of the defensive league established to counter Persian interference in the Aegean Sea, in part a consequence of the great naval victory which Themistocles had achieved in 480 BC at Salamis. But Pericles also witnessed the loss of an expedition of 200 ships sent to assist the rebellious Egyptians against the Persians. He is perhaps best remembered for the rebuilding of the temples on the Acropolis, including

The Athenian leader Pericles, who was elected to an almost continuous generalship from 455 BC onwards. But his popularity was not enough to save him from the payment of a fine in 429 BC, when his political enemies accused him of misusing public finds.

the goddess Athena's great temple, the Parthenon, the ownership of whose great marble frieze is now a matter of dispute between the United Kingdom and Greece. Finally, Pericles guided Athens through a conflict with Sparta which ended in 445 BC with a 30 years' peace.

Although this peace settlement meant that Sparta recognised the existence of an Athenian empire, a grave danger in the division of the Greek world into two mutually suspicious blocs was political instability in either Sparta or Athens.

Pericles' behaviour

Because he really appreciated this danger, Pericles did his utmost to minimise friction. And the peace Pericles sought to maintain lasted down until 431 BC, when the Peloponnesian War began. His ability to steer the Athenians away from conflict with Sparta and its allies for so long was quite remarkable, considering how he needed to manage popular opinion in order to remain in office year on year. It has to be said that Pericles kept himself very well informed about Spartan affairs. But his close friendship with King Archidamus of Sparta was to cause him serious embarrassment when at last war came. Archidamus led the attack on Athens, and Pericles was afraid that his friend would bypass his own fields while destroying those of other Athenians. In order to thwart the Spartans, whose army was still second to none, he had persuaded the Athenians to abandon their homes in the countryside and seek refuge within the city's fortifications, which reached down to a harbour where the fleet lay anchored. From there food from abroad could be brought in to feed the refugee population. So as to deflect criticism, Pericles was forced to make a public statement. He admitted his friendship with Archidamus but denied that it was ever made to harm Athens. Then he turned over his private property to the state, asking that no suspicion should fall on him because of it.

But the outbreak of plague in 430 BC, within the crowded city, momentarily broke Athenian morale, and Pericles was driven from office after being convicted and heavily fined. As he had been in office without interruption for many years, bolstered by his prestige and a reputation for honesty, Pericles must have had no small task in accounting for the use of public funds during this long period of time. The jury was obviously not fully convinced of Pericles' guilt, for the crime of embezzlement carried the death penalty. Within a year he was elected again as a general, but he too had contracted the plague and died shortly afterwards.

Outcomes

After the death of Pericles no leader or party was able to control Athens, as different groups held sway on different occasions. Perhaps for the first time the Athenians experienced the problems inherent in truly democratic rule in time of war. Pericles' strategy of rejecting battle on land and abandoning the countryside to Spartan devastation was forgotten, as was his advice to avoid imperial expansion when in 415–413 BC an even greater expedition than the Egyptian one was lost in Sicily. Yet Athens might still have resisted Sparta had it not been for internal trouble. There were two short periods of revolution in 411 and 404 BC. Democratic sentiment was not permanently destroyed, although the general sense of unease weakened Athens to the point of defeat. What was left of the empire was liquidated on the Athenian surrender in 404 BC, the city's fortifications were pulled down, and a ban imposed on possessing a fleet.

The Peloponnesian War of 431–404 BC was like no other in ancient Greece. Its unprecedented length was actually due to the strengths and weaknesses of each side: Sparta was all-powerful on land, while Athens ruled the waves. Each side tried to find ways out of the stalemate but, as Pericles understood, stalemate meant an Athenian victory, for Athens had only to survive, Sparta had to win if it was to keep its land-based supremacy intact. Once

Sparta agreed to give the Persians a free hand with the Greek cities of Asia Minor in return for money to develop a fleet capable of fighting the Athenians, the end of the struggle was in sight. A brief tyranny ruled in Athens after its surrender, until in 403 BC the Athenian democracy was restored. Power politics dictated this gesture of friendship, for Sparta wished to use Athens as a check on the growing power of Thebes in central Greece. The end of Spartan domination indeed was to be the work of two Theban generals, Epaminondas and Pelopidas, who in 371 BC at the battle of Leuctra together defeated the Spartans and their allies.

Why does it matter?

Integrity and the exercise of power

The power of Pericles was not uncontested during the period of his supremacy, but it was his friends who usually fell foul of his political enemies. His close friend, the philosopher Anaxagoras, had to hastily leave Athens before being charged with impiety for asserting that the sun was a molten rock the size of the Peloponnese. For, as Pericles' admirer the historian Thucydides put it, 'Athens, though still in name a democracy, was in fact ruled by her first citizen'.

Yet even though there is no doubt that the Athenians believed wholeheartedly in democracy, neither in the legislative nor judicial sphere did they entirely trust individuals. Ostracism, banishment for a decade, was the weapon that the Athenians used against overbearing leaders and would-be tyrants. That Pericles never suffered this harsh political fate says something about his leadership – his acumen, his sensitivity and his timing. As the fine imposed on him in 429 BC shows, the Athenians were never gentle when it came to politics, which in their view was the chief reason for living in a city-state. Forty days a year the citizen assembly met to determine policy in Athens and at these meetings every citizen was guaranteed the right to speak freely and to vote as he wished. The behaviour of all the leaders they elected to office was, therefore, under almost constant public scrutiny.

To use power responsibly is perhaps the greatest challenge of leadership. For some people, power is a highly desirable aim in itself, and the exercise of power can be a source of great satisfaction for some leaders. An ability to identify and understand the sources of power, and appreciate the likely effects of its application are significant capabilities for a leader. Most theoretical models draw a distinction between those sources of power which are derived from the position that the leader holds in an organisation, and those which are related more to the leader's personal skills, attributes and knowledge. 'Position power' has as its basis the authority accompanying the role and status that the individual has; as well as the potential this gives the leader to coerce by threat or fear; or to reward through praise, recognition, pay, privileges or increased responsibility.

Identifying the sources of 'personal power' demands a more subtle analysis, for here one is drawn into an examination of the personal qualities of leaders and their influence on the respect which other people have for them or the esteem in which they are held. It was obviously 'personal power' which kept Pericles so long in office. Although successful leadership like his is partly determined by skills and behaviour which can be learnt and developed, there remains a feeling that certain innate personal qualities play an equally important role too. The extent to which an individual's personal qualities will stand up to the test of leadership is difficult to predict: as the Roman historian Tacitus notably said of the short-lived emperor Galba, 'Nobody doubted his capacity to rule until he became emperor'.

Of the personal qualities or characteristics which people in an organisation will highlight as being important in their leaders, integrity is frequently mentioned, but often in a somewhat imprecise way. As Thomas Teal writes in *The Human Side of Management*:

Another characteristic of great managers is integrity. All managers believe they behave with integrity, but in practice, many have trouble with the concept. Some think integrity is the same thing as secretiveness or blind loyalty. Others seem to believe it means consistency, even in a bad cause. Some confuse it with discretion and some with the opposite quality – bluntness – or with simply not telling lies.

For Teal though, genuine integrity is difficult to define, but 'it comes very close to what we used to call honour'. With a similar feel, *The Oxford English Dictionary* defines integrity as, 'soundness of moral principle; the character of uncorrupted virtue; uprightness, honesty, sincerity'. What we admire about a leader such as Pericles is that in using his power consistently for the public good he was truthful, ethical and principled in his behaviour. The telling description of the interrelationship of power and integrity, which figures in an article by Suresh Srivastra and David Cooperrider entitled 'The urgency for executive integrity', might well be applied to Pericles when they write:

Executive mind is impotent without power, power is dangerous without vision, and neither is lasting or significant in any broad human sense without the force of integrity.

Honesty

In their book *The Leadership Challenge*, James Kouzes and Barry Posner summarise the results of a survey they have repeated with managers in many different countries over a period of more than 20 years. The survey asks managers to identify the features they most look for and admire in their leaders. The results have varied from survey to survey and only four characteristics have consistently been recorded by more than 50% of the respondents. The qualities highlighted are that people want leaders who are honest, forward-looking, competent and inspiring. Honesty has always recorded the highest percentage score, and has increased from 83% to 88% from 1987 to 2002. The surveys also highlight some intriguing cultural comparisons, with honesty as a leadership quality being most highly valued in Australia, with a 93% rating, while being rated at a significantly lower level in Japan and Singapore (67% and 65%, respectively). James Kouzes and Barry Posner further examine the reasons for honesty being accorded such importance and ask how respondents measured the presence of this quality in their leaders.

Just how do constituents measure a characteristic as subjective as honesty? In our discussions with respondents, we learned that a leader's *behaviour* provided the evidence. Regardless of what leaders say about their own integrity, people want to be shown, they observe the behaviour.

In this, and other analyses, employees seem to see honesty as inextricably linked to integrity, and to what they often refer to as 'character'. People look for leaders who consistently behave in a way that reflects their stated values and standards: this is what they conceive of as being an 'ethical' leader. After the first Gulf War in 1992, General Norman Schwarzkopf, commander of the American ground forces, gained public notoriety for his high-profile leadership of the campaign. Questioned subsequently about his approach to leadership, he identified 10 golden rules, several of which relate centrally to this notion of being honest with the people in the organisation. He avows, for example, that leaders must 'Let people know where they stand', and that they must 'Do what's right – the truth of the matter is that you always know the right thing to do. The hard part is doing it'. Perhaps more telling, however, particularly given his role at that time, is his injunction that a leader should 'Never lie. Ever'. It was something that Pericles was never accused of doing. That he moved so fast in 431 BC to assure the Athenians that his friendship with King Archidamus of Sparta was never made to cause them any harm reveals the value he personally placed on an honest reputation.

Ethical leadership

In the July 2005 edition of *Management Today*, Richard Reeves summarises the results of a survey, entitled 'Ethics at work' – carried out by the Institute for Business Ethics and *Management Today*. Encouragingly, 64% of those surveyed agreed that their manager set them a good example of ethical business behaviour, yet only 43% thought that their organisation was always honest in its business practices. The survey showed, too, that employees' attitudes to honesty, and their perception of the impact of unethical or dishonest behaviour, varied depending on the seniority of the staff member concerned. As the authors remarked:

The power wielded by CEOs, their capacity to make or ruin lives, means they have a disproportionate ethical responsibility. Cooking the books or 'borrowing' from the pension fund is light years from the question of whether Jim is right to claim an extra £1.50 on his taxi fare.

Inevitably there are occasions when there is a tension between a business's obligations to be ethical and its aim to be financially successful. It has been said that competition brings out the best in products and the worst in people. But it is the prime responsibility of leaders to set the standards for their organisations. Recent corporate scandals, such as those affecting Enron and WorldCom, will have reinforced the impression among some that in reality there is little place for genuinely ethical behaviour in a typically competitive private sector business. Little wonder that the study of business ethics is one of the fastest growing fields of study in management education. In *Complete Leadership*, Susan Bloch and Philip Whiteley contrast the ideals of trust and integrity in the business world with the public perception of the business leader, when they write:

It's very difficult to shake from the Western psyche the image of the successful business leader as a buccaneer; a ruthless warrior . . . too many leaders go collecting enemies, engaging in gratuitous office politics, imagining that putting someone down increases their power.

Nevertheless, a strong business case can be made for senior managers leading their organisations in a fundamentally ethical manner. This is reinforced by the 2001 Hay Group survey of entrepreneurs, which found that successful business pioneers scored much higher on issues of probity and ethics than the sample of corporate managers which also featured in the survey. It noted how:

Well over three-quarters of those interviewed (successful entrepreneurs) displayed high levels of integrity. This means they are prepared to stick to their principles, even when that might mean taking a financial loss.

Maintaining the public reputation of a business is, of course, a very significant concern for senior managers, just as it was for Pericles and his democratic political programme. Perhaps the most remarkable instance of sound corporate ethical behaviour in recent times was the way in which Johnson & Johnson responded in the 1980s to the crisis generated by the incidents of Tylenol poisoning of their products in the United States. The company immediately acknowledged the gravity of the situation, removed products from sale, and was scrupulously honest with the public – by providing news briefings at least once a day at the height of the crisis. Its factories and packaging plants were opened to media scrutiny and senior staff made themselves available to speak to consumer groups in an attempt to maintain public confidence in their products. It should be noted that remedial action was initiated by a regional executive in Chicago, who later said that he dared to act on his own initiative because of the emphasis always placed by the company on care for its customers.

Such a crisis can quickly undo years of good public relations. Shell, for instance, had carefully constructed its image as a more considerate, thoughtful and environmentally sensitive oil company than its rivals over a number of years. It promoted an awareness of its social responsibility and was fashionably multicultural. Nevertheless, in 1995, its reputation suffered a series of body blows from which it took a long time to recover. Firstly, its plans to dispose of the massive Brent Spar oil rig by sinking it in the North Sea enraged environmental activists who successfully orchestrated a highly damaging media campaign. This, despite the fact that Shell's decision was probably the least environmentally damaging disposal option. Secondly, the corporation's involvement with a series of high-profile government scandals in Nigeria, which culminated in the execution of poet and opposition activist Ken Saro-Wiwa, highlighted some deeply questionable company policies in that part of the world. What seemed to be missing from Shell's response at the time was a clear, decisive and unambiguous voice from the top to explain the company's position and plot a course forward.

What does it mean for you?

On the 14 July 2005, the BBC Business News website carried the following story.

WorldCom's ex-boss gets 25 years

Former WorldCom boss Bernard Ebbers wept openly as he was sentenced to 25 years in jail for his part in the scandal that brought down the firm.

Mr Ebbers was found guilty of fraud and conspiracy in March, following revelations of an $11bn (£6.2bn) accounting fraud at WorldCom in 2002.

As the 63-year-old Ebbers was taken from court to begin his 25-year sentence, it was incredible to recall that in 1999 WorldCom had been one of the most profitable and fastest growing in the United States, and that President Bill Clinton had said of him, 'He is the symbol of 21st-century America and the embodiment of what I want for the future'.

Bernard Ebbers' working life had begun with jobs as a bouncer, a basketball coach and a milkman, before he set up a small chain of hotels. From this modest start, his business career blossomed through the creation of WorldCom, which expanded with astonishing speed through a series of take-overs which saw some 50 other small telecoms companies absorbed by WorldCom. In 1998 he purchased MCI, the second largest long-distance carrier in the United States in a $40 billion acquisition, which was the largest purchase in corporate history at the time. Not that everyone shared Wall Street's love of Ebbers: there were, even then, some commentators who felt his aggressive and autocratic leadership style would sow the seeds of future disaster.

Throughout his trail, Ebbers argued that he was unaware of the fraud being carried out; that as CEO he didn't really understand the details of the company accounts. Not surprisingly, the jury rejected these claims, holding him responsible for the biggest bankruptcy in corporate history, which left 2000 people jobless and shareholders with losses amounting to some $180 billion.

The Ebbers trial is, of course, just one of a series of high-profile legal cases relating to company fraud on a massive scale. Several of Ebbers' former senior colleagues are due in court soon, as are three of Enron's executives and the former chief of Tyco, Dennis Kozlowski, accused of extracting $600 million from the company.

The reaction of the US administration to these cases of corporate fraud and deception has been to strengthen the regulatory frameworks under which such corporations operate. Do you believe this will have an impact on other business leaders who might be tempted to break the law in pursuit of personal success? Just consider how remote they are from scrutiny in comparison with Pericles, who faced in the Citizen Assembly, a forest of eyes. Ancient expectations of openness, and especially in democratic Athens, meant that leaders were never out of the public gaze for a moment. No doubt Pericles took care to cultivate an acceptable image as a democratic statesman, but he remained the subject of an intense examination from his fellow citizens, whom he had to persuade directly in open debate. They heard what he had to say, listened to his political opponents' views, and then took a vote. The Athenians kept their leaders on a tight rein and could easily become suspicious of tendencies to arrogance, as happened to Themistocles after the naval victory he masterminded over the Persians at Salamis in 480 BC. He was banished, a fate Pericles never suffered. This is all rather different from today, when corporate statements in times of crisis are made, usually by a spokesperson, well away from the sanctuary of the CEO's office suite.

8

Taking Decisive Action: The Critical Decisions of Epaminondas

What happened?

The leader

Along with his fellow general Pelopidas, it was Epaminondas (pronounced 'Ee-pam-in-on-das') who was responsible for ending the Spartan hegemony of Greece at the battle of Leuctra in 371 BC. Their subsequent invasion of the Peloponnese freed Greece from the hated domination of Sparta, which had lasted since the defeat of Athens in 404 BC at the end of the Peloponnesian War.

The historical setting

In 404 BC people expected that Sparta would take over something of its defeated rival's greatness, as it certainly took over much of Athens' power. But, as the philosopher Aristotle sagely remarked, an exclusively military training produces brutes, not men who can control either themselves or other men and, in the end, even leads to military failure. The squalid story down to the battle of Leuctra shows how right he was.

Just as the Spartans used repression at home to hold down an enslaved peasantry, the helots, so abroad they relied on the force of arms to get their way. In 424 BC we know that a cull of 2000 of the strongest helots occurred at a time when the war against Athens was not going well for Sparta. Once Athens had surrendered, however, there seemed no reason why the use of tough tactics should not keep the other Greek city-states in a similar sub-servience. So, Spartan officials, backed by troops, issued orders to allies and enemies alike. The reluctance of Thebes to obey these orders without question annoyed the Spartans to such an extent that they seized its citadel without declaring war. This act shocked the Greek world, especially as it was accomplished by means of treachery.

The chief city in central Greece, Thebes, unlike Sparta, had developed itself politically and militarily since the Peloponnesian War. It now led there a league of city-states whose existence the Spartans could not accept. When asked if Thebes would relinquish this leadership and allow league members full independence, Epaminon-das answered with this question: 'Would Sparta allow the cities of the Peloponnese independence?' The defeat of the pro-Spartan faction in Thebes, and the expulsion of the garrison from its citadel in 378 BC, thus set the scene for a showdown between the Thebans and the Spartans.

Epaminondas' behaviour

Although some Thebans broke the safe conduct given to the Spartan-led garrison occupying the citadel and set

The monument set up at the battlefield of Chaeronea to commemorate the destruction of the Sacred Band in 338 BC. Prior to this overwhelming Macedonian victory, Theban generals like Epaminondas used this crack force to dominate Greece.

upon these hated enemies, there was little Epaminondas could do but save more than a few of them. When the Spartans had learned what had happened, they determined on revenge. But the decisive encounter only took place in central Greece at Leuctra in 371 BC, by which date Epaminondas and Pelopidas as annually elected generals had built up the strength of the Theban army. Whereas Pelopidas commanded the Sacred Band, a 300-strong body of shock troops, Epaminondas exercised overall control of the soldiers fielded by Thebes and its allies.

Prior to the encounter at Leuctra there was concern among Thebes' allies about the wisdom of fighting the unbeaten Spartans in a set-piece battle. Epaminondas, realising that only his Theban troops were really trustworthy, gave leave to any who did not wish to fight to withdraw, and a few allies did so. He also reported favourable oracles, which encouraged the troops. As they were outnumbered by the enemy, Epaminondas explained his tactics by this device. He caught a snake and likened it to their opponents. Then he crushed its head, which represented the Spartans. The troops immediately understood that they had only to beat the Spartans in order to sweep the field.

Epaminondas' skilful use of cavalry and infantry disconcerted the Spartan king Cleombrotus, who in adjusting the line of his own troops offered Pelopidas a perfect opportunity for a sudden attack. At the head of the Sacred Band he dashed forward and engaged the Spartans while they were still disordered. King Cleombrotus fell along with 400 of the 700 Spartan citizens present; the remainder eventually gave way and retreated, in good order, to their camp. Little action happened elsewhere on the battlefield, as neither the allies of Sparta nor Thebes had much of an appetite for fighting. After the surviving Spartans and their allies had limped home, the Athenians endeavoured to broker a peace. This did not appeal to the Thebans, who still distrusted Spartan intentions. In 370 BC, therefore, Epaminondas led an army into the Peloponnese in order to break Sparta once and for all. He did this by ravaging the Spartan countryside and freeing the helots in Messenia, an area from which the Spartans drew much of their wealth.

On their return to Thebes, however, Epaminondas and Pelopidas were charged with extending their generalships beyond the recognised time limit. Though they accepted the democratic validity of this restriction, the military advantage in a prolonged invasion of the Peloponnese had seemed simply too good an opportunity to ignore. At the trial Epaminondas admitted his guilt and accepted the death penalty prescribed, only asking that a record of his deeds be inscribed on his tombstone: 'That the Greeks should know how he had compelled the unwilling Thebans to ravage Sparta, which had been free from devastation for 500 years, that he had caused Messenia to be resettled after 230 years, that he had gathered the Arcadians together and organised them into a league, and that he had given the Greeks their autonomy'. Upon hearing this request, the jury threw out the case amid laughter.

Outcomes

Both Pelopidas and Epaminondas were later killed fighting Thebes' enemies. But neither their new tactics nor the political impetus they had given to Thebes through weakening Sparta were enough to create a lasting hegemony. Real power, real energy had shifted to other, larger states on Greece's borders, chief among them Macedon. While no single Greek city-state could reach such a height of military power that it could permanently dominate the others, King Philip of Macedon schemed and fought his way into central Greece to end this political stalemate. With the aid of his son Alexander, the future conqueror of Persia, he won in 338 BC the decisive battle of Chaeronea, where the Sacred Band of Thebes was annihilated.

Why does it matter?

Decision making in organisations

Epaminondas' liberation of Messenia in 370 BC destroyed the Spartan military system, which for centuries had relied on the agricultural labour of the enslaved helots there in order to free Spartans to concentrate on warfare. No longer could Sparta devote its time almost exclusively to training its men as soldiers. Sparta's later revival, limited though it was, remained a humiliation for what had once been the most effective military power in Greece, since it depended now on the hire of mercenaries. The Thebans had once and for all exploded the myth of Spartan invincibility on the battlefield.

Like Epaminondas, effective business leaders take critical decisions, their organisations act on them, and then move forward. At least that is what we expect them to do. Arguably it is in their different approaches to decision making that individual leaders most clearly and dramatically show their personal perceptions of their role and their preferred style of working. Furthermore, an examination of the ways in which decision making is pursued within an organisation will highlight the extent to which real leadership is seen as the prerogative of the chief executive or senior team, or as an attribute to be encouraged and nurtured throughout the management of the business.

Surely management is all about decision making? This is why managers spend so many hours analysing data and reports, and why meetings absorb so much of their diary time. The whole process is geared to analysing a problem or an issue, examining and weighing the different options before selecting the best solution and communicating that decision for action. But is that really the case? In some instances, meetings can seem to be a way of delaying any real decision while the need for ever more complex data and statistics can also serve as an excuse for further procrastination. As Paul Taffinder points out in *The New Leaders*,

The evidence around us shows that managers spend extraordinary amounts of time engaged in meetings of one kind or another, or in sorting data, analysing, examining options, coming to decisions. Or do they? In the real world meetings drag on without conclusion, data is passed up and down without decisions and without resulting action.

The skills of decision making

Decision making as a key leadership skill is perhaps most fully examined in a series of highly influential studies by Henry Mintzberg in the 1970s and beyond. Mintzberg, the professor of management at McGill University, repeatedly stresses the complexities of managers' jobs and seeks to define the characteristics of managerial work. Among the variety of tasks he sees facing managers decision making has a central position. In his influential 1973 book entitled *The Nature of Managerial Work*, Mintzberg develops a model which identifies a distinct set of what he calls 'decisional skills', functions to do with the systematic use of information and data to reach decisions. His analysis further subdivides this skill set into four decisional roles, which an effective manager must take on at appropriate moments. These are that of 'entrepreneur' (focusing on activities relating to adaptation and change), 'disturbance handler' (concerned with responding to externally imposed changes and pressures), 'negotiator' (balancing different interests) and 'resource allocator' (ensuring the optimum use of resources).

This last role actually highlights a key issue in decision making. Where within an organisation can decisions actually be taken and who is empowered, or authorised, to take decisions on which issues? The trend from hierarchical to flatter organisational structures, and the concern with 'de-layering', is, in part, a recognition that decisions need to be taken as close to the customers or clients as possible, by the deliverers of the service or product as far as is practicable. De-centralisation, the push to divide large and complex businesses into smaller operating units with considerable decision-making power and authority, is an expression of the same outlook. Within such organisational structures decision making is a key leadership competency and the emphasis is clearly on such skills being deployed by managers at a range of levels.

Of course, decisions always need to be taken at different levels within an organisation and the extent of their impact will be very different. Epaminondas' tactical decision at the battle of Leuctra to take decisive action when an opportunity presented itself is, of course, very different in character from his decision to prolong his generalship and invade Sparta, although both decisions illustrate his faith in his own intuition and his willingness to take calculated risks. His two decisions were based partly on good intelligence, but he was not content with simply responding to events since he sought to anticipate future challenges and position himself to meet them. Firstly, he beat the Spartans on the battlefield. Then, secondly, he destroyed their military system through his immediate invasion of the Peloponnese, Sparta's stronghold.

Decision making through consensus

In some organisational cultures it is seen as vital to achieve consensus among all the parties engaged in a problem-solving activity before a decision is finally agreed. Toyota, for example, promotes a particular approach to decision making that is extraordinarily thorough and exacting, with all possible options analysed in great depth and detail, with the aim of achieving both group consensus and management approval. Executives adopting the Toyota approach will acknowledge that the processes can be detailed, slow, cumbersome, time consuming and, consequently, expensive. However, in the company's judgement, the high quality of the decisions arrived at more than justifies the investment in time and effort. Very significantly, the company also believes that how you arrive at a decision is as important as the decision itself. The exhaustive and highly systematised Toyota approach to decision making might appear to be a straitjacket for their managers, and an undesirable constraint on creativity and decisiveness. But in practice the Toyota manuals and decision-making models are more flexible than they may at first appear, acknowledging that in different contexts decisions need to be taken in distinctively varied ways. Nevertheless, Toyota's apparent capacity to deliver a smooth and almost flawless implementation of new initiatives time after time owes much to the care and attention that is paid to an up-front planning process in which every detail is attended to. As Jeffrey K. Liker describes the process in *The Toyota Way*:

Thorough consideration in decision making includes five major elements:

1. Finding out what is really going on.

2. Understanding underlying causes that explain surface appearances – asking 'Why' five times.

3. Broadly considering alternative solutions and developing a detailed rationale for the preferred solution.

4. Building consensus within the team, including Toyota's employees and outside partners.

5. Using very efficient communication vehicles to do one through four, preferably one side of one sheet of paper.

Decisiveness

At the most senior level, decisions which are likely to affect the future of the business can be a daunting task. From the ancient world a further example of the way leaders sometimes arrive at a critical moment in their careers, where a choice between available options will determine the future, not just of themselves but of their organisations, has come down to us in the expression, 'crossing the Rubicon'. In this case it was Julius Caesar who, knowing that to cross this muddy river with his army in 49 BC would inevitably lead to civil war, faced the crunch decision with all its attendant risks. Once he ordered his troops across, they were illegally in Italy and became a direct threat to the Roman republic. As David Taylor says of decision making in *The Naked Leader*:

A decision, a true decision, means quite simply to close off all other options. And that is not an easy thing to do, because to move away from where you are at the moment ... may mean leaving something behind you.

Epaminondas' decision to invade Sparta, then, was of a similarly critical nature to his city-state, but the outcome illustrates a further aspect of the practice of decision making. Though he was successful, Epaminondas had exceeded the authority granted to him by his fellow citizens in Thebes, whose laws were unforgiving – he was to be executed. Modern business theory would claim to encourage the development of a 'no blame' culture, encouraging managers to take decisive action even if it carries risks with it, and standing by them even if things go wrong. In ancient Thebes, like other Greek city-states, it appears that even in a case where things had gone decidedly right (as they did as a result of Epaminondas' invasion decision), the sanctity of the rules and regulations could have led to his punishment. That Epaminondas was able to demonstrate the wrongheadedness of applying the rules so inflexibly is a strong indication that he had instinctively grasped another vital factor in effective decision making: he knew he had secured the support, the 'buy-in', of the Theban people in order to deliver the results that would arise from his decisive action.

What does it mean for you?

Playing hardball

In the April 2004 edition of the *Harvard Business Review*, George Stalk and Rob Lachenauer of the Boston Consulting Group created a considerable stir in business circles by writing an article entitled 'Hard ball', since it provocatively challenged much of the prevailing thinking on management purpose and practice. In their essay, they vigorously asserted the validity, indeed the necessity, of an approach to doing business that was uncompromisingly aggressive and ruthless, and focused single-mindedly on securing and maintaining competitive advantage over rivals. According to their analysis, the purpose of being in business was always to win, by destroying the competition and achieving market dominance through any means that were not actually illegal.

Stalk and Lachenauer examined the 'hardball' strategies of successful businesses, such as Dell, Southwest Airlines and Wal-Mart, companies that make no apologies for playing rough, and very explicitly contrasted their approaches with others which based their business practices on softer, more accommodating practices. The authors also claimed that management training and education must bear some of the blame for encouraging softball businesses which may be fortunate enough to survive, but don't really compete in the real world.

This may reflect the recent emphasis of management science, which itself has gone soft. Indeed, the discourse around a constellation of squishy issues – leadership, corporate culture, customer care, knowledge management, talent management, employee empowerment, and the like – has encouraged the making of softball players.

'Hardball' is indeed a challenge to those who have invested money or careers in supporting corporate developments based around such issues as those listed above! Some may interpret Stalk and Lachenauer's powerful account of a 'hardball' approach as little more than advocacy of unrestrained free enterprise, a mode of operation that is no longer either acceptable or effective. But perhaps their justification of this style of working is only a fundamental reaffirmation of what has always been done in the cause of good business – to win markets at the expense of others.

Stalk and Lachenauer offer five key elements in their hardball manifesto and suggest five basic strategies. These are summarised below:

The Hardball Manifesto

Focus relentlessly on competitive advantage
Exploit competitive advantage ruthlessly and remorselessly. Aim to widen the performance gap between yourself and your competitors. Look for tomorrow's opportunities today.

Strive for extreme competitive advantage
The ultimate endgame is to create an unassailable market position, so far ahead of the opposition as to be untouchable.

Avoid attacking directly
Somewhat paradoxically, they insist that direct assaults on rivals are often counter-productive. It

is better to tease out opponents' weak points well away from their power centres by careful use of intelligence.

Exploit people's will to win
Appoint and keep action-oriented people and don't ever let them become complacent. Maintain a continual sense of urgency in the organisation.

Know the caution zone
Operate close to the limits of acceptable, legal behaviour, but be quite clear where the boundaries are and never try to cross them.

Strategies

Devastate rivals' profit sanctuaries
Identify where rivals make their easiest profits and use aggressive pricing to attack them there.

Plagiarise with pride
Steal any good idea that is not patented, and improve on it. Remember that good ideas can be transplanted both geographically and commercially.

Deceive the competition
Mislead and 'wrong-foot' the opposition in order to keep them off balance.

Unleash massive and overwhelming force
When the opportunity is there for a decisive advantage, apply all the available resources in a focused, direct and swift attack.

Raise competitors' costs
Manoeuvre your rivals into a situation where their own costs increase.

To what extent is your own organisation a 'hardball' business?

What sort of leadership do you think is needed in such an organisation?

9

Influencing People: Alexander's Multi-ethnic Kingdom

What happened?

The leader

King Alexander III of Macedon was called the Great on account of his conquest of Persia. He was born in 356 BC, the son of King Philip II and Olympias, one of seven royal wives. Olympias' relations with Philip were strained, but there is no reason to suppose either she or her son had any connection with the king's assassination in 336 BC. Alexander inherited his mother's mystical interests as well as his father's practical approach to life.

The historical setting

The sight of Philip being killed by one of his bodyguards must have haunted Alexander for the rest of his life. The memory made him aware of the constant danger of assassination, and of the fact that in the last resort even a Macedonian king could not even trust a chosen bodyguard. Having been confirmed as the next ruler by the citizen army, Alexander executed those involved in his father's death and then set off to campaign in the Balkans.

He had already been accepted as leader of the Greek city-states, a position occupied by Philip as a result of Macedonian prowess on the battlefield. With this recognition went the post of commander-in-chief of the forces then being assembled for the war against Persia. But as Alexander was completing the military operations in the Balkans, which he felt were necessary for a long absence in Asia, he learned that the central Greek city of Thebes was in revolt and the Macedonian garrison in its citadel was in danger. By a lightning march he reached Thebes before troops from Athens, and other sympathetic Greek city-states, could aid the rebel Thebans. After Thebes had fallen to the Macedonians amid much bloodshed, Alexander was content to accept the suggestion that the Thebans be enslaved. This was the first and perhaps the most striking of his acts that filled the Greeks with fear.

In 334 BC Alexander crossed to Asia Minor at the head of an army of 32,000 infantry and 5100 cavalry. First to land, he drove his spear into the soil and proclaimed that he accepted Asia as won by the spear, a gift from the gods. It was a prophetic claim, for his later policy showed that he intended that his Asian subjects were to be free and neither part of a Macedonian empire nor slaves to the Greeks. On Alexander's part it was both belief and propaganda, and it was destined to win many Asian hearts. Also unnoticed, at the time of the landing, was his intention of conquering more than just Persia.

But first Alexander had to defeat the armed forces of Persia, which he did in three pitched battles. In the first he used only his Macedonian troops and some Greek horsemen. In the second and third his army consisted of Greeks, Balkan troops and Macedonians. Alexander himself was the spearpoint and the Macedonians the

A youthful portrait of Alexander carved in ivory. It was found in the royal Macedonian graveyard in northern Greece. Alexander's body was hijacked on its way there in 323 BC and taken to Alexandria by Ptolemy, one of his generals. When Julius Caesar was in the city with Cleopatra in 47 BC, the Roman dictator could not resist touching the preserved body whereupon part of the nose broke.

spearhead in battle, but the other forces were indispensable for the fulfilment of his grand ambition. Once Persia was overthrown, he began to recruit Asians as soldiers. When he reached India in 326 BC his army had grown to 120,000 men, of whom the Macedonians were one-eighth, the Greeks one-third, and the Balkan and Asian troops more than half.

Alexander's behaviour

It was the Macedonians in Alexander's army who ultimately decided the limits of his conquests, however. They felt they had been misled, since the end of Asia was nowhere in sight. It has to be said that Alexander himself was baffled by the sheer size of the Indian subcontinent. Though he still wished to advance eastwards, Alexander recognised that this was now impossible with his Macedonians refusing to march, and so he agreed to turn back, much to their delight.

On his return to Babylon in the summer of 323 BC he prepared for an invasion of Arabia. To keep order in his Asian kingdom he planned to leave behind a multi-ethnic army, which would be built around a core of Macedonian foot soldiers. For this purpose he arranged for 30,000 young Persians to be trained in the Greek language and Macedonian weapons so that they could be integrated into this new army. Another 20,000 Persians were also recruited as auxiliaries.

To underline his idea of a multi-ethnic kingdom, albeit organised on European lines, Alexander made it plain that every person was to be judged in terms of worth, irrespective of parentage. He also insisted that he and 80 of his closest companions married the daughters of Persian noble families. Soldiers' Asian women and their children were made legitimate and educated at Alexander's expense, many of them settling in the 70 new cities he founded in Asia. Quite apart from the pressing need to augment his armed forces and find a way of bringing stability to his vast conquests, the greatest ever achieved by an ancient leader, Alexander firmly believed he had a divine mission to fulfil, which worried some of his Macedonian and Greek followers. As the historian Plutarch commented, 'Alexander considered that he had come from the gods to be a governor and reconciler to the world. Using force of arms when he could not bring men together by reason, he employed everything to the same end, mixing lives, manners, marriages and customs, as it were, in a loving-cup'. Possibly the innovation that the Macedonians disliked most of all was the court ceremonial Alexander decided to adopt, since it included the Persian custom of prostration. Though he could have practised one form of ceremonial for the Macedonians and another for the Asians, his insistence on the new one shows the extent to which his mind was set on treating all his subjects alike.

Outcomes

That Alexander grew up with a sense of mission was certainly to be expected. For he believed that he was descended not only from the semi-divine hero Herakles, but also from the chief deity Zeus, a fact which seemed to be confirmed on his visit to the oracle at Siwah in Egypt. There he was addressed by the priests as a son of the god.

Only Alexander's sudden death from a fever, at the age of 33, cut short his great multi-ethnic experiment. When the dying conqueror was asked to whom he left his vast realm, he replied 'to the strongest', correctly anticipating the prolonged struggle between his senior commanders. Their wars ensured the division of Alexander's conquests into a number of new kingdoms. But one of these new kingdoms, founded by Seleucus in 305 BC, stayed close to the idea of a multi-ethnic society. At his eastern capital, Seleucia on the Tigris, in present-day Iraq, a suburb was named Apanea after Seleucus' Asian wife, whom he had married at Alexander's behest. This marriage lasted, unlike others between senior Macedonian commanders and Asian brides, and Apanea was the mother of Seleucus' eldest son and most able successor Antiochus I.

Why does it matter?

The art of persuasion

Before he set out on his first Asian conquest in 334 BC, Alexander must have asked himself whether he was indeed a 'son of a god', capable of heroic achievement. He seems to have thought he was. Following his victories on the battlefield, and his reception at the Siwah oracle, he no longer had any doubts about his parentage. And it remains a fact that very many of his followers came to the same conclusion themselves, which was fortunate for Alexander. For whatever the direction that a leader sets for a team or organisation, the success of the journey will ultimately depend to a large extent on the willingness of colleagues and staff to take the chosen route with enthusiasm and commitment. Rarely, if ever, can a leader have taken his people on such an ambitious and challenging journey as the one on which Alexander led his Macedonian army, eastwards right across the known world, and even into the unknown.

As with Alexander, the *sine qua non* of any attempt by a leader to persuade the staff within an organisation of the way forward, is that the leader himself believes in it wholeheartedly. For Alexander's spiritual and religious beliefs gave him an unassailable conviction that he was destined to conquer Asia, and that he effectively communicated this belief to his army is evidenced by the determination they showed throughout the campaign, often against extraordinary odds. Yet contributing also to their sense of resolve was their confidence in their own preparation, training and equipment; their belief that they comprised the best fighting machine in the ancient world, a judgement which had been tested many times in battle before the invasion of the Persian empire. In the world of business the significance of the quality and quantity of resources available is, of course, a key determinant of the motivation levels within a team and of their likely future success. Like the Macedonians, you have to be prepared for all eventualities.

Changes in the prevailing organisational structure of businesses, the move away from hierarchies to networking and cross-process, cross-functional working, mean that the effectiveness of leaders increasingly depends on their ability to influence, persuade and convince people. In terms of changing the working practices or principles of an organisation, it is perhaps a leader's own behaviour that influences most powerfully whether others will adopt new ways of working or not. It is obvious that Alexander intuitively grasped this from the very start of his reign. A highly competitive individual from an early age, his need to perform at the highest level manifested itself in everything he did. He was determined to outdo everyone else. His courage was exemplary, and he always led his army from the front, exposing himself to huge risks in the process. It was a matter of pride that he shared the dangers and discomforts of his soldiers, suffering wounds, living on the same rations and walking the same paths as they did.

In seeking to influence others a leader can use a range of tactics. These were well summarised by researchers,

Yukl, Falbe and Youn in an article which was published in 1993. These leadership tactics are

- Rational persuasion – presenting a variety of logical arguments, facts and statistics to support a particular view of an issue.

- Inspirational appeals – focusing on values, ideals and aspirations as well as aiming to build the self-confidence of others.

- Consultation – showing a willingness to modify a viewpoint in dealing with the concerns or opinions of others.

- Ingratiation – using praise, flattery, friendship or assistance to predispose others to comply.

- Personal appeals – calling upon loyalty or friendship to secure compliance.

- Exchange – offering the prospect of shared benefits to accomplish an objective.

- Coalition tactics – seeking the aid of others to present the fact of their support as a reason for others to comply.

- Pressure – using demands, threats, constant checking or reminders to produce compliance.

- Legitimating tactics – claiming authority, right of legitimacy or verifying the consistency of a request or demand in line with organisational policies, rules, practices or traditions.

At different points in Alexander's amazingly short but successful career one can identify most of these leadership tactics in action.

Knowing your audience

In seeking to persuade and convince other people of a course of action effective leaders will adopt different approaches and techniques depending on key contextual issues, such as the readiness of the organisation to change, and on the particular audience with which they are communicating. Even with a shared sense of purpose or vision, any organisation is likely to be composed of groups and individuals with very different and often conflicting interests and priorities, who are likely to respond to different elements of the message. A good leader needs to know enough about those anxieties and aspirations felt by the people in the business, which are most likely to affect their response to his or her message, and have the capacity to modify its style and content accordingly. At its worst, this capability is about what has become known in the world of politics and the media as 'spin', the triumph of presentation over substance but, used legitimately, it reflects an honest acknowledgement that people's responses to a piece of communication are affected by a variety of intrinsic and external factors which need to be considered in planning how best to get the message across.

This skill is, at its heart, about empathy. Empathy, in this context, is not about some therapeutic 'I'm OK, you're OK' mode of thought, but rather, it is concerned with thoughtfully considering the emotional needs of others, their distinct feelings and perspectives, in the process of making intelligent decisions. Daniel Goleman, the key promoter of 'emotional intelligence' in management, describes the role of empathy in leadership in *The New Leaders*, when he argues that:

Leaders with empathy are able to attune to a wide range of emotional signals, letting them sense the felt, but unspoken emotions in a person or group. Such leaders listen attentively and can grasp the other person's perspective. Empathy makes a leader able to get along well with people of diverse backgrounds or from other cultures.

Cultural sensitivity was absolutely critical to Alexander's success. The respect with which, as victor, he treated the defeated Persians was very different from the behaviour shown by other leaders in ancient wars; for, as well as showing an intuitive grasp of the fragility of his own position at the head of a relatively small army many miles from home, it reflected a genuine conviction that the survival of his newly won empire required the commitment of the people he had conquered. As he said to the Persians, 'You are each to observe the religions and customs, the laws and conventions . . . which you observed in the days of Darius. Let each stay Persian in his way of life, and let him live within his city'. There was no question of enslavement, no threat to traditional values. All his subjects were to live together in peace.

Leadership style

Alexander had very different roles to play as the king of Macedonia and as the king of Asia, and they caused him great problems. His leadership style with the Macedonian army had to conform to the democratic principles of the Greeks. This meant that he not only shared their hardships, but also enthusiastically joined in their festivals and drinking parties. As Nicholas Hammond puts it in *The Genius of Alexander the Great*:

He led them not by fiat but by persuasion, and a crucial element in that persuasion was that he should always tell them the truth. Thus he respected the constitutional rights of the Macedonians, and his reward was that he was generally able to convince them in their assemblies that they should accept his policies.

This consultative and democratic style of kingship was unfamiliar to the Persians, and so Alexander's behaviour as their new ruler had to mirror their quite different expectations of a king. Living in a court of extraordinary opulence and splendour he became, in their eyes, the sort of autocratic, demanding and unapproachable 'Great King' they had always known and obeyed.

Many experienced leaders today are able to adopt different styles to suit a variety of circumstances but, if not handled with great tact, this can lead to the dangerous perception that they are inconsistent or cynical in their approach, resulting in their employees feeling both confused and distrustful. A democratic style of leadership works well when employees are already highly motivated and have clear goals which they understand and value. If not precisely 'democratic' in his manner of leadership, Alexander's natural style was certainly 'affiliative', relying on the maintenance of bonds of loyalty and trust with the Macedonian army. For he knew that his Macedonian soldiers were his power base. That is the reason why Alexander had no choice but to call off the conquest of India when they refused to march eastwards.

The dissonance between this way of working and the tone he adopted at his Persian court led to tension which came to a head in 324 BC. Then Alexander proposed to send back to Macedonia several thousand veterans who were considered unfit for active service through injury or age, and to replace them with Persian recruits, trained in Macedonian warfare. He expected that this suggestion would be greeted enthusiastically, but, in the event, the Macedonian soldiers felt humiliated and resisted the idea very forcibly: to the extent that Alexander had to have 13 of the leading dissidents executed! He had gravely misread the situation. Evidently, Alexander's consultative style of leadership did have its limitations.

Leading a team

Teams are now used to meet a wide range of purposes in organisations, including collecting and sharing information and ideas, managing and controlling work, coordinating tasks and problem solving. It is in the context of heading up teams that many managers have a first experience of leadership. The pervasive use of teams means that these skills need to be deployed throughout the organisation, and developed by a wide range of staff with supervisory responsibilities. Among the skills of team leadership are the following:

- Gate-keeping – seeing that everybody has a fair opportunity to contribute to discussions by 'gate-keeping' to encourage the participation of quieter members and limiting the contributions of the more dominant ones.

- Compromising – being willing to yield one's own status or argument, if necessary, in order that the group as a whole may achieve progress, rather than sticking stubbornly to one's own point of view or privileges.

- Harmonising – acting as a mediator when differences of opinion obstruct the group; reconciling different points of view; smoothing ruffled feathers.

- Supporting and encouraging – reinforcing good contributions; giving credit to others; acting in an encouraging way, particularly towards newcomers.

- Relieving tension – asking people to say how they're feeling, or publicly stating one's own feelings; calling for a break in activity at appropriate times; using humour constructively; changing physical arrangements.

- Contributive listening – following others' contributions non-verbally and weighing up the arguments in one's mind; respecting silently the contributions of others.

- Summarising – making sure that everyone is clear about the process used, decisions made and follow-up actions.

It is a characteristic of a well-led, high-performing team that the collective identity of the group influences the work of team members whether they are working collaboratively at a given time or not, or whether they are actually gathered together in a meeting of some sort. Nevertheless, the most obvious context in which the sort of leadership skills highlighted above can be deployed and developed is within a meeting. The meetings at which Alexander learned that the Macedonians refused to consider any further campaigning in India must have been a particularly tricky time – what a shame the minutes have not survived down to our own time! At the first meeting Alexander made his intention of going on quite clear; at the second he said that any who wished to leave their king and go home, while he went on, could do so. Then Alexander withdrew to his tent for three days, presumably in the hope that the Macedonians would change their minds. On the fourth day, hearing of no alteration, he sacrificed and discovered the omens were unfavourable. Calling his commanders together for a third meeting, he declared that he had made the decision to turn back, an announcement that was greeted by the Macedonian army with shouts of joy and tears of relief.

What does it mean for you?

Influencing is a much sought after skill in a modern matrixed organisation where people need to achieve results across different locations and functions, without having direct power.

Alexander brought about considerable changes, but so too do leaders in today's world where we experience unprecedented change across every aspect of society. To understand the validity of the power of influence, it is important to understand the steps that people go through before they strongly support change.

- **Innocence** – this is the stage of being blissfully unaware of impending changes, a state sometime referred to as ignorance.

- **Awareness** – at this stage people have had the changes communicated to them, and the likelihood is that they will not have grasped the full magnitude of what is likely to happen. The changes may well be seen as something in the future – nothing to worry too much about. At this early stage the leader will be using various communication skills such as presentation meeting and discussion skills.

- **Understanding** – now people have grasped what is going to happen. At this later stage the leader sets out to change the thinking of the people involved, giving them every opportunity to experience what they are going to have to go through. This could be to arrange visits to other organisations that have already gone through these changes. Although people have reached understanding, they may still be negative about the end goal. To cope with any reluctance the leader will employ influencing skills such as questioning, listening and observing. This could also take the form of expressing empathy for the situation people find themselves in and understanding their legitimate concerns.

- **Commitment** – the next stage is dealing with the emotional level – feelings. To get people through to positive commitment towards the project requires them to alter the way they feel about the changes and here influencing skills play a critical role.

- **Action** – this final stage is all about changing behaviour, since people are now doing things differently, and the project is about to be passionately supported.

What often happens in real life is that changes are just imposed on people and they are not given the opportunity to go through the stages of change outlined above. A good leader will carefully follow through each stage in order to ensure full commitment to change. Persuasion yes, compulsion no! Only a leader who knows how to effectively influence people's outlook can ever hope to emulate Alexander, notwithstanding his problems with the Macedonian army in India.

Take a typical case study from today's world of work.

A manufacturing organisation plans to reduce the level of supervision in its factories and empower the shop-floor operators to be multi-skilled. In the past these changes would be planned behind closed doors and, finally imposed on the organisation, with considerable resistance from all levels and failure to deliver the anticipated savings. See Table 9.1.

Table 9.1   Five steps of change

	Innocence	Awareness	Understanding	Commitment	Action
Senior mangers	Appreciate need to change	Project meetings	Lead the projects	Walk the talk	Walk the talk
Middle managers		Road shows	Project teams	Re-training	Lead the change
First line managers		Road shows	One-to-one consultation	Re-training	Exit or new job
Shop-floor operators		Team briefing	One-to-one consultation	Training	Do multi-skill jobs

For change to work effectively, each and every person in an organisation needs to be convinced that it is the right thing to do. With so much change happening in the world today, influencing people has become one of the key skills that a leader needs to mature and grow, if he or she is to have any hope of surviving our ever changing times.

In setting out an influencing strategy, you need to take into account the varying levels of power of the people that you are intending to influence. To spend a disproportionate amount of time influencing people with low levels of power will only backfire when the powerful people you have ignored finally decide to block your projects.

Power can, therefore, be summarised like this:

- little power or influence;

- some – the voice of reason;

- influential and local power – can get people thinking;

- highly influential – can sway the vote;

- ultimate power.

Good advice, when trying to initiate change, is to be aware of exactly where the power lies. Always start to persuade those with high power and influence at an early stage. Let them contribute during the time you are shaping your solution, because if they feel the end product has been influenced by them, they can be powerful allies in persuading other people to commit to your project.

To summarise, *influencing* is achieving a result through persuading people when you have no direct authority, and you do this by

- questioning, listening and observing;

- showing empathy;

- guiding people one by one through the five stages of change;

- making use of the power and influence of others.

It is a skill which leaders can develop, but really effective leaders instinctively know how, and when, to influence others. Without this inner awareness, this understanding of other people's needs and aspirations, Alexander would never have become the Great.

10

Leaving a Legacy: The Abdication of Candragupta

What happened?

The leader

Candragupta (pronounced 'Can-dra-gup-ta') was the first Indian ruler to found an empire. Having seized power from a Nanda king in Magadha, a major state in the lower Ganges valley, he built up a powerful army before extending his authority by force into the Punjab. Candragupta's conquests there in the 310s BC gave his dynasty, the Mauryan, an empire which stretched right across the northern plains of India.

The historical setting

The establishment of Mauryan rule happened at a time of acute disturbance in the Indian subcontinent. Buoyed by his defeat of the Persians, the Macedonian king Alexander the Great had marched his forces as far east as India, which he invaded in 326 BC. Then Alexander thought he was entering the last country of Asia. His tutor, the philosopher Aristotle, had told him that the subcontinent projected eastwards into the great ocean which surrounded the lands of the world, in the same manner that the Chersonesus, the Gallipoli peninsular, jutted into the Aegean Sea. One of the surprises for the Macedonian king and his men was the sheer size of India, the scale of its kingdoms and their populations. Although he conquered the whole of the Indus river valley (modern Pakistan and parts of northwestern India), Alexander was unable to get his army to enter the Ganges river valley. His Macedonian troops, the core of his army of 120,000 men, refused to march any further east. Possibly Alexander acquiesced with this mutiny because of the realisation of how great were the military resources of the Indian kings who still chose to oppose him. Despite being overshadowed by the splendour of its successor, the Mauryan dynasty, the Nanda kings then ruled over a large state. News had already reached the Macedonians that the Nanda army comprised 200,000 infantry, 20,000 cavalry, 2000 chariots and 4000 elephants.

Four years after Alexander headed west, Candragupta extinguished the Nanda dynasty and founded the Mauryan empire. According to one ancient writer, he 'overran and subdued India with an army of 600,000 men', of which 30,000 were cavalrymen. War was always a serious business in India. Alexander's brief intervention of 326–325 BC was not so much a military revelation to Indian rulers as a stimulus to someone like Candragupta to set off on his own campaign of conquests. Megasthenes, a Greek ambassador who attended Candragupta's court, was amazed at the professionalism of the Mauryan standing army. It was organised under a committee of 30 senior officers, divided into subcommittees which controlled the infantry, chariots, cavalry, elephants, navy and supply trains.

Candragupta's behaviour

The emergence of Magadha, the present-day Indian state of Bihar, had begun under the Nanda kings around the

This coin, issued around 300 BC by Seleucus I, refers to the war elephants received from Candragupta as part of the settlement of the Indian border. In 301 BC these great animals gave to Seleucus a great victory at the battle of Ipsus in Asia Minor by scaring away his opponent's cavalry.

time Persia first subdued the upper reaches of the Indus. The willingness of rulers in that river valley, like the king of Taxila, to accept Alexander's authority two centuries later, indicates a tradition of foreign overlordship which started with the Persians in 530 BC. It was the failure of the successors of Alexander to hold on to this rich area and its passing under Mauryan control which led to Megasthenes' embassy to Candragupta in 303 BC. A new western border was then agreed for Candragupta's empire, which incorporated much of modern Afghanistan. In return for acquiring this vast tract of land, Candragupta was pleased to give as a present 500 war elephants: they were soon to have a decisive impact on the battlefields of the eastern Mediterranean.

Candragupta was assisted by more than able commanders, however. He found in the Brahmin Kautilya a minister of outstanding worth. For the surviving writings of Kautilya show him to have been a great political and economic thinker. He understood that the Mauryan empire's stability depended on well-paid civil and military officials, whose salaries came from an efficient taxation system. The predictability of state revenue derived from agriculture was regarded as the basis of fiscal security, but Kautilya also pointed out the need to keep an eye open for new sources of tax, such as trade. His linking of taxation, administration and military power was crucial to the establishment of India's first centralised empire. Even though it is doubtful whether the Mauryan dynasty ever exercised the level of regulation that Kautilya envisaged, the advice which the minister gave to its founding emperor Candragupta led to the political unification of much of the Indian subcontinent, and the ensuing security provided by a stable government encouraged a massive expansion of trade.

Yet at the same moment that the political landscape was undergoing this great change, another transformation thoroughly reshaped religion. Two beliefs, Buddhism and Jainism, were then making startling headway. Traditional religious practices were being challenged by the teachings of the Buddha, who had died in 479 BC, and the Jaina saviour Mahavira, his contemporary. No less open to their influence than his subjects was Candragupta. Finding himself unable to save his empire from the ravages of a famine, he abdicated in 297 BC in favour of his son Bindusara, and travelled to southern India where he became a Jain recluse. A bas-relief there today at Sravana Begola records Candragupta's life, including his final act of renunciation, the Jaina rite of starving unto death.

Outcomes

Notwithstanding the terrible famine, the empire Candragupta handed on to Bindusara was a remarkable achievement, and a complete break from the Indian past. Yet Bindusara did not espouse the non-violent doctrines of Jainism so beloved of his father. Quite the reverse, his belligerent foreign policy earned him the nickname 'slayer of foes'. Religious scruples were to trouble Bindusara's successor Ashoka, however. Although he did not abdicate like his grandfather Candragupta, Ashoka became shortly after 260 BC the world's first Buddhist ruler. It seems that the unprecedented bloodshed involved in a campaign in Kalinga, a part of modern Orissa, proved to be a turning point, for Ashoka afterwards suffered a severe crisis of confidence in Mauryan aggression. To pull himself together, the third Mauryan emperor embraced the Buddhist faith, and for the rest of his life he endeavoured to conquer through righteousness rather than warfare.

Why does it matter?

Planning a career

Perhaps because Candragupta was such a new phenomenon in Indian politics – the usurper of power over an extensive area of land that before was a patchwork of squabbling kingdoms – he could safely indulge his own preference of Jainism, an even more austere faith than Buddhism. Its ideas were located right at the impersonal end of the spectrum of ancient belief, far removed from western notions about the survival of the personality. Only through an act of sustained self-renunciation could the soul of a Jain make its escape from the sufferings of the world.

That Candragupta could abdicate and leave his imperial legacy intact says a great deal about his competence as a ruler, and something about the quality of the officials who served him as well. To his astute minister Kautilya he owed much, but there can be no question that it was the loyalty he inspired in his subjects for the newly founded Mauryan dynasty that really permitted Candragupta's successful abdication. He knew when he could safely relinquish imperial authority and devote the rest of his time to religion. Candragupta's rise to power showed him to be a leader of great determination and drive, and in the subsequent maintenance of his empire he demonstrated an instinctive grasp of some key leadership principles. His logical and rational approach to organising the administration of the empire has some resonance with what was the original modern 'system' of management, the approach that became known in the early part of the twentieth century as 'scientific management'.

Scientific management rested on principles first developed by F.W. Taylor. It was based on the idea that work should be organised for maximum efficiency, emphasising a division of labour by specialisation and ability, with output maximised through incentive payments, and the whole regime directed by skilled and trained managers. These theories found their most obvious expression in the corporate creations of such industrialists as Henry Ford at the Ford Motor Company, and Alfred Sloan at General Motors during the 1920s and 1930s. 'Scientific management' systems also tended to produce a certain type of manager, someone dedicated, hard-working and rational, and, above all, someone utterly loyal to the company: what later became known as 'corporate man'. As a pioneer of the telecommunications industry in the 1930s, Chester Barnard encapsulated the virtues of corporate man when he wrote that, 'the most important single contribution required by an executive, certainly the most universal qualification, is loyalty, domination by the organisation's personality'.

One of the most influential creators of corporate man was IBM, within which, as Stuart Crainer describes in *Key Management Ideas*, 'corporate culture and the individuality of managers became intertwined in a way never envisaged when the manager was a mere supervisor'. The popular stereotype of the IBM manager – sober suits, white shirts, plain ties and company songs – was not far distant from the reality. It is now quite difficult to imagine how thoroughly the large corporations once controlled the careers and lives of their managers. Some of Charles Handy's books include a telling account of his early career at ICI, and powerfully illustrate this phenomenon; how his career path was mapped ahead for him by the company with development opportunities and likely promotions factored in to give him a foundation for an executive position. And it was not just his career that was planned for him; ICI would also dictate the style and content of his social life, and even manage his matrimonial prospects. Such powerful corporate cultures were often the expression of their founder's personality. As Thomas Watson Junior said of his father, the creator of IBM: 'The beliefs that mould great organisations frequently grow out of the character, the experience and the convictions of a single person'. Just as Candragupta discovered that the growth and success of his empire depended on a professional military and civil administration, so sustaining the strong corporate cultures which once characterised large, multinational corporations also required a loyal group of functionaries and administrators, whose years of service would be rewarded with the certainty of a job for life and, ultimately, with a generous company pension as well.

Nowadays, this close association of an individual's career with one business throughout a working life is not the dominant model. In the 1980s corporate loyalty took a back seat to the notion of individual initiative in advancing a management career, and self-managed development became the norm. Professor Edward Schein of the Massachusetts Institute of Technology coined the phrase 'the psychological contract' to describe the implicit agreement between an individual and an organisation about the way they should be treated and the extent of obligations to the organisation. In Schein's analysis these respective obligations and expectations became much looser in the 1980s. This development was largely brought about by the fundamental changes to the prevailing organisational structures, which occurred during this period, changes that were further accelerated by the advent of new technologies. These changes are well summarised in the image which Charles Handy develops of a 'shamrock organisation', with the three leaves representing a lean core of permanently employed staff, a flexible labour force and a 'contractual fringe' of outsourced specialists brought in to meet particular needs. In such organisations, a management career takes on a radically different shape with many ambitious young managers seeking a career path outside of large organisations altogether, moving readily from business to business, and often ending up working as freelance suppliers to their previous employers.

Succession planning

A leader who has made a large personal and professional investment in the development of an organisation may well have serious anxieties over the direction it is liable to take under a successor's control. It is doubtful, for example, that Candragupta could have predicted the very different ways in which his empire was to be led by his heirs. This can be as true for a department head or a branch manager as a powerful CEO and, in all these cases, there can be a dangerous tendency for the individual to stay in post too long. Allen Gilmour, former CEO of Ford, described the dangers this can bring to an organisation when he said:

I had a belief, which I still do, that people can stay in a job too long – in part because they may run out of ideas and vitality but more important, because of the need for vibrancy in an organisation. Bringing younger people along and giving them opportunities doesn't work as well if the top-level jobs are filled for a long time.

Planning a change at the top can be a difficult and time-consuming business for a leader. A change of leadership may, in some circumstances, be a direct outcome of a persistent record of underperformance but, even in the case of a successful organisation, the retirement or resignation of a leader can be seen as an opportunity for a thorough review of the strategic direction, purpose and working principles of a business. The key decision in such a situation is whether to select someone from within, or appoint from outside. The basis of such a decision says a great deal about the culture of the organisation. In some commercial sectors or public sector professions there is a particularly strong predilection for bringing in new blood from outside the organisation, with the expectation that this will re-energise things. The trend in recent years to appoint senior managers from the private sector to executive positions in the public sector provides a particularly intriguing instance of this approach, and the varying success of some of these appointments raises very difficult questions indeed.

Growing your own talent

Other organisations take the view that they should retain, groom and promote their own top performers from within. Marshall Goldsmith analyses a range of strategies to retain the highest quality people in an essay entitled

'Retaining your top performers'. In summary, he emphasises the following tactics:

- Clearly identify which employees you want to keep.

- Let them know that you want to keep them.

- Provide recognition.

- Provide opportunities for development and involvement.

- Challenge the compensation plan (be flexible and responsive about pay, rewards and benefits).

- Relax the culture (let them express themselves in their own ways).

- Provide 'intrapreneurial' opportunities.

In recent years there has been intense interest in the management principles underpinning the sustained success of the Japanese car manufacturer Toyota. In terms of leadership development and planning, Toyota believes in growing its own leaders rather than purchasing them, a view expressed in the company principle – 'Grow leaders who thoroughly understand the work, live the philosophy and teach it to others'. At the most senior levels of Toyota, succession to executive posts for a long time tended to rest with members of the founding Toyoda family, but others began to take on such positions as the company began to expand greatly. In the company's history it is no accident that key leaders have been found from within to shape the next stage in its development. In stark contrast to car manufacturers in other parts of the world, Toyota does not buy in solutions. Jeffrey K. Liker makes this clear in his account of Toyota, entitled *The Toyota Way*, when he writes:

Their leaders must live and thoroughly understand the Toyota culture day by day, since a critical element of the culture is *genchi genbutsa*, which means deeply observing the actual situation in detail. Leaders must demonstrate this ability and understand how work gets done at a shop floor level.

Toyota does not like radical shifts in culture, and a key responsibility of its leaders is to teach their subordinates 'The Toyota Way', so that potential future managers absorb the ethos of the business and are thoroughly familiar with its ways.

Work–life balance

In what are increasingly pressurised working environments, much attention is now being paid to the importance of maintaining a healthy balance between working life and life outside the organisation. This concern now figures in the work of a significant number of management writers and researchers; focusing on the idea that leaders, in particular, will contribute more effectively and creatively in the workplace if they have interests beyond work, and the time to engage in them, which satisfies other parts of their personalities. They need, in essence, to renew themselves each day. So the theory is that maintaining this variety of work-related and social activity ultimately benefits the business in that the individual becomes a more balanced person, better able to cope with the inevitable stress that comes with holding down a senior post in an organisation. This view does run counter to the notion that work itself can, at its most motivating, create a climate of, which psychologist Abraham Maslow has called, 'self-actualisation'. This means that the individual's highest level and most subtle needs are actually met through engagement with the work undertaken.

The idea of someone leaving office because they wish to spend more time with their family has, of course, become something of a cliché, and has often been used to conceal a more complex reason for a resignation. Nevertheless, the very real difficulties involved in juggling family commitments with the responsibilities of a senior post in an organisation really do highlight the challenging complexities of maintaining an appropriate work–life balance. The particular conundrum arising from this question of work versus family is, inevitably, one that has impacted particularly, but not exclusively, on women executives and leaders. Many managers, both male and female, will sympathise with Deborah Coleman of Apple Computers, when she said, 'If I work less than 60 hours a week, I have a twinge of guilt'. Yet women are likely to share an especially strong bond with Brenda Barnes who, on resigning from a very senior post with PepsiCo in 1997, commented,

I hope people will focus on the fact that I've been with the company for 22 years, and I hope that people might say, 'Isn't it great that she could work so hard and make such a contribution to her company?' Every time you would miss a child's birthday, or a school concert, or a parent–teacher discussion, you'd feel the tug.

Retirement offers the hope of time and space for a leader to find genuine self-fulfilment, but this dream is not often realised. Only an exceptional leader, such as the first Indian emperor Candragupta, can make a clean break from the organisation that has absorbed so much energy and embrace an entirely different mode of life. For the rest of us there is always the prospect of going back to the organisation in some form of consultancy role in retirement, a bizarre career twist given that so many executives, while in office, would share the view of consultants expressed by Scott Adams, creator of the Dilbert cartoon strip: 'A consultant is a person who takes your money and annoys your employees while tirelessly searching for the best way to extend the consulting contract'.

What does it mean for you?

What are people going to remember about you when you move on to your next challenge, be it a new job, a new company or retirement?

Planning on leaving a legacy is a good idea, if it means that you really will be 'letting go' and avoid becoming possessive. It also implies that you believe you can take the organisation to a certain stage and then hand it on to the next leader.

Leaving a legacy is about ensuring the long-term survival of your organisation rather than just tearing it apart for short-term gain.

So think of leaving a legacy as a good thing, and not just about personal ego.

At the end of PepsiCo's leadership development programme, Roger Enrico asked all the participating executives to imagine, not how high they would rise, but rather the legacy they would like to leave at the end of their careers. For organisations that remain successful over the long term, that legacy is often the creation of leaders who surpass their predecessors.

The directors of KPMG's leadership development programme felt they had made a major contribution to the firm because 'when the time comes to turn over the leadership of the firm, we feel we will have played an important role in passing the baton to a more capable pair of hands'.

Stephen Covey's book *The Eighth Habit*, launched in 2005, covered getting from effectiveness to greatness. 'To live, to love, to learn and to leave a legacy'. He recognised that in today's challenging and complex world, being highly effective is the price of entry to the playing field. To thrive, innovate, excel, and lead is this new reality, and we need to reach beyond effectiveness towards fulfilment, contribution, and greatness. His research, however, showed that the majority of people are not thriving. They are neither fulfilled nor excited. So the chances are that they will not leave a legacy.

There are opportunities for people in all areas of the business to leave a legacy and the first stage of the journey is wanting to do so.

This case study relates to such a person.

Anna somehow had always believed that if an organisation were to thrive it needed to have the right people in the right jobs at the right time. She had chosen sales as her career, largely because she liked the contact it gave her with people. She had been headhunted by a fast-moving consumer goods company operating throughout Europe and she had been told, at the interview stage, that her biggest challenge was going to be developing her team. Its members were described as mostly middle-aged, and survivors of multiple mergers, and as a result they were shrewd operators who knew how to block the way for the bright young things that joined the organisation.

By the end of the third month she had met and spent quality time with all of the team. She had also met the next two levels down, and so had a pretty good idea of where the talent was in the organisation. The team were good operators, and they turned in good results, but they weren't really great results. Anna reasoned that she would be in this job no more than three years, by which time she would need to reinvigorate the structure, implement changes, get the results and leave an organisation for a successor, ready for the next challenge.

She got to know Massimo, one of the HR managers, and he had some good ideas on how to bring about the changes she wanted. They took all the organisation charts and against each of the positions identified an immediate successor or someone who could be ready for promotion within two years. Then for each job they used a colour code, green if a move was planned within the next 12 months, amber if within 12 to 24 months, and red if there were no plans for a move at all. Once this was done, they placed all the organisation charts on the wall so they could keep the whole situation under review. It was too much for Anna when she saw the end result. 'There is a solid band of red across all of my direct reports', she said in despair. 'Obviously this is creating a barrier to progress'.

Within the next three hours, Anna made the big decision that would refresh the organisation, create career paths, and result in a twenty-first century sales force that the organisation could be proud of.

Anna had decided to go for a flat and flexible structure, moving away from five direct reports to 12. This meant some tough decisions had to be made and four of her direct reports were encouraged to take early retirement. She knew who she wanted to appoint but, to ensure fairness and encourage participation from other senior managers, she decided to run an assessment centre with the assistance of Massimo.

The changes were made and, after an initial period of settling down, the team got going. All new appointees were told that they should expect to spend no more than two years in their new positions, so they needed to have successors in place to free themselves up for their next challenges.

Because the business was going through a phase of rapid growth, with a number of new products that had taken the market by storm, having in place a young and not so young team that was highly motivated proved nothing less than a magic injection for the business.

Anna's next big opportunity came within two years and, true to her plan, she had her successors in place and was free to move on.

It can be seen from the case study how leaving a legacy can be built into the way leaders operate, making sure each aspect of what they do is self-sustaining.

11

Representing the Business: Hannibal's Invasion of Italy

What happened?

The leader

Hannibal was the scourge of republican Rome. He was responsible for the start of the Second Punic War (218–201 BC), which subjected Italy to more than a decade of devastation.

The historical setting

It was Phoenician traders from Tyre who founded Carthage in about 814 BC, not far from the modern city of Tunis. The new settlement acted as an anchorage and a place of supply for vessels plying the length of the Mediterranean in search of gold, silver, copper and tin. Clearly Carthage had the makings of a state in itself, something the influx of settlers from Africa and other places soon turned into a reality. The lure of wealth here, as in Rome, supplemented the population and under its early kings Carthage became the dominant trading power in the western Mediterranean. In a treaty of 506 BC the

Romans had to accept that their ships were not allowed to trade freely either around the islands of Sardinia and Sicily or along the coast of Africa.

Conflict between Carthage and Rome began in 264 BC as a result of a Roman attempt to gain a foothold in Sicily by forming an alliance against Syracuse with Messana, present-day Messina, although this Greek city had previously had a Carthaginian garrison. The First Punic War was largely fought in Sicilian waters and ended in 241 BC with Rome expelling Carthage from Sicily. The renewal of conflict occurred because of competition in Spain, where Carthage had built up another empire. There Hannibal had married a Spanish princess and set about enlarging Carthaginian holdings. But his campaigns brought him into conflict with Rome's ally, Saguntum, a city near present-day Valencia. Possibly the oath of eternal hatred to Rome which his father had made him swear before leaving Carthage fuelled Hannibal's military ambitions, because in 219 BC he took Saguntum by siege knowing that its capture might well lead to war again. The Romans immediately ordered the Carthaginians to hand over Hannibal to them, or face them in arms. Their overconfidence was soon deflated when Hannibal marched over the Alps and inflicted three major defeats on Roman forces in as many years.

Hannibal's behaviour

Before setting out on his epic march to Italy, Hannibal had sent messengers to the Gallic inhabitants of southern France, seeking assistance for the passage of his army through their territory. They promised support not only for his march but also for his Italian campaign, since many of them willingly joined the ranks of the Carthaginian army. But not all the Gallic tribes saw Hannibal as a saviour from Roman domination, and he was obliged to battle his way through hostile territory several times.

Images from coins showing Hannibal and the Roman general Scipio Africanus who defeated the Carthaginians at Zama in 202 BC

From a treaty drawn up between Carthage and Macedon, Rome's enemy in Greece, we know that the aim of Hannibal's invasion of Italy was breaking up the Roman confederation of allied states. If Hannibal could get its allies to declare their independence, then Rome would be once again no more than one among a number of states, and not the dominant partner among the Italian cities. He was encouraged to pursue this strategy by rumblings in a number of Rome's allies. In Capua, for instance, the citizens of this great southern city had openly begun to query whether the alliance with Rome was of any real benefit. After the Roman defeat at Cannae in 216 BC, Capua immediately defected to Carthage. The same sort of political uncertainty existed in other cities such as Tarentum, the modern port of Taranto, whose prosperity had declined as a result of Roman hegemony.

Hannibal knew that Rome's authority was sustained by her legionaries. By adopting a manoeuvre-based approach for the destruction of the Roman army, he intended to unsettle Rome's allies and preserve the strength of his own limited forces. A war of manoeuvre demands a high level of generalship but this was exactly what a skilled tactician like Hannibal could provide. At first he was brilliantly successful in a campaign little short of a 'blitzkrieg'. In late 218 BC he smashed two Roman armies at Trebia in northern Italy; in early 217 BC another two Roman armies were nearly destroyed at the lake of Trasimene in modern Tuscany; and in the summer of 216 BC at Cannae, near the Adriatic coast, he inflicted on the Romans the worst defeat they had ever known. At Cannae Hannibal encircled two armies and slew 80,000 men. 'The morning after the battle', the historian Livy relates, 'the Carthaginians applied themselves to collecting the spoils and viewing the carnage, which even to an enemy's eye was a shocking spectacle. All over the field Roman soldiers lay dead in their thousands, horse and foot mingled together, as the shifting phases of the battle, or the attempt to escape, had brought them together'.

Livy goes on to say that had Hannibal moved onto the city of Rome straight away, the war would have been over. But the Carthaginian general felt there was no immediate possibility of conducting a siege, and so a shaken Rome managed to adopt a war of attrition against the invaders and those Roman allies who had gone over to their side. Gradually it won back most of the important ones, Capua and Syracuse in 211 BC, and Tarentum in 209 BC. Hannibal's problem was in fighting so far from home, without the possibility of regular supplies and reinforcements. Roman supremacy at sea meant he had to feed himself, and especially after the Roman counter-attack in Spain. The end was in sight once Rome moved directly against Carthage.

Hannibal was recalled and in early 202 BC faced the Romans at Zama, south of the city of Carthage. Prior to the engagement, Livy tells us, 'exactly half-way between the opposing ranks of armed men, each attended by an interpreter, Hannibal and the Roman commander Scipio met . . . For a moment mutual admiration struck them dumb, and they looked at each other in silence . . . But at length the negotiations failed, and the two generals returned to their armies with the news that the issue must be settled by arms. Each side had to accept the fortune which the gods chose to give'. At the end of the battle, the Romans had lost barely 2000 men, but on the Carthaginian side 20,000 men lay dead on the ground, and many more were taken prisoner. The Second Punic War was over.

Outcomes

After the end of hostilities Hannibal settled down to a political career in Carthage, but Roman suspicions were aroused by his enemies, who told visiting envoys that he was scheming with the Seleucid ruler Antiochus III. Whatever the truth of the accusation, Hannibal fled to Antiochus' court in Syria and played a minor role in the struggle between Antiochus and Rome. After Antiochus' defeat, a fugitive Hannibal sought refuge in a number of places before taking his life in 182 BC, so as to avoid a Roman extradition order.

During the half century after the battle of Zama Carthage survived as a commercial centre, until in the Third Punic War (149–146 BC) Rome decided to totally destroy the city. Even though the Carthaginians were no longer a threat, the Romans could never forget that Hannibal had nearly brought them to their knees.

Why does it matter?

The leader as figurehead

After the defeat at Zama, Hannibal told the Carthaginian government that he had lost not only the battle but the war, and there was now no option other than suing for peace with Rome. Perhaps this frankness impressed Publius Cornelius Scipio Africanus Major (to give the Roman victor his full name), as he made no move to curtail Hannibal's freedom. He may have also acknowledged then his continued respect for the Carthaginian general, since Rome's enmity towards Hannibal was still to come.

Some of the best known and most widely recognised companies have achieved their notoriety in the eyes of the public not simply through the quality of what they do or what they produce (although that does help), but because they have leaders who have very deliberately developed a distinct public persona, rather like Hannibal. If successful, these individuals become inseparable in the public mind from the companies they lead. They have become not just figureheads but the image of their organisation in the wider world. Richard Branson of Virgin, for example, has cultivated the image of a powerful but relaxed, unorthodox and approachable chief executive; an image which is mirrored to a significant extent in the working principles and goals of his businesses. Bill Gates of Microsoft has created a similarly influential personal image, since it is hard to think of the organisation without the physical image of the man appearing in your mind. This image is carefully maintained by the man himself, and managed by the company. As Paul Moritz, head of Microsoft's development division, put it, 'We use his celebrity shamelessly'.

Leaders such as these have more than a little of the showman about them, they are comfortable and accomplished with the media and are drawn to making dramatic public gestures of their commitment to their businesses, particularly when new products are launched on the world or when their organisations' reputation is under threat. Leaders are watched very carefully and their behaviour is often mimicked by their subordinates. To the marketing professional, this highlights the need for leaders to think carefully about the way they develop and present a personal 'brand' in their relationships with their employees and with external stakeholders. This is not to say that all chief executives have to promote themselves so assiduously, or that this is an essential ingredient in creating a successful business. Not all leaders are comfortable with such high-profile exposure, and many prefer to work behind the scenes in order to set the direction for the organisation and to secure its reputation in the wider world.

Creating an image

Of course, the notion of a leader building a public image is not a new one, and virtually any period of history and any geographical area can be mined to find examples. In early nineteenth-century Britain, for instance, there was Nelson, who had decided as a teenager that he was going to become a national hero, took huge risks to achieve his goal, and consciously promoted a public image based on his naval successes by using the media in a highly sophisticated manner; and there was Lord Byron, whose public persona ('mad, bad and dangerous to know') made him a superstar of his time, as well as the most widely read poet in Europe. In some cases the association of a leader with their organisation in the public mind can endure for a long time, but rarely as long as Hannibal's image has done for a personification of Carthage. Few people today would be able to identify the location of ancient Carthage, or indeed be familiar with anything significant about its history or culture. Except, of course, for the picture of Hannibal and his elephants struggling to cross the Alps!

An image made familiar to generations of children through their school history textbooks, this heroic crossing has somehow become widely embedded in the public consciousness; the noble and brave Hannibal, wrapped in furs, probably astride his elephant, driving through a snowstorm, surrounded by his loyal troops. And this reflects what little we may know of his organisation, the city of Carthage itself, proud, courageous, independent and determined to resist the power of Rome. For the Romans too, Hannibal's image continued to exert a powerful influence for years after his invasion of Italy, but for them he was the epitome of the aggressive, calculating and untrustworthy neighbour who would turn against Rome given a suitable opportunity. It is also important to note that at different times people have found very different things to admire about Hannibal. Machiavelli, in his famous manual of guidance on practical politics in the Italian Renaissance entitled *The Prince*, is drawn, as others have been, to the remarkable way that Hannibal kept his multinational force together overseas for some 15 years without a single mutiny. For Machiavelli, however, it is the total ruthlessness of the man that provides the lesson from which others can learn. He writes:

When the prince is with his armies and has under his command a multitude of troops, then it is necessary that he does not worry about being considered cruel; for without that reputation he will never keep an army united or prepared for battle. Among the praiseworthy deeds of Hannibal is this; that, commanding a very large army in foreign lands, made up of all sorts of men, there never appeared the slightest dissension, neither amongst themselves or against their leader, including the times of good fortune and bad. This could not have arisen from anything other than his inhuman cruelty, which, together with his other outstanding qualities, made him respected and terrifying in the eyes of his troops; and without that, to achieve the same effect, his other qualities would not have sufficed.

Leaders as ambassadors

Rather than the cruelty so beloved of Machiavelli, it may have been Hannibal's tactical genius and gift for planning that kept his mission alive for 15 years in enemy-dominated territory, but it was his role as ambassador for Carthage which put him in a position to contest the field with Rome in the first place. His outstanding reputation drew allies to him from the wide range of peoples who felt themselves to be the natural opponents of Roman expansion. No organisation is a closed system. All businesses are influenced by government policy and legislation, affected by swings in public opinion and taste, and struck by changes in the marketplace stemming from the actions of their competitors. Leaders need to network effectively with opinion-formers and stakeholders on behalf of their organisations. In presenting the interests of their business, it is not unknown for pragmatism to replace honesty. Reflecting on his posting to the court of Venice in the late sixteenth century, Sir Henry Wotton, an experienced Elizabethan diplomat and politician, described this tension when he said: 'An ambassador is an honest man sent to lie abroad for the good of his country'. The remarkable success of Chong Chuyong, for instance, in creating the Hyundai corporation in Korea owed much to his superb ambassadorial skills, his networking with political leaders firstly from Japan, and later from the United States, but as Andrew Brown explains in *The Six Dimensions of Leadership*:

Within Korea itself the success of Hyundai was intimately tied to the wrangling, bribery and influence-peddling – all norms of the Korean construction industry at the time – of which he was an impressive exponent.

Chong Chuyong started out with a small but prosperous machine and automobile service shop. Though tiny by any measure of business success, he was ready for the post-war boom that the departure of the Japanese and the arrival of the Americans brought about in Cold War Korea. The colonial rule of Japan had begun Korean industrialisation, which accelerated after the outbreak of the Sino-Japanese War in 1937. So it was that first Japanese military needs, then American ones, were successfully exploited by entrepreneurs like Chong Chuyong.

In Hannibal's case, despite repeatedly beating Roman armies sent against him, conditions in Italy never allowed him to bring about the mass defections of Rome's allies and friends which he had envisaged would flow from sustained military success. Stubborn Rome was ultimately too strong, or too bloody minded, to concede. At the very time that Hannibal eventually, but rather ineffectually, arrived at the walls of Rome itself, the land on which his camp was sited a few miles away, was being auctioned at a price which took no account of the Carthaginian army currently based there!

Securing resources

A key function of a leader is to secure the resources required to support the business plans of the organisation. In the private sector, investors need to have confidence in the leader and to believe that the company has the potential to grow and create a profit; while in the public sector, leaders are well used to a competitive process of lobbying for funding from official budget-holders. Despite his high-profile leadership style and his ingenuity in finding the resources to endure for so long in the field, Hannibal progressively found an adequate level of support increasingly hard to secure. His political masters in Carthage failed to provide him with the resources in terms of reinforcements and supplies that he needed to complete his daring mission. His position was analogous to a chief executive who cannot get the board to commit the level of support needed to turn a plan into reality. Rome, on the other hand, had the wherewithal to create new armies and keep them in the field.

The differing approaches which leaders in the same industry can adopt in securing resources for their business ventures is well illustrated in the contrasting stories of two highly individual tycoons in the very competitive field of newspaper publishing. In his early publishing career, Robert Maxwell showed an innate skill in networking with political leaders, particularly in Eastern Europe and Russia, which led to the rapid growth of his Pergamon Press empire. During takeover negotiations with Leasco, an American financial and data-processing group, in 1969, doubts began to emerge about Maxwell's business dealings. A subsequent enquiry by the UK's Department of Trade and Industry found that he, 'is not a person who can be relied on to exercise proper stewardship of a publicly quoted company'. Few business people could expect to recover their career after such damming comments, but Maxwell's ambitions were fierce and by the 1980s he had rebuilt his empire and was desperate to add a national British newspaper to his publishing activities. Twice thwarted by Rupert Murdoch, the Australian media mogul, Maxwell eventually became the proprietor of the *Daily Mirror*. But this purchase, and that of the Macmillan publishing house, dragged him into colossal debt. Despite maintaining his confident public profile and his lavish lifestyle, he was utterly desperate for finance, which he could no longer secure from legitimate sources. The extent of his desperation did not become clear until his mysterious death in 1991, at which time it was revealed not only that his company was some £2 billion in debt, but that £400 million was missing from the company pension funds, destroying the financial security of thousands of Mirror Group workers.

Intriguingly, Rupert Murdoch, now one of the highest profile and most influential global media leaders, faced a similar crisis in 1990, at the very moment that Maxwell's business was sliding rapidly into insolvency. Having overstretched himself in expanding so quickly, Murdoch found himself with no less than $7.6 billion of debt and 146 creditors! Murdoch's considerable ambassadorial skills were put to a severe test as he tirelessly flew from country to country to meet his main creditors face to face. He was fortunate, in the end, that Citibank agreed to reschedule his News Corporation's massive debts. Since then Murdoch has never looked back. In business terms you either have it, or you don't!

What does it mean for you?

'Superheads'

The New Labour government, which came to power in the UK in 1997, had famously declared that its priorities were to be, 'education, education, education'. By the end of the decade their drive to improve educational standards faced a major obstacle from the failure to turn around a 'rump' of seriously underperforming secondary schools, many of which were in deprived inner city areas. These schools seemed impermeable to the effects of a flood of policy initiatives and additional funding. Judged as 'failing schools' by OFSTED, the school inspectorate body, they typically showed the following characteristics:

- poor SATS and GCSE exam results;

- high levels of truancy and 'unauthorised absence';

- low teaching standards;

- weak management;

- low teacher morale;

- high turnover of staff resulting in lack of continuity.

The government's solution to this problem was to relaunch the weakest schools, usually rebranded with new corporate images and logos, through a programme entitled 'Freshstart'. In the opinion of its educational advisers, the poor performance of these schools was often a result of weak leadership. One response to this conclusion was the creation of a new kind of school leader, the so-called 'superhead'. With a well-proven track record of success in large secondary schools, a superhead was thus appointed on a high salary and charged with a mission to turn the school round, quickly and decisively. The performance of such a headteacher quickly became the subject of intense scrutiny from the local and national media, parents and the teaching professionals. If they were successful in bringing about a real transformation in the school's performance, then their achievements would be trumpeted as a vindication of educational policy.

Typically, these 'superheads' are people who relish a challenge and, almost without exception, they are great communicators, charismatic, visionary and inspirational, and more than happy to take on the role of figurehead for their recreated schools. In fact, they are the sort of leaders that any organisation could justifiably feel proud of having at the top. However, a spate of resignations (three of the first group left their schools in the space of a few weeks in 2005), accusations of professional malpractice in the case of one high-profile individual, and less than enthusiastic results from research carried out by university academics, have all combined to take the gloss off the 'superhead' revolution. So, what issues are actually emerging and what lessons can be drawn from the experiment?

Pressures on the individual

Being a headteacher in a large secondary school is no sinecure at the best of times, but in the case of a 'superhead' in a school already identified as failing, and with all the attendant scrutiny from OFSTED and the local education authority, the challenges of the role can be overwhelming. By necessity, the individual is firmly in the public gaze and the ambassadorial aspects of the job can be extremely demanding. Although the local community is likely to be encouraging and supportive, and especially the parents who are desperate to see the successful rebirth of their local school, other interested parties will be scrutinising every event for signs of impending failure.

Lasting change

The evidence suggests that, despite rapid and impressive improvements in performance and quality in the early days, lasting change is very much harder to embed. Several of the 'Freshstart' schools have, in fact, drifted back towards their previously poor standards after the initial burst of enthusiasm, particularly once the 'superhead' has moved on to another job. Keeping up standards over time is enormously tough, once failing schools have been raised from the lowest level.

Careers, salaries and conditions

The opportunity to take on the leadership role in a 'Freshstart' school is not one that successful headteachers have always seen as an irresistible career move! A previously strong career record could lose its lustre, if such a move went badly wrong. So in spite of highly attractive pay and incentive packages, 'superhead' posts have not always proved easy to fill. The pay and conditions package itself has also been a cause of dissent in schools whose staff may feel embittered at a new headteacher being 'parachuted in' with a remuneration deal to which they could never aspire themselves. In a culture where salary scales have traditionally been in the public domain, this has been an extremely difficult change to accommodate.

Alternatives and the future

That many education professionals are so uncomfortable with the notion of 'superheads' reflects the fact that the style of leadership implicit in their creation is still not a familiar one in schools. Interestingly, the National College for School Leadership (NCSL) carried out a survey of newly appointed headteachers in November 2005, which showed that the most respected leadership style was the 'courageous servant leadership' approach of Gandhi, over what they perceived as more aggressive or coercive styles. As Alison Kelly of the NCSL put it, 'Coaching and democratic styles enable headteachers to work with others to bring about improvements in schools that are sustainable over the long term'. As an alternative to the 'tough-guy' approaches that characterise the 'superhead' phenomenon there is a growing interest in the notion of 'distributed leadership' as an alternative to investing so much in the performance of one leading individual. In such a model leadership roles and responsibilities are shared by different people in the organisation, thus giving a team a shared stake in improving the performance of the school. On the other hand, there is continuing concern in official circles of a shortage of effective leaders in schools, with suggestions of creating 'hyperheads', capable of acting as CEOs of whole groups of schools. It does not help, of course, that they are likely to be called unofficially big, big heads.

What issues does this account of educational change raise for the leadership of your own organisation?

12

Creativity: The Resourcefulness of Zhu Geliang

What happened?

The leader

A distinguished mathematician and inventor, Zhu Geliang (pronounced 'Zoo-gee-lee-ang') was renowned for his ability to solve apparently insoluble problems. Something of a legend in his own lifetime, this minister put his quick-wittedness at the service of Shu, one of the three states into which ancient China disintegrated after the fall of the Han dynasty in AD 220.

The historical setting

The crisis which overtook the early Chinese empire had been developing for a century. No longer were emperors able to control powerful families who had acquired great estates. They could not even conduct a survey of cultivated land for the purpose of reassessing the land tax, the empire's basic revenue. As a result of this central weakness, there occurred a gradual resurgence of feudalism. Peasants were once again tied to the land, either as sharecroppers or labourers, while artisans and scholars were compelled to associate themselves with local magnates strong enough to offer protection against bandits and rebellious soldiers. Once conscription was abolished, the imperial government had to depend on regular troops and the retainers of powerful families, a military weakness that encouraged raids from the nomads living north of the Great Wall. Eventually China found it impossible to cope with these foreign people when they became allies of the various factions during civil disturbances. But prior to the foreign occupation of the northern provinces in the fourth century the Chinese empire briefly split into what are known as the Three Kingdoms.

Although a contributory factor in weakening the imperial regime was unrest among the peasantry, goaded into revolt by foreign incursion and the greed of wealthy land-owning families, the immediate cause of the overthrow of the Han dynasty was the rivalry that bedevilled the palace. Against powerful families, who tended to dominate both the military and civil arms of government, late Han emperors were tempted to employ eunuchs, whose own ambitions soon made them yet another faction in the contention for power. The killing of one general at court by the eunuchs in 189 brought a brutal response from his troops: they stormed the palace and slaughtered every eunuch in sight. The beneficiary of this military coup was another general by the name of Cao Cao, who assumed authority in all but name. When in 220 his son, Cao Pi, deposed the last Han emperor and founded a dynasty of his own, the Wei, his two chief rivals set up their own houses in western and southern China.

Against the southern kingdom of Wu, Cao Pi had no success, but against the smaller, western kingdom of Shu his forces made greater headway. It was fortunate that the ruler of Shu found in Zhu Geliang a very capable minister. Despite its relative weakness in terms of population, Shu pursued an aggressive policy towards both Wu and Wei, the strongest of the Three Kingdoms.

Zhu Geliang, the ingenious Chinese minister, sitting on a chariot-like wheelbarrow. His leadership ensured the survival of the Shu state during his period of office.

Zhu Geliang's behaviour

Zhu Geliang's efficiency in war and diplomacy ensured that Shu remained independent during his lifetime. One of Zhu Geliang's inventions, the wheelbarrow, was used for transporting military supplies. Its large central wheel permitted one man to wheel a heavy load over otherwise impassable tracks. Yet his undoubted ability to discover ingenious solutions to apparently insoluble problems went beyond such practical aid.

When in 222 AD the king of Shu chose to ignore Zhu Geliang's advice and launch an ill-prepared attack on Wu, the resourceful minister devised a scheme which baffled the advancing enemy. On the line of the inevitable retreat of the Shu army, Zhu Geliang built a marvellous city in the form of a maze. When the victorious forces of Wu reached this incredible construction, they turned back rather than risk disaster in exploring its layout. Five years later, after the collapse of another Shu army during an equally ill-prepared invasion of Wei, Zhu Geliang saved the day by means of a similar ruse. He ordered the gates of the city into which the defeated Shu soldiers had fled to be thrown open, while conspicuously on the undefended battlements he strummed a lute. So at odds with the military situation was the joy of the music that the Wei commander decided to withdraw in case a trap was being set.

The rivalry between the Three Kingdoms was a function of a shift in economic strength southwards and westwards. The ancient heartland of China, the northern plains of the Yellow river valley, temporarily found itself unable to dominate the whole of the country. What Zhu Geliang achieved until his death in 234 was the effective direction of Shu's resources, not withstanding the unnecessary aggressiveness of its ruler.

Outcomes

The struggle between the Three Kingdoms was ended in 280 by the Western Jin dynasty, which had toppled the Wei house 15 years earlier. The first Western Jin emperor, Sima Yan, was a soldier in the mould of Cao Cao, but he outdid him by briefly ruling all China. What stood behind his triumph was a great concentration on agricultural productivity and water transport as a means of strengthening military power. Local magnates were stripped of their retainers and extra manpower came from foreign migrants who were permitted to settle within the Great Wall. This policy of foreign settlement was to have the same dire military and political consequences it had in the Roman empire. The Western Jin dynasty lasted only until 316, the year in which most of the northern provinces passed in the hands of people from the steppe and the remnant of Sima Yan's line fled southwards to the Yangzi River valley and founded the Eastern Jin dynasty. A combination of external and internal pressures caused this collapse and ensured that China should be divided for 273 years.

Why does it matter?

The need for innovation

Against all the odds, Zhu Geliang preserved the independence of Shu. He had to make the best of this kingdom's scant resources and minimise the impact of the ill-judged military actions ordered by its aggressive ruler. As long as he remained a minister Shu managed to keep rival kingdoms at bay. In the end though, demography brought about defeat: there were not enough people to stand against the northern state of Wei.

Like Shu's brief period of brilliance under the guidance of Zhu Geliang, small companies have similarly come and gone. In June 2005 *Business Week* produced its annual survey of the 100 best small companies in the USA. The article by Arlene Weintraub and Peter Burrows highlighted the achievements of a wide range of businesses, some household names such as Pixar, the film production company, and many less well-established or familiar companies. The list also highlighted the volatility of the small business sector, with some companies that had featured in previous years as hot prospects disappearing from the scene altogether. There, however, some common features of companies appearing in the list.

What these companies prove is that talent, teamwork and *creativity* often win out, even against tough foes like a struggling economy and fierce competition . . . Some are famous names. But many have toiled in obscurity for years – even decades – tweaking their business models multiple times before finally hitting on winning formulas.

Anyone familiar with the world of small businesses will recognise the years of toil which often precede overnight success! It is also very significant that creativity is picked out as such a vital ingredient in the recipe for success. In many cases it is the initial creative spark which inspires an individual to become an entrepreneur and develop their own business in the first place, often driven by the need to see an idea for a new product or service from conception to production. In the United States small companies are a major source of innovation, producing 13 times as many patents as large companies do. In the UK the emphasis that government policy places on small and medium sized businesses as the key driver of economic growth and employment reflects a similar profile of activity.

Creativity is an essential precursor to innovation and the inextricable links between the two are most obviously demonstrated in the development of successful small businesses. For the leaders of businesses, such as those analysed in the *Business Week* article, creativity is a determining feature of their personality. In *The New Alchemists*, an intriguing study of the creative and entrepreneurial process, management thinker and writer Charles Handy profiles a variety of successful leaders in the private sector and the 'not-for-profit' arena in London. He identifies some common threads in their stories, including their dedication, doggedness and 'difference'. Creativity is central to the accounts of their business lives and tends to make them non-conformist in their attitudes and beliefs.

Creative people, other research suggests, like to cultivate their difference, by which they mean their particular edge or talent, while the rest of us are still wondering what is different about ourselves, what talent we can lay claim to.

Although some of the individuals profiled have gone on to develop their organisations into large-scale undertakings, such as Richard Branson of Virgin and Charles Dunstone of Carphone Warehouse, Handy suggests that these are not people who would easily fit into a corporate environment (unless they had created it themselves).

None of our group would fit easily into the ranks of a large organisation. They would be very uncomfortable subordinates, since their delight in difference makes them intolerant of both conformity and assumed authority.

Corporate creativity

This points up an important concern for larger and more mature organisations. There may be an aspiration to appoint and develop genuinely creative managers and, indeed, an acknowledgement that drawing on the creative talents of people throughout the organisation is a significant factor in keeping the business forward looking and competitive in changing times but, even given that awareness, how can such personalities be accommodated in a complex organisation? For many writers, such as James Kouzes and Barry Posner in *The Leadership Challenge*, that is a key issue for leaders today. They claim:

Leadership is inextricably connected with the process of innovation, of bringing new ideas, methods or solutions into use.

The sort of ingenious solutions to the problems facing the state of Shu, which Zhu Geliang devised, are remarkable examples of 'thinking outside the box'. They clearly relied on deploying resources in highly imaginative ways. That such radical solutions were actually permitted clearly says much about the gravity of the situation facing the state, but without the creativity of Zhu Geliang nothing could have made a difference. Zhu Geliang's actions were, of course, highly unorthodox, have an almost mythical feel to them, and may seem far distant from the realities of modern life.

Yet it is possible to find examples of such radical thinking in response to crises in more recent times. A principal objection to the choice of the Normandy beaches as the point of invasion of German-occupied Europe in 1944 was the absence of a natural harbour to use for the vast number of reinforcements and supplies that were to be needed in the first few weeks of the battle. The solution? Construct a huge portable concrete harbour, the 'Mulberry' harbour, and take it in sections across the Channel with the invasion force. Although considered crazy and a huge waste of precious resources by some military planners at the time, the plan was championed by Churchill and others and it worked, to the consternation of the Germans. It was worthy of the inventiveness of Zhu Geliang. Turning to one's own creativity in order to anticipate or solve problems depends on a leader being questioning about the status quo and open minded about possible options. This mindset is well described by Hilarie Owen and Vicky Hodgson in *The Leadership Manual*, when they write:

Thinking in both a creative and critical way requires not only a will to challenge your own ideas and beliefs, and those of other people, but also an ability to think laterally, questioning and changing ideas and research and testing new ways of doing things.

A creative environment

In contrast to methodical and systematic approaches to problem solving, the learning models of decision making that characterised management training at one time, the emphasis has shifted in recent years to developing processes which encourage creativity and ingenuity. Techniques such as 'mind mapping', 'creative brain showers', and 'process flow diagrams' typically stimulate a flow of ideas at an individual level which are then tested and refined through team interaction, discussion and challenge. Yet some managers, even those who are highly creative themselves, can find it difficult to develop creativity in others by listening, encouraging and discussing. They may also, unintentionally, overwhelm people with ideas. To value creativity does need a particular sort of environment to be effective and not all businesses can provide this. Alan Robertson and Graham Asbbey point up the differences between the rhetoric and reality of creativity as it is commonly applied in *Managing Talented People*:

Surely all organisations are unequivocal in calling for innovation and in encouraging creativity? Surely this is what underpins the demand for continuous improvement? In theory, yes. But in practice, do managers consistently welcome that creativity? Do their actions support the organisational rhetoric?

Some organisations remain understandably anxious about the directions in which unfettered creativity might take them were they are able to create the right conditions for its expression. An underlying fear of anarchy can lie close to the surface, for, as Michael Bakunin, the nineteenth-century anarchist, said, 'The urge for destruction is also a creative urge'. In fact this might not seem too distant from the thinking of some high-profile management gurus of recent times. As the highly influential Tom Peters says in *Thriving on Chaos*:

Following and administering rules might have been dandy in the placid environments of yesteryear. Not today. Managers must create new worlds. And then destroy them; and then create anew.

How ready are the leaders of our own organisations to take that forward? And how many have the advantage of a Zhu Geliang to overcome inevitable setbacks?

What does it mean for you?

Take any large organisation that has regularly registered patents over the years and you will find one key change between now and (say) 50 years ago. Seldom today is one person nominated on patents, and this is largely because now whole teams, even multiple teams, work on new ideas, whereas in the past it was more likely to be one person or just a few people who had worked on a breakthrough. So, as leaders in an organisation, there are a number of key drivers of creativity that they can sensibly put in place. The first is an environment which encourages creative thinking.

A supportive environment

If innovation and creativity are really important to your organisation, as they are to most present-day organisations, then say so! Let people know via your vision and values, inductions and team meetings that both are a priority. Then reinforce this message by allocating budgets which enable creativity and innovation to thrive.

Words extolling creativity in the workplace are never enough unless they are reinforced by senior manager behaviour. This means allocated resources, supporting time away for thinking, and allowing people to take risks.

Organisations that thrive on creativity have this supportive environment, in stark contrast to those organisations that have failed to innovate themselves to cope with changing business conditions. In non-innovating organisations you always find an environment of risk aversion, where sticking your head above the parapet becomes a dangerous pastime. So often here you encounter an over-bearing bullying senior management team which is forever connected to a traditional business model.

So if you want innovation to thrive make is easy for people to participate and not put themselves at risk. Otherwise, nothing at all will happen. The second thing most likely to influence innovation and creativity is appropriate project selection.

Pick the right project

The next important step is to make sure you pick the projects that are really going to make a difference. The need for getting innovation quickly on the market means that organisations have to find ways of allocating scarce resources to what really matters.

So be clear about which market you are in, have a real picture of where you are going, and identify the three to five key areas that you want to operate in. This is another reason why small companies so often thrive as innovators, because they can only afford to operate within a narrow area, and this provides them with a real sense of focus.

Large companies, however, have found ways over the years to address some of these constraints. In the past innovative projects that had progressed beyond a certain stage were almost unstoppable. As a result of this head-long rush, this project-driven dynamic, products were often launched onto the market only to be discontinued shortly afterwards. It is worth reflecting on the whole process of innovation. Have a look at this model.

Today projects go through a number of stages where they have to meet rigorous criteria before they can move on to

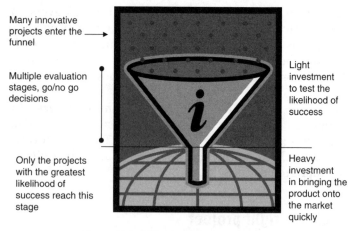

Figure 12.1 The innovation process

the next stage. Then what finally emerges out of the funnel at the end are those projects most likely to succeed, and these will receive the heavy investment required for speed to the market.

Teach creative methodology

Brainstorming, team facilitation and creative techniques can all be taught and should be taught if your organisation truly values creativity. Here is a relevant case study.

Barefoot on a Beach is a holiday company focusing on exclusive beach vacations around the world. They have always prided themselves on being ahead of the competition, both with creative ideas and new products.

The company recognised some years ago that they needed to have a way of harvesting great ideas from their staff, customers and partners and had, therefore, invested in training a team of internal facilitators who could run an innovation process for the business. Having identified six people with the right personalities and skills to take on the challenge they worked with an international 'ideas company' based in Singapore which, to preserve commercial confidentiality, worked with only one client in a given market sector at any one time. They set out to train the facilitators to run the innovation process.

The process incorporated the following steps:

- Selecting the right project

- Picking the right team for the job including a board sponsor

- Creating the right environment

- Gathering the right data

- Using the right tools

- Validating ideas

- Turning ideas into products

What made the process successful was that, although being simple and fun to use, it was still a highly effective way of turning ideas into real products. People learnt the process through their participation in its methods and were then able to use it in their daily roles. In this way some of the key tools and concepts became second nature to them and were embedded within the organisation.

The innovation team were supported by a sponsor on the main board, who had ensured support for the project at the highest level. Once the training had been completed the team presented themselves to the board, explaining the rigour of their process and winning their support for the difficult start-up phase.

They all agreed that they needed a few quick wins to build up the confidence of the organisation in the team and the process.

As their first real project they selected the Maldives, which has some of the best resorts in the world. Customers in the UK complained that their dream holidays were being ruined by the difficulties of getting there and back. Direct flights to Male were hard to come by and it was not unusual to have to endure an 18-hour three stop return flight which tended to negate the benefits of the relaxing holiday.

To fully appreciate the problem the project team were flown in to the Maldives from various destinations across Europe so that they had first hand experience of getting there. During their short stay they met representatives from the leisure industry and spoke to as many customers as possible. They then went through the gruelling journey home, gathering as much relevant information as possible.

Once back in Europe with the help of two of the facilitators they set out to resolve the problem and came up with a headline that was going to transform their approach to this route. They labelled the project as 'The Joy of the Journey' and, instead of making it an ordeal, they looked for ways of making the trip a real pleasure. This alternative approach won huge support from management and was soon implemented across the business.

Recognise creativity

The final ingredient that needs to be put in place is timely recognition. People have to feel that their exceptional contributions to the organisation have not gone unrecognised, especially when they are most needed.

Recognition can be as simple as just saying thank you, a simple technique that many managers never bother to use. Or there could be a formal recognition scheme culminating in a recognition celebration of the most successful creative contributions of the year. Whatever you set up though, it must be seen to be fair, and the nominations as well as the recognition need to be valued by all of those participating. Such schemes also have to run consistently year after year to build up their credibility and acceptance.

In conclusion, successful organisations are those which are able to harness the creativity of all their people, and capitalise on the innovation that emerges. To get to that point takes a lot of hard work, establishing the right environment and investing in ways to engage the drive of your employees. However, if you don't do it, the chances are you will at a later stage pay an even higher price, when your organisation fails because you have not found ways of competing in an increasingly fickle marketplace.

13

Learning: Li Shimin and Wei Zheng

What happened?

The leader

The man who did most to preserve a reunified China was Li Shimin (pronounced 'Lee-she-min'), the second emperor of the Tang dynasty. It was his straightforward and economical government that confirmed the Chinese people's belief in the value of unity. He came to the throne in AD 626 and took the reign title Tai Zong, 'Great Founder'.

The historical setting

At the end of the ancient world the situation of China was totally different from that of Rome. Both of these extensive empires had endured foreign invasion, but in the western Mediterranean all the Roman provinces were lost as the invaders carved out for themselves separate kingdoms. An attempt from Constantinople to reconquer Italy, Spain and Africa in the sixth century had only mixed success.

Although the northern provinces of the Chinese empire were similarly overrun and settled by foreign invaders in the fourth century, so strong was the absorptive power of Chinese culture that these nomadic people eventually abandoned their own customs for those of China. This Sino-Turkish synthesis led to a reunification of the whole country, since in 589 a Chinese-speaking Turkish general from the north conquered the Chinese ruler of the south. The new dynasty was called the Sui and it ruled until the foundation of the Tang dynasty in 618. Its downfall was caused by a popular rebellion, a disastrous war against Korea, excessive labour on public works, and harsh punishments for any show of disobedience.

It was at this troubled time of uncertain loyalties that Li Shimin grew up in northwestern China. He was a younger son of an old noble family, descended from a celebrated general who four centuries earlier had served the Han emperors, almost the last rulers of an undivided empire. From an early age Li Shimin became familiar with warfare. In spite of a prophecy to the effect that a new dynasty was about to be founded by a family with the surname Li, there was no possibility that Li Shimin's easygoing father would become its first emperor had he not had such an able younger son. But in 618 Li Shimin captured the capital city of Chang'an, present-day Xian, and placed his father on the throne. Then he set off as commander-in-chief of the new dynasty's forces to subdue the rest of China and gain recognition for his father's rule.

Although he had achieved this aim by 623, Li Shimin received scant thanks from his brothers and especially the crown prince, his eldest brother, who was totally without talent. As Li Shimin's father was by now credulous and ageing, the Tang dynasty looked as vulnerable as the Sui one it had recently replaced. Intrigue at court nearly cost Li Shimin his life through poison and, when this attempt

Li Shimin, the Tang emperor Tai Zong, with his senior officials. His trusted prime minister Wei Zheng is the figure on the far left, next to the emperor.

failed, the crown prince tried to have him arrested on the charge of treason. In 626 Li Shimin struck first, putting his brothers to death and forcing his father to abdicate in his favour. It was fortunate for the new emperor that he was then popular with the army and admired by people at large as the hero of the age.

Li Shimin's behaviour

The tragic story of the quarrel between the brothers revealed the problems inherent in palace politics. It also revealed, however, Li Shimin's inexperience of such intrigues because only at the eleventh hour did the efforts of his devoted followers galvanise him into taking decisive action. In later life, when his experience as a ruler had opened his eyes to the political methods of control in use at court, did Li Shimin have reason to regret the resort to naked violence which had gained him the throne.

Instrumental in this realisation was Wei Zheng (pronounced 'Way-zern'), his most valued counsellor. The military background of the imperial family made Li Shimin very sensitive to dangers from generals and led him, on Wei Zheng's recommendation, to shift the balance of power from the military to the civil arm of government. Therefore he increased the number and frequency of official examinations for entry to the imperial civil service and instituted a scholarship system to promote learning. Examinations had been held by the Sui emperors, but the aristocracy only began to decline in influence under Li Shimin, when its place in government was gradually taken over by professional scholar-bureaucrats recruited on the basis of personal talent and education. The rise of men committed to the service of the empire changed the position of the ruler: he was no longer the chief aristocrat whose pedigree, as in the case of the Li family, was modest; on the contrary, with no aristocracy to challenge his authority, and with a loyal and hard-working bureaucracy, the imperial clan became set apart from ordinary people in quite a new way, and the emperor started to gather powers that could lead to despotism.

Wei Zheng set himself the task of resisting this dangerous political trend. When asked after Li Shimin had been on the throne for a decade, whether government was better conducted than it had been before the emperor first took over the administration, Wei Zheng replied: 'In the beginning you feared that we would not dare to tell you of your mistakes; later you received our admonitions with pleasure; now one must say you accept them with difficulty'. At Li Shimin's request Wei Zheng gave specific instances of what he meant and the emperor remarked: 'I would never have known my character was changing, unless Wei Zheng had proved it to me by these personal instances'.

Like the first Han emperor, the commoner Liu Bang, Li Shimin appreciated his own need for good advice: he knew that he had to learn more about leadership. So just as Liu Bang had turned to Lu Jia for help, Li Shimin asked Wei Zheng to write a manual for him and his sons. It was entitled *A Record of Good and Evil Rulers from Antiquity*, and the examples Wei Zheng chose under-scored his own views on responsible government. For he was keenly aware how during Li Shimin's reign prece-dents and patterns were being set which would affect the conduct of state business for generations to come. He believed that the emperor's power had to be contained and the ruler–minister relationship of shared decision making vigorously reaffirmed. However, the ruler-minister relationship was not always so smooth as Wei Zheng hoped. Yet he was never overawed by the emperor's powerful personality and was completely unafraid of him, even when he heard that in a towering rage Li Shimin had cried out, 'I am going to have to kill that old country bumpkin!'

Outcomes

Wei Zheng's daring independence rested on the unshake-able conviction that the fall of the previous Sui dynasty was attributable to its reluctance to heed the advice of loyal officials. He believed that its inability to deal with internal difficulties resulted from a preoccupation with foreign conquest, a belief which led him in 640 to oppose an expansionist policy in Central Asia, much to Li Shimin's annoyance. Five years later, renewed conflict with Korea turned into a disaster when a great blizzard caught the imperial army on its march home. Remem-bering the prudent advice he had always received, Li

Shimin sadly commented, 'If Wei Zheng were still alive, he would not have allowed US to do this'.

Why does it matter?

Self-awareness

From Wei Zheng's rapid rise to the highest civil service post, the modern equivalent of prime minister, and the reliance Li Shimin placed on him for 17 of the 23 years he reigned, it might be thought that he really did enjoy a special relationship with the throne. Yet nothing could be further from the truth, if this is assumed to mean good personal relations. For the emperor's relations with his chief minister were often strained and stormy, not least because Wei Zheng always stuck to his principles. But Li Shimin was still prepared to listen, even when, as a result, he had to acknowledge his own errors. One clear day in 636 the emperor climbed with his minister to the top of a new tower in the grounds of the imperial palace, from which it was possible to see the splendid mausoleum recently built for the deceased empress. To Li Shimin's consternation Wei Zheng said his poor eyesight prevented him from seeing anything. When at last he was pointed in the right direction, the minister commented: 'Oh, that's it then ... I thought Your Majesty was looking at another tomb'. Realising that Wei Zheng referred to the poor resting place provided for his own father, the first Tang emperor, Li Shimin wept and ordered the observation tower to be demolished at once – the Confucian minister had touched that potent Chinese nerve, filial piety.

Most analyses of leadership rightly draw attention to the significance of being able to manage oneself. In the seminal research on leadership carried out by American academic and writer Warren Bennis, 'management of self' features as one of the four leadership competencies, together with 'management of attention', 'management of meaning', and 'management of trust'. Similarly, Daniel Goleman, the populariser of emotional intelligence, suggests a model of leadership competencies with four domains – self-awareness, self-management, social awareness and relationship management. For Goleman, the very concept of an emotionally intelligent leader is founded on self-awareness, as he summarises the point in *The New Leaders*:

Self-awareness – often overlooked in business settings – is the foundation for the rest: without recognising our emotions, we will be poor at managing them, and less able to understand them in others. Self-aware leaders are attuned to their inner signals. They recognise, for instance, how their feelings affect themselves and their job performance.

A high level of self-awareness implies that a leader is able to identify his/her key strengths and deploy them effectively to the wider benefit of the organisation. It also means that a leader has a realistic sense of the limitations to his or her abilities, and knows how to improve skills and knowledge in these areas. Self-awareness is a key quality in leaders, especially as their own behaviour is so closely scrutinised by other people. Being in the spotlight means, for instance, that leaders with an inflated sense of their own abilities are readily exposed to criticism, or even ridicule, undermining the trust and confidence upon which effective working relationships are constructed.

A realistic awareness of self also needs to be translated into action in relationship building; self-awareness needs to create a facility for self-control in leaders. The alternative can be highly damaging for their businesses. Warren Bennis expresses this concern powerfully in *Managing the Dream* when he writes:

Management of self is critical; without it, leaders and managers can do more harm than good. Like incompetent doctors, incompetent managers can make life worse, make people sicker and less vital.

Reflection and feedback

In developing an accurate appreciation of their strengths and weaknesses a good leader is likely to draw on two key sources of learning, firstly on experience and, secondly, on the advice of other people. As Li Shimin struggled to come to terms with palace politics early in his career, and later greatly regretted the violence with which he had sought to resolve his family problem, so many leaders make serious errors of judgement at the start of their working lives (and sometimes later as well). They are fortunate if the businesses for which they work understand that the occasional mistake is inevitable and support the individual through the pain of this realisation. The biographies of high-profile business leaders often include accounts of such early disasters. It is a truism to say that such failures can provide a learning experience, but this is only really the case if the individual has the motivation to reflect honestly on the experience and then identify the extent of their personal responsibility. Or, if like Li Shimin, they have the very good fortune to encounter an adviser as honest, reliable and straightforward as Wei Zheng.

It is also true that, as Yoshisha Tabuchi, the former CEO of Nomura Securities, put it, 'past success can be as much a trap as failure'. Nomura was once a symbol of Japan's economic success, the largest and most profitable securities house in the country. But the late 1990s brought a spate of allegations of dealings with corporate racketeers and this together with a series of disastrous overseas investments made at the time of a major slowdown in the

East Asian economy, saw the company plunge into the red to the tune of $1.77 billion. For Tabuchi the underlying cause of the disaster was that the belief had grown within the organisation that they were effectively untouchable, that their track record of rapid growth was bound to continue. This proved to be a fundamental misunderstanding of their real situation.

The second crucial source of learning in relation to leaders developing their self-awareness lies in the way they listen to, and learn from, the perceptions that other people have of them. Most organisations now have well-developed schemes of performance management, and most leaders are well used to taking part in them as an appraiser or reviewer of colleagues. Not all leaders, however, are as enthusiastic or comfortable about being the subject of a performance review themselves, particularly if the programme incorporates an element of 360-degree assessment, which inevitably provides an opportunity for structured feedback on their performance from colleagues and subordinates as well as from their own bosses. Nevertheless, many organisations now use frameworks of management competence which identify the skills which they want their managers to demonstrate, and which now form the basis for evaluating the progress of even the most senior staff.

This type of formal review does not, of course, provide the only means by which a leader can gain the feedback from other people that is so important in planning his or her own subsequent development. Without access to this perspective, the inevitable loneliness of leadership can be further exacerbated. The fact that leadership can be a very solitary business is well evidenced by the growth in 'executive coaching', programmes whereby an experienced consultant from outside the organisation spends time with a senior postholder in order to open up a discussion of problems and issues, and assist the individual to find solutions appropriate to their position and personality. If leaders are lucky, they may have people within their own businesses who are able to play the role of 'critical friend' in this way, as indeed Li Shimin found in his redoubtable minister, Wei Zheng. A particularly telling criticism which the minister made of this ruler, to the effect that he found it increasingly difficult to accept criticism from others, marks a familiar phenomenon in leadership: namely, that as leaders grow in experience and authority they are sometimes less than ready to take note of how they are perceived by others, or to actively seek real feedback on their performance or on their leadership style. If they are blessed with someone like Wei Zheng, whose outspokenness is sufficient to keep their feet on the ground, then they are likely to prosper. It needs to be recognised, however, that it was the uncertainty of Li Shimin at the beginning of his reign which put Wei Zheng in such a strong position as a personal adviser in the first place.

Self-managed development

As with staff throughout an organisation, the pace of technological, commercial and structural change means that training and development has become an integral part of the process of maintaining a leader's effectiveness. In terms of development, managers were once firmly in the hands of their organisations and, as their careers developed into leadership roles, they would assemble lists of courses and qualifications through which they had been sponsored. The extent to which these development activities actually impacted on their performance was frequently less carefully monitored. Yet many companies would micro-manage the training route that they had designed for the individuals who had been identified as offering the potential for a senior post. Today, by contrast, the emphasis has firmly shifted to managers taking over responsibility for their own learning. As Stuart Crainer explains it in *Key Management Ideas*:

Managers and their companies now realise that developing managerial skills and techniques is not simply the responsibility of the company. Managers, too, have a role to playing being proactive and identifying areas in which they need to develop ... Rather than having their development mapped out for them, managers are managing it for themselves.

Underlying this shift in emphasis is the realisation that learning is, in itself, a vital component in successful leadership; that curiosity, open-mindedness and a thirst for new ideas, knowledge and skills, mark out the most effective leaders now, and in the future. A leader demonstrating this kind of outlook is also much more likely to inspire an organisation to be adventurous and questioning, and to create a culture where all staff are constantly seeking to change and improve the way in which they work. This sort of thinking provides the foundation for creating that much sought-after, but rarely achieved entity – the 'learning organisation'.

Charles Handy, the influential British writer on organisational development, has written a great deal about this type of learning and its relevance to the changing world of business. In *The Age of Unreason* he seeks to distinguish between formal training and learning when he notes that:

Learning is not the same as study, nor the same as training. It is bigger than both. It is a cast of mind, a habit of life, a way of thinking about things, a way of growing ... Learning is not finding out what other people already know, but is solving our own problems for our own purposes.

Handy also identifies in those individuals who take their own learning seriously a characteristic he calls 'a proper selfishness', a justified obsession with one's own development. He suggests that those who learn best and most are those who take responsibility for themselves and for their future; have a clear view of what they want that future to be; want to make sure that they get it and believe that they can.

Wei Zheng's *A Record of Good and Evil Rulers since Antiquity* was a stopgap for Li Shimin. It provided the emperor with a useful perspective on leadership, but his real learning, his growth in self-awareness, came through listening to the views of Wei Zheng and other ministers on the decisions he considered taking.

What does it mean for you?

Chartered manager

The Chartered Manager award has been developed by the Chartered Management Institute (CMI) as a benchmark against which individual professional managers can assess and accredit their own competence against the highest national standards. The scheme is promoted as the 'hallmark of the professional manager', and 'the ultimate benchmark for practising professional managers'. Gaining the status of 'Chartered Manager' is intended to 'open doors to new levels of professional achievement and personal satisfaction'. At its heart, the scheme is intended to be an acknowledgement that, at the highest levels, management, regardless of sector or setting, deserves to be recognised as a distinct profession which is as critical to organisational success as any other, and is as demanding on any individual who seeks to manage a career path within it. The performance standards that underpin the Chartered Manager scheme are certainly rigorous, and to attain them is an endorsement of effectiveness at a very serious level. The Chartered Management Institute also suggests that the Chartered Manager scheme will help to transform organisations, the working practices of managers and their careers.

The Chartered Manager process is composed of the following elements:

1. **An approved entry qualification**
   A professionally recognised qualification at degree or equivalent level, in a management or business discipline. If an individual is working towards a suitable qualification, they can also embark on the Chartered Manager scheme, provided that the qualification has been attained at the time a final submission is made.

2. **Full Institute membership**
   This demonstrates the practice and experience of an operational manager along with active involvement in ongoing professional development. One of the qualifying criteria for full membership of the CMI is that you must have at least three years' operational experience as a practising manager.

3. **Online assessment**
   The Chartered Manager Assessment Questionnaire is based on the six core management skills of leading people, managing change, meeting customer needs, managing information and knowledge, managing activities and resources and managing yourself. This online questionnaire initially seeks the individual's self-assessment and is subsequently sent to six nominated colleagues who are asked to assess the candidate's abilities in these key topics. Among the six nominees should be the candidate's line manager, two colleagues and three direct reports. An evaluation is generated from the combined inputs of all those nominated.

4. **Online CPD submission**

   This submission should demonstrate the individual's learning and development, including an account of specific learning activities and how they have helped improve performance. The submission needs to contain:

   – what you set out to learn and develop, and for what purpose;

   – how you carried out activities to meet your learning and development needs;

   – what you have learned as a result;

   – how you have used the learning to improve performance at work;

   – clear, demonstrable evidence that learning has taken place in at least one of the Chartered Manager Skill areas;

   – how you intend to continue to develop as a manager.

The submission also incorporates a business impact submission to show how you have made a significant difference in real terms to the success of your organisation, as a direct result of applying the Chartered Manager Skill areas of leading people and managing change.

An online assessor will scrutinise the submission and, if successful, the candidate will be invited to a panel interview. Candidates are then required to make a 15-minute presentation based on the business impact submission. The purpose of the panel is to confirm that candidates have made a significant impact on, or contribution to, their organisation, and to evaluate their communication skills. It is also designed to assess whether they are working in accordance with the Institute's Code of Professional Management Practice.

In what ways do you think the Chartered Manager scheme could contribute to your own learning and development?

14

Change: Sulla's Constitutional Reforms

What happened?

The leader

Lucius Cornelius Sulla was a member of an old but not very prominent aristocratic family in Rome. He managed to combine as a young man 'a dissolute way of life', much to the amazement of the historian Plutarch, with 'winning a good name for himself on military campaigns'. Felix was added to Sulla's name because a soothsayer had predicted his future happiness, and the ending of his life at the height of good fortune.

The historical setting

What distinguished Rome from its ancient enemies was a capacity for virtually continuous warfare. The long contest with Carthage, the great Phoenician colony in present-day Tunisia, had transformed the Roman army from an essentially part-time force of farmers into an almost professional organisation in which it was not uncommon to serve abroad for years on end. And no one was allowed to hold a political office at Rome until they had completed 10 annual military campaigns. The expansion arising from this glorification of war did not stop with the annexation of Carthage and Greece in 146 BC, as Roman influence was progressively extended over Asia Minor, Syria, Spain, France, Libya and Egypt.

But this republican empire was acquired at a very high price, because the economic and political problems it threw up combined to undermine Rome's political institutions. The immediate issue that fuelled civil unrest was the plight of non-Roman Italians who did not enjoy the privileges of Roman citizenship but had to carry many of the burdens, and were being increasingly evicted from their lands to make way for the settlement of veterans or for the big estates of the aristocracy. The land problem was not solved by a four-year war between the Romans and the Italians but, at its end in 87 BC, Roman citizenship was granted to most of the inhabitants of Italy.

Sulla fought successfully in this conflict and was rewarded with command against King Mithridates of Pontus, a state in northern Asia Minor. Anti-Roman sentiment in Greece had encouraged Mithridates to challenge Rome in the eastern Mediterranean. In the Roman province of Asia, today the Aegean shore of Turkey, he symbolically ended Rome's imperial greed by forcing one of its captured officials to drink molten gold. Another 80,000 Roman and Italian settlers followed him to the grave. Against Mithridates Sulla was supposed to march but his command was transferred to his bitter rival Marius. When he refused to accept this, he marched with the support of his troops instead on Rome, which fell without a blow. Marius fled to Africa.

Sulla's behaviour

After passing several laws by threat of force, Sulla left to deal with Mithridates, whom he defeated in 85 BC after

A rare portrait of the Roman dictator Sulla. The gilded equestrian statue of him in the centre of Rome was torn down and destroyed in 48 BC by ordinary citizens, when news arrived of Julius Caesar's victory over senatorial forces under the command of Pompey in Greece.

hard fighting. The brutality of his generalship was notorious. Plutarch noted how in central Greece fallen troops of Mithridates 'filled marshes with blood and lakes with their corpses, so numerous were they that later many bows, helmets, shreds of breastplates and swords were found buried in the mud, even though two centuries had passed'. So angry was Sulla with the Athenians, who had thrown their lot in with Mithridates, that he was only dissuaded from ordering wholesale slaughter or enslavement by the pleas of Athenian exiles in his retinue. As it was, Sulla had already cut down all the trees belonging to the Academy and the Lyceum, two of the ancient western world's foremost centres of learning, for timber for his siege engines. He told the Athenians that they were a worthless lot and that he only spared them because of the achievements of their ancestors.

The moderate peace terms Sulla imposed on King Mithridates were dictated, not by any mildness in his character, but the fact that he could no longer afford to be absent from a Rome dominated by his political enemies. Outlawed, he returned and overcame his opponents, becoming in 81 BC dictator, an old office of unlimited powers that was supposed to be occupied for only six months at a time of crisis. Revenge could only be taken on Marius' exhumed body, as this arch enemy had died while Sulla was away.

Sulla has always tended to have a bad press. It is probably due to his impatience at opposition: rather than try his enemies individually in order to establish the strength of each one's opposition to his constitutional plans for Rome, on one occasion he grew tired of such judicial arrangements and had 12,000 of them rounded up in one place and executed. When Sulla offered to spare one man because of a past kindness shown to the dictator, the offer was refused and he died along with the rest. This savagery was not an isolated occurrence, but part of a general massacre of his political opponents. Up and down the Italian peninsular the dictator's agents hunted his enemies. In the absence of any clear criteria as to who was hostile to Sulla's political programme, it was not surprising that matters quickly got out of hand. Many agents were far too enthusiastic, with the result that friend as well as foe went in danger of assassination. But with his political opponents either killed or scattered abroad, and their property confiscated, the dictator was free to reshape the Roman constitution, enhancing the role of the aristocratic senate but placing restraints on the authority of chief office-holders. On one hand his reforms sought to end the popular disorder fomented by Marius' supporters; on the other, he was determined that no one should imitate his own use of military force. An ailing Sulla died in 78 BC, shortly after stepping down as dictator. Plutarch recounts how he burst an internal ulcer by shouting too loudly when he had a corrupt official strangled in front of him.

Outcomes

Sulla's constitutional reforms failed to resolve conflict in Rome. Cicero endeavoured to put together in the 60s BC a political programme aimed at stability, but the intense rivalry between two generals, Julius Caesar and Pompey, brought about another civil war. Caesar's victory in 48 BC over Pompey at the battle of Pharsalus in Greece made him supreme, and he became dictator for life. There is a distinct possibility that Caesar intended to assume the status of king and god, prior to his assassination by senators in 44 BC. But the cry of 'freedom from tyranny' then was little more than a cover for preserving their own power and privileges. It made no difference to Octavian, Julius Caesar's heir, as he went on to become in 31 BC Augustus, Rome's first emperor.

For in the spectacular failure of the Roman republic Sulla had himself set the pattern with a military coup. It was he who seized absolute power and then tried to change the way things were done by force of arms. That he could not discover a sure method of preventing others from following his example was the fundamental problem.

Why does it matter?

The process of change

When in 88 BC Sulla put himself at the head of an army in order to lead it against his political enemies in Rome, he revealed to his fellow citizens where power really lay – with those who bore arms. Five years later, on his return from Greece, he confirmed this political fact by starting Rome's first civil war. Sulla struck his contemporaries as a man easily capable of winning friends: the intense loyalty of his supporters was matched by his own unchanging kindness to them. But there was another side to his character, for cherish though he might his friends, Sulla also nursed injuries and was utterly ruthless in seeking revenge from those responsible for them.

The radical change which Sulla sought to introduce by force of arms was extreme. Such a change was nothing less than an urgent response to the political circumstances in which he found himself. In the context of business practice, however, there was a time when change within any organisation was simply seen as a planned movement from one familiar, well-established and stable position to an improved and more efficient situation through the implementation of new systems or processes. You could determine if the change had been managed successfully by the way that the organisation absorbed the new procedures smoothly into its routines and settled into a durable new way of working. In this context the change process tended to impact only on one or two particular areas of the business at any one time. The understandable resistance to change which some employees would show in these circumstances could be explained and dealt with and the expectation that things would soon settle down again provided enough reassurance to help most people cope. But now the situation is somewhat different, if not perhaps as extreme as it was in Sulla's Rome.

Change or transformation?

For change has come to mean something very different to many organisations. Rather than a localised and timebound procedure which can be managed through a period of development, testing and, finally, implementation, for many businesses change is today a constant process which continually challenges the underlying strategy, the fundamental working principles, and culture of the organisation. Change is a process, not a destination. It is undoubtedly true that some companies have suffered grievously from an over-zealous enthusiasm to respond to every new organisational fad, repeatedly changing their structure and form; and in such settings the change process itself has destroyed their effectiveness. But most forward-looking organisations now see that constant and discontinuous turbulence in the external environment (commercial, technological, legal and political) means that they must constantly review and reinvent themselves to remain competitive and efficient. If change happens as a last resort, forced on a reluctant business because of market pressures, plummeting profitability or corporate scandal, it is in all probability already too late! The transformation of Korea's Samsung Electronics into a world-leading corporation, for instance, owes much to the leadership of Jong Yong Yun. He has focused attention on the need to embed change in the organisation's thinking. Quoted in an interview in *The Sunday Times* in August 2005, Jong Yong Yun commented, 'At times of crisis you have to change. And in order to keep on succeeding, you need to change even without crises'.

There is a temptation for managers to believe that change can be managed through small incremental improvements rather than major shifts in attitude or behaviour. Among the key proponents of the latter approach is Richard Pascale. This Harvard Business School professor and influential consultant analysed the process of corporate transformation in two major books, *The Art of Japanese Management* and *Managing on the Edge*. He insists that organisations have to distinguish between 'change' (gradual improvement) and 'transformation' (a fundamental shift in capability). For Pascale it is vital that a business adopts a constant process of self-questioning, particularly about its competitive situation, to establish whether continued incremental improvements will be adequate to sustain its viability or whether a real transformation of its thinking and behaviour – its culture – is needed. Pascale has shown that changed organisational structures do not necessarily change the culture of an organisation. Culture change is a delicate, lengthy and time-consuming process which needs leadership skills of a high order.

Sulla's failure

In Pascale's terms, it is clear that Sulla's military coup was concerned with transformation rather than change. The title he assumed on taking control of Rome in 83 BC translates as 'dictator with supreme power to reorganise the state'. There could have been no clearer indication of the scale and scope of his intentions. Although he restored order and some of his constitutional measures lasted long after his death, Sulla patently failed to achieve his ultimate goal of establishing a radically reformed and stable state. If we think of Sulla as a 'change agent' in contemporary terms, then he was clearly a failure. There was scarcely an element of the existing Roman power structure which was not directly challenged by Sulla. As a result, he was unable to gain sufficient support to take his initiatives permanently forward. Because he challenged deeply rooted traditions, many people saw his determination as serving perhaps his own political ambitions, rather than bringing any significant benefits to the Roman republic. And of course his policies were all forcibly imposed at the time.

Change agents

People in Rome at the time of Sulla must have experienced similar responses to those working in organisations implementing major change programmes today. Uncertainty about the direction in which change would take them and anxiety about the threat to their status, role and prestige and to their established working relationships would have made it tough for a leader to gain the 'buy-in' to make the change really work. So what does make an effective 'change agent'? In their essay, 'The way chief executive officers lead' in the *Harvard Business Review on Leadership*, Charles Farkus and Suzy Wetlaufer summarise their analysis of the different approaches that CEOs adopt, and present five distinct models. One of these, the 'Change Approach' is characterised by individuals who seek to

create an environment of continual reinvention, even if such an environment produces anxiety and confusion, leads to some strategic mistakes, and temporarily hurts financial performance.

Typically such CEOs are only marginally concerned with reports, strategic plans and policies; their time is spent 'in the field', meeting stakeholders within and beyond the business. Communication is something of an obsession and they spend large amounts of time building consensus for the desired change, using a wide range of media. In their working relationships seniority matters little; they are focused on working with colleagues with passion and energy, whoever they are in the organisation. They are often given to occasional dramatic public gestures to demonstrate their commitment to change.

Change strategies

There are echoes here of the work of Harvard Business School's John Kotter, who, in *Leading Change*, identifies eight steps in the process of leading successful change. They are the appointment of a leader

- with a strong track record;

- with an outsider's openness to new ideas;

- who creates a sense of crisis;

- who creates and communicates a new vision and new strategies;

- who acts as a role model;

- who involves others in key positions in the push for change;

- who encourages these key players to influence people throughout the business;

- who produces tangible results within two years to build the momentum for change.

Jack Welch, former CEO of General Electric, has a formula for the successful leadership of change which encompasses some of the same thinking but has a harder edge! He writes:

There are really just four practices that matter: communicate a sound rationale for every change. Have the right people at your side. Get rid of the resisters. And seize every single opportunity, even those from someone else's misfortune. That's it.

Change: a function of managers or leaders?

A familiar debate, which runs through the literature of business management, revolves around the perceived differences and similarities between the concepts of 'management' and 'leadership'. No topic throws this discussion into sharper relief than the issue of organisational change. Who is responsible for implementing effective change? Is it peculiarly a function of a strong leader at the top of the business or a role for managers throughout the organisation? Is a ruthless individual like Sulla ever enough to guarantee significant change? No matter how powerful or persuasive, can a dictator effectively determine events now and in the future? How can he or she secure a thoroughgoing transformational change?

For John Kotter management and leadership are not the same; rather they are distinctive but complementary systems of action, both vital to the success of an organisation. The growth of management as a specialism within business is a response to the growing complexity and size of enterprises. It is concerned with activities such as planning, budgeting, organisation, staffing, controlling and problem solving. Leadership, by contrast, is centrally about coping with change. If change is now inescapable and discontinuous, as indeed it seems to be, then we desperately need leaders as never before.

What does it mean for you?

Just think of the changes that have happened over the last decade wherever you may live in the world.

Computing power has grown enormously, and systems have become a lot smarter. Take Dassault Aviation. By the use of computer simulations for aircraft design, and for the design of the manufacturing facility, this company no longer has to produce a physical prototype before going into full manufacture of an aircraft.

The Internet has also changed our lives. We buy our books online from Amazon, we also buy low-cost flights, hotels and hire cars. We bid for products through online auctions and we download music (either legally or illegally) to our iPods.

The world's manufacturing base has transferred to China and other low-cost manufacturing nations, and the new sweatshops are the telephone call centres, scattered around the world thanks to modern technology.

Advances in telephony have been amazingly huge. The cell phone has transformed remote and poor areas of the world, which were previously cut off, and personal computers using high-speed broadband through existing copper wires has already transformed the way we work. Indeed, some people no longer need a workplace at all. The home office now has new meaning!

In this rapidly changing world, the key skills needed by leaders, therefore, are:

- to know when a change is required;

- to understand and manage the impact of change on people;

- to manage the change itself;

- to start looking for the next change, immediately afterwards.

Know when a change is required

As leaders, we have to be constantly vigilant to the changes that are taking place around us and now at such a rapid rate. Here we have to avoid the mindset of:

- this will not apply to our organisation;

- not invented here syndrome;

- it's a short-term trend, which we will ride and survive;

- the consumer is loyal and will continue to buy our product, even if it is more expensive.

Invariably the household names that have failed over recent years have been driven by an arrogant board that has failed to respond to the above changes.

Understand and manage the impact of change on people

Today people tend to be more able to adapt to change, but getting them to a point where they are committed to it, that takes real leadership.

Figure 14.1 illustrates the different stages of change programmes. The most likely first stage of any major change programme will be to deny it exists, and assert that it will just go away. Treat it as another fad or fantasy of the CEO, and don't become too involved, because there is bound to be something else coming along. So just duck your head and it will pass over, you hope!

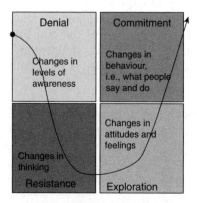

Figure 14.1 Stages of change programmes

The next stage is resistance, and here people resist for a variety of reasons. These are usually

- lack of information;

- no obvious benefits seen for themselves or the organisation;

- a low level of trust for management;

- traditional, custom-bound work practices;

- fear of . . .

    - the unknown;

    - failure;

    - looking stupid;

    - losing status or job;

    - losing skills or power.

It is important, when handling change, to give people the opportunity to explore its implications, as a way to get them over their initial fears and resistance. Early participation in the design of the end solution, creating the opportunity to express an opinion, and running pilot studies, are the best ways of getting people on board.

Changes happen faster, last longer, when all the stakeholders to a change are committed, but getting people there takes real leadership. It takes insight and courage (I know we need to do this), humility (I don't have all the answers) and tenacity (but we are going to do it, however).

Manage the change

As leaders, we need to manage the change through to completion, and there are a number of steps we absolutely have to take in order to achieve this. First of all:

- Set up open, honest and easily understood two-way communication.

- Then make sure people understand:

  - why you are making changes;

  - their urgency;

  - their importance to the organisation.

- Communicate in person.

- Be specific about the implementation, who does what and the personal impact on individuals.

- And walk the talk throughout the change process.

- So that you can find ways to change resistance into support, always:

  - listen;

  - involve;

  - encourage;

  - show empathy for the feelings of your people; and

  - communicate progress and, as importantly, celebrate success.

Start looking for the next change

Don't allow yourself the comfort, after completing the implementation of any change, of a false sense of security. Your competitors will be working 24 hours a day to overtake you. So start looking at once for the next moves that you will have to make in order to maintain the health and success of your organisation. Change never ends: the leader who understands this is the successful survivor.

15

Networking: Cicero's Efforts to Find Allies

What happened?

The leader

Marcus Tullius Cicero was a prolific author as well as an active Roman politician. Typical of his outlook was the approach he took to Greek philosophy, which many Romans feared might challenge and undermine society. For Cicero philosophy's chief role was to furnish the traditional order with secure intellectual foundations. Thus he could argue that proper conduct upheld the regime of property, privilege and power enjoyed by the Roman aristocracy.

The historical setting

Overlooked by Cicero, however, were the endemic violence and corruption of Rome's highly competitive political system. The perpetual drive for fame and fortune, the gruelling life reserved for men who belonged to the ruling class, was something that moulded the behaviour of the aristocracy in the final years of the Roman republic. Some aristocrats, in disgust at the state of Rome's politics, even opted out of public life altogether. Cicero was never tempted to take such an action, although he admitted that death and age had carried off most of Sulla's heirs. There were few left by the 60s BC who felt any esteem for the constitutional reforms which Sulla had introduced during his bloody dictatorship 20 years earlier.

It might be said that Cicero himself contributed to the disorder in 63 BC, when as consul, the highest office in Rome, he insisted that the conspirator Cataline should be executed without trial. In the final debate in the senate one of those who spoke against it was Julius Caesar, the future dictator. Even though a sentence of death was finally agreed, the conspiracy was not the tremendous crisis from which Cicero claimed to have saved the state, but a relatively minor upheaval connected with Cataline's proposal to cancel debts and redistribute land. Only the support of discounted veterans for this political reform made it into an issue. What may have caused Cicero to insist upon the death sentence for Cataline was the office he held, the consulship. Election to it delighted Cicero because he was afforded the rare opportunity to take the lead politically in Rome. He must have felt then that he was the saviour of the republic itself.

In fairness to Cicero though, it was true that soldiers, recruited from the poorest classes in Italy, were ceasing to feel any allegiance to the constitution. Military service had become a means of livelihood and no longer part of a citizen's duty. The demands of an empire and the ambition of generals led to extraordinary commands in the provinces, like that of Pompey in the eastern Mediterranean and Caesar in Gaul, present-day France. Soldiers now tended to look to their commanders for rewards when campaigns were over: they expected not just a share in the spoils but also land on which to live in Italy. So a successful general had to be good at domestic politics as well as military strategy.

As Cicero was to find at his personal cost, oratory alone could not save Rome from dictatorship. In 43 BC his head and hands were cut off on Mark Antony's orders, presumably because what he said and wrote had offended this hardened soldier.

Cicero's behaviour

In an attempt to deal with the growing instability caused by army commanders and their political agents, Cicero tried to put together an alliance of interest and sentiment which embraced both the upper classes and the well-to-do. But it remained an ideal rather than an effective programme and no political party ever formed under his leadership. Possibly Cicero believed that he could manage with oratory and intrigue, the usual methods of Roman politics. For he had a high opinion of his own abilities as a speaker, whether he chose to offer advice to statesmen or generals. As a result of this excessive self-belief, however, Cicero made serious mistakes.

His refusal to cooperate with Caesar, Crassus and Pompey in what became known as the First Triumvirate effectively pushed him to the political margins. Their blatant use of force revealed how Rome, instead of being controlled by an oligarchy of nobles, was really in the hands of three ambitious men. And since Caesar relied on street gangs to represent his interests during his absence from Rome, Cicero became an easy target and suffered exile. Cicero's return to Rome from exile in 57 BC was little short of a triumph, the parade only accorded by the senate to a victorious general. 'Nobody of any rank', Cicero noted with satisfaction, 'failed to come to meet me, except for those enemies who could not conceal or deny the fact. When I came to the Porta Capena the steps of the temples were thronged by the common people, who welcomed me with great applause, the same throngs, the same applause, followed me to the Capitol, and there was an amazing crowd in the Forum and on the Capitol itself'. Such a reception persuaded Cicero that his moment of political influence had come, but he was soon brought down to earth with a bump. To his dismay, he discovered that his house was demolished, his statues and furniture were scattered, and a temple was built on his land. Cicero tore down the temple and managed to rebuild his house, but not without the protection of gangs of gladiators loyal to Pompey, the powerful sponsor of his recall from exile.

The growing animosity of the two warlords, Caesar and Pompey, following the death of Crassus on campaign in 53 BC, placed Cicero in a political dilemma. Neither of them could claim to be the guardians of republicanism, despite the senate's support for Pompey on the outbreak of civil war in 49 BC. The clearer it became that Pompey would abandon Italy to Caesar, the more agitated Cicero became, troubled about what he should do and what was the right time for action. He may still have hoped for a compromise peace. Once he had gained control of Italy, Caesar endeavoured to win Cicero over to his side or, at least, secure his neutrality. He failed in both aims when finally Cicero joined Pompey in Greece. After Pompey's defeat there, Cicero returned to a Rome subject to the will of one man, Caesar.

The assassination of that man in 44 BC by a small group of senators shocked and delighted Cicero. He even suggested that Mark Antony, Caesar's chief lieutenant, should be killed as well. For in vain Cicero had begged Antony to 'remember the state: think of your ancestors, not your associates . . . I scorned the daggers of Cataline, so I shall not tremble before yours'.

Outcomes

These were brave words, because Cicero's suggestion of violence against Antony did not go unnoticed. On the formation of the Second Triumvirate, in 43 BC, between Octavian, Caesar's heir, Antony and Lepidus, Cicero was marked down for elimination. The historian Plutarch relates how 'by Antony's orders his murderers cut off Cicero's head and hands'. Presumably the latter were also singled out for punishment because his writings as much as his speeches had caused offence to those who sought to usher in a post-republican order. The problem for the Roman republic was that Cicero proved to be a flawed champion, a politician perhaps more interested in words than deeds. And Cicero's late arrival at Pompey's camp in Greece did not impress every republican, despite his claim to be the spokesman of liberty.

Why does it matter?

Building relationships

Cicero's contemporaries were never enthusiastic about his politics, since he had a reputation for vacillation and compromise. Yet it was not unreasonable that he sometimes found it difficult to decide on a particular course of action in what were very confused times. Unfortunately, his manoeuvring too often appeared tactical rather than a matter of principle, despite his life-long belief in republican government. And Cicero conspicuously failed to find staunch political allies. He was very bad indeed at networking.

The attention paid to trends such as the 're-engineering' movement has tended to focus organisations on developing sophisticated formal structures to facilitate and support networking by managers: to create the opportunities for cross-functional dialogue and communication through devices such as project teams, liaison meetings and task groups. Whether these structures work effectively or not, leaders still tend to rely more on strong networks of informal relationships to help coordinate leadership activities, perhaps reflecting an underlying frustration with the pace and style of work within the formal channels and a feeling that, 'it's not *what* you know, but *who* you know that matters'. In this context, networking is about creating and maintaining connections to build up a web of contacts. It is also concerned with building and sustaining relationships with people whose interests and concerns are similar, or who share common aspirations for the development of a particular organisation, or who, more broadly, have a shared interest in promoting a particular commercial or industrial sector. In late republican Rome Cicero's political programme could have obviously done with such support.

In building these informal networks within an organisation, leaders will frequently be seeking 'intelligence' from a range of people whose jobs give them an unorthodox perspective on the way that the business is performing, rather than depending exclusively on the views of senior managers or their direct reports. In his highly influential book, *In Search of Excellence*, management writer and consultant Tom Peters coined the phrase 'Management By Walking About' (MBWA) as a way of capturing this mindset. According to Peters, this type of active and subtle networking is critical to successful leadership, a view he rehearses in his subsequent book, *A Passion for Excellence*, when he writes:

The number one management productivity problem in America is, quite simply, managers who are out of touch with their people and out of touch with their customers. And the alternative, 'being in touch', doesn't come via computer print-outs or the endless stream of overhead transparencies viewed in ten thousand darkened meeting rooms stretching across a continent.

If you were to replace the reference to overhead transparencies with 'PowerPoint slides' or even 'emails', one could legitimately question whether things have really changed since Peters' passionate advocacy of 'MBWA' in 1985! The message from Peters' analysis of successful companies is that leaders need to keep away from their offices, limit the time they spend in meetings, and remain in direct physical contact with the people throughout the organisation. Importantly, he also emphasises the need to extend this networking beyond the boundaries of the business and adopt a similar approach to communicating with external stakeholders and, particularly, with customers and clients. Reflecting this thinking, it is now fairly common practice in some organisations for senior staff, for instance, to participate directly in focus group meetings of customers, to take a turn on the customer service helpline or pay regular visits to major customers, all as a means of keeping in touch with the market.

Networking requires sophisticated social and communication skills and among the key attributes of a successful networker are the following:

- Treating other people as you would like to be treated.

- Developing a process of 'give and take' in relationships.

- Seeking points of shared interest and partnership working.

- Keeping in touch, even when communication does not have a definite or short-term objective.

- Building bridges.

- Cultivating contacts.

We expect our leaders to be good communicators, and many tend to value the 'productive' communication skills of writing and speaking more highly than the 'receptive' skills of reading and listening. Leaders, for example, often have very highly developed presentation skills, and many aspiring senior executives are now coached and trained in this area of competency. But it is the receptive skills, particularly the ability to listen attentively and sensitively to the experiences, views and opinions of others, which really mark out the best networkers. It is this skill which allows a leader to pick out the underlying messages in what they are hearing, identify the significant issues emerging from the dialogue, and plan accordingly.

In Cicero's time, oratory, the art of public speaking, was a critical skill for a politician, and Cicero himself was by all accounts a master of this skill, a judgement he seems to have shared. For he assumed that his position and influence would enable him to draw together an alliance representing the old aristocracy and the newly wealthy in a shared effort to save the traditional values of the republic which were then under threat. However, Cicero badly miscalculated the complex and mutually suspicious nature of the relationships between the various interest groups which he sought to bring together as partners. Perhaps the confidence he clearly had in his skills as an orator deluded Cicero into thinking that his audience were bound to go along with him, and perhaps he, like some of our current leaders, might have benefited from a higher level of skill in listening. 'This man's works, so many and so fine', a contemporary commented, 'will last for ever and there is no need to speak about his great abilities and capacity for hard work. Yet it remains a pity that he could not have been temperate when things went well and stronger in adversity'. What an epitaph for poor Cicero!

Interdependence

Cicero's self-belief was such that he did not feel it necessary to identify in any detail the common ground that he and his potential political partners might share, or the detailed aims around which they might collaborate. He assumed a shared perception that things were deteriorating in the Roman republic would lead to their acceptance of his leadership and the solution he could offer. Here Cicero revealed an underdeveloped social awareness, without which networking will create little real impact. The familiar contemporary model of 'emotional intelligence', developed from earlier psychological research by Daniel Goleman, is one approach which emphasises the importance of social awareness in leadership and management. The concept of emotional intelligence can be defined as the ability to perceive, understand, integrate and manage one's own and other people's feelings and emotions. A person with a high degree of emotional intelligence will have both self-awareness and empathy with others. Within what Goleman describes as the 'social awareness' domain, organisational awareness sits as a distinct set of competencies which is vital for leaders who wish to develop an understanding of the political forces at work in an organisation and detect the crucial social networks and power relationships. Without these skills, they will be unable to identify the guiding values that operate among people in the organisation and, moreover, they will be unable to select appropriate ways of taking them forward. Networking is an expression of this aptitude in action. As Goleman says in *The New Leaders*:

That is why socially skilled leaders tend to have resonance with a wider circle of people and have a knack for finding common ground and building rapport. That doesn't mean they socialise continually; it means they work under the assumption that nothing gets done alone. Such leaders have a network in place when the time for action comes.

For an effective leader, networking is not simply about maintaining social relationships but has very distinct aims. Networking helps leaders to build their knowledge base, come to understand the processes through which they can promote their values and interests, and then translate their understanding into action. Specifically, leaders who take networking seriously are acknowledging the interdependence of different functions, skills and departments in modern organisations. In the current context of volatility, uncertainty and complexity, organisations face a huge variety of challenges. The experience, information and wisdom locked in different parts of the organisation must be harnessed and directed purposefully, and networking is a tool to achieve this. Effective networking reduces the likelihood of inflexible or categorical judgements being made and helps to ensure that the organisation develops visions which are linked and compatible. Partnership working is an aim for many large organisations and the globalisation of the market makes it even more of a priority. Working globally means working with partners sensitive to the cultural contexts of different markets. As Paolo Fresco of General Electric said of the rapidly developing market of the Indian sub-continent, for example:

The best way to enter the Indian market is with Indian part-ners, and the best Indian partners get taken very quickly. Coming in late with a partner who is not as strong is a serious double whammy.

'Knowledge capital' and networking

The shifting image of the organisation has moved from the traditional pyramid, symbolising the importance of hierarchy and structure, and emphasising the significance of control, bureaucracy and status, to symbols such as cobwebs, grids and networks, which reflect newer, more integrative and empowering ways of organising activity. The development of such structures is a reflection of the belief that knowledge has become the most valuable capital resource in organisations. Although the capability of a business will continue to be expressed in terms of the goods it produces or the services it provides, the most important capability of any organisation relates to its ability to maximise the benefits accruing from the com-bined knowledge of its personnel. As Professor Dave Ulrich of the University of Michigan explains it in an essay entitled 'Organising around capabilities', published in a collection produced by the Drucker Foundation entitled *The Organisation of the Future*:

As organisations become flatter, capabilities must also change. The hierarchy was established to preserve a set of cherished capabilities: clear accountability, legitimate authority, estab-lished routines, division of labor, and specialization. In a world of unpredictable change, globalization, dynamic technologies, and educated employees and consumers, these capabilities will not work.

Ulrich is an advocate of what he terms the 'boundaryless organisation', which lives on networks and within which 'talented individuals provide expertise regardless of hierarchy, function or position'.

At its best, technology both mirrors and drives this sort of corporate networking. The investment in technological support for the creation of a networked business goes beyond email, websites, groupware and intranets. The ambition for businesses committed to this way of working is to develop the infrastructure to ensure everyone has access to the organisation's store of knowledge and can add to it in a systematic way. A pioneering example of such a 'knowledge management system' would be Anderson Consulting's Xchange system, but many corporations are seeking to develop such approaches. In an article entitled 'New competencies for a new world', Iain Somerville and John Edwin Mroz, summarise the implications of this networked way of working for leaders:

... the systematic acquisition, synthesis, and sharing of insight and experience is critical to the success of almost all organisations. The role of the top executive becomes that of the knowledge capitalist who creates a market that evaluates, recognises, rewards – and thus shapes – the knowledge assets.

What does it mean for you?

How many of us have attended conferences where the topics looked interesting but the speakers were definitely not. Yet we return to our work and tell our colleagues that what made the conference still worthwhile was the opportunity it provided to network with like-minded people. If you find two or three people who have experienced similar challenges to the ones you face, then soon you have a wave of email sharing. This kind of sharing usually continues for a number of months and then comes to an end.

So how do we network effectively in the twenty-first century, with so much change, and with such amazing technology at our fingertips? Let's look at a case study of networking in a large multinational pharmaceutical business, for some ideas.

It was with networking in mind that Mayling caught her flight from Beijing Capital Airport to Miami. Mayling worked for a major multinational. Born, brought up and educated in Hong Kong, she had joined Mani Pharmaceutical as a chemist and had the good fortune to spend five years working for Xiao Qiang, the renowned director of the Hong Kong facility. Xiao's career had rocketed and his latest promotion had seen him moved to Miami as vice-president for Africa and Asia. A year ago, when he was on a visit to Hong Kong, he had dropped a huge challenge Mayling's way. Recognising her ability to work well at all levels within the company, and the way she got things done through people, he had offered her the top human resources job in Beijing.

She had taken up the challenge, and spent her first 100 days just soaking up as much as she could. The operations staff were delighted to have someone from the sharp end of the business in HR, and when the HR team had got over their bruised egos, and realised what a genuine and talented person Mayling was, they were equally supportive. Now 12 months later, Mayling was on her way to the annual human resources conference at the company headquarters in Miami.

As the plane touched down at Miami International Airport, Mayling had set herself a key objective to meet as many people as possible, and in particular to find out which countries were leading in the adoption of the new leadership initiative and talent pool management.

The conference was packed with content, presentations, networking and social engagements. There was not a minute that was not accounted for, and the week went by with the speed of light. Mayling had got to know and like a group of eight people, all like-minded and all the countries they represented were in actual fact at very similar levels of HR development. Everyone swapped business cards and swore loyalty to the informal network that they had just set up, and everyone departed for home the morning after a fun-filled last night in Miami.

Mayling's background as a chemist had given her the experience of working in 'virtual groups'. There were already established systems in the organisation that supported collaboration in the research and development area. Even though these systems were available to everyone, they had tended to be seen as being for the benefit of the boffins and not for ordinary folk to use. But as Mayling had given her commitment to her Miami network, she would make use of these systems to keep their new network alive.

Often organisations hide behind technology, saying that they will start effective networking as soon as they have the right technology. Yet 80% of good networking is people related, and only 20% technology. Meeting one another, getting on and having mutual respect for each person are all very powerful reasons for having a network. The willingness to give as well as to take, and recognising that sometimes the need to sacrifice self-interest for the benefit of the whole group, is something very special in good networking.

Mayling had suggested that they focus on one aspect of the talent pool management: the method used to identify talent within the organisation. So she undertook to set up a virtual conference within the first week of her return. The company had a Webex system which allowed people to meet as the advertising blurb read 'with anyone, anywhere, anytime using on-demand web meeting applications. Share documents, presentations, and other applications over the web and enjoy rich interaction, as if you were face to face'. As an experienced Webex user Mayling employed the early sessions to break her HR colleagues from around the world into the new technology. Within the first three months everyone gave the impression of being seasoned veterans but more importantly the project had really taken off. All eight countries had made considerable progress in their approach to talent management.

The network continued to thrive, and started to draw in new members and run subgroups. The annual HR conference thus became an opportunity for a reunion, where friendships were renewed, new networkers recruited, and the network itself reinvigorated.

Learning from Mayling's experience, we can summarise the secrets of good networking as follows:

- People joining a network should have a real willingness to share, as there always has to be give and take.

- You need to physically meet at some point, and if you have the luxury of an annual reunion so much the better.

- It helps if you all get on well, and have respect for one another.

- You need to formulate common goals and objectives.

- Everyone must be willing to accept assignments and then complete them on time.

- Throughout the process find ways to keep things as simple as possible.

- Make use of technology, virtual meetings, collaborative sharing, telephone and video conferences to keep people connected.

- Make sure people are trained to use these system well.

- Celebrate your success publicly.

16

Dealing with Conflict: The Policies of Vespasian

What happened?

The leader

The founder of Rome's second imperial dynasty, Titus Flavius Vespasianus, was born in AD 9, the son of an Italian tax-gatherer. The future emperor came to notice as a legionary commander during the conquest of southern Britain in 43–47. One of the strongholds which Vespasian's legionaries stormed was situated on White Horse hill near Uffington in Berkshire. He had sent a column against it along the Ridgeway from the Thames at Goring. Later as governor of the province of Africa, present day-Tunisia, his administration was praised, because he did not use his position greatly to enrich himself.

The historical background

Vespasian (pronounced 'Ves-pay-see-an') was the governor of Judea, when in 68 he heard of the suicide of Nero. The news caused him to halt his military operations against the rebellious city of Jerusalem, since he needed confirmation of his governorship from the new emperor Galba before launching an all-out attack. This assault occurred in the ensuing year, when the city was sacked and the temple destroyed. The campaign was largely directed by Titus, Vespasian's eldest son and his successor as emperor.

For by that date, Titus had persuaded his 60-year-old father to seize the imperial throne. It was the extravagance of Nero that really brought an end to Rome's first imperial dynasty, which nearly a century earlier Augustus had established after his naval victory at Actium over Antony and Cleopatra. So short of cash was Nero that he squeezed every penny he could from the provinces. The revolt of Judea was actually caused by the forcible removal of money from the temple treasury. Unconcerned by widespread signs of discontent, Nero found pleasure in his magnificent new palace in Rome, where he said that at last he could live comfortably. Opposition to Nero's rule first emerged, however, during an imperial tour of Greece in 67. No amount of prizes awarded for his poetry, acting and chairoteering could disguise an increasingly unpopular reign. At Olympia, where a special games was put on for his benefit, Nero won the prize for chariot racing, although he fell out of his 10-horse vehicle and failed to finish the race. Handing out death sentences to his army commanders was a policy hardly calculated to impress their troops, even though the legions were slow in abandoning Nero.

But mutinies among the legions in Gaul, modern France and in Germany finally persuaded Nero to end his own life. The way was open for the accession of another emperor and this was Galba, whom the senators invited to return from his governorship in Spain. Nearly 70 years old at the time, Galba soon discovered that the politics of Rome were beyond him. A marked reluctance to spend money displeased the soldiers, while the sending out of special commissioners to recover the lavish gifts distributed by Nero annoyed many others. Galba even made the

In 69 Vespasian was the fourth Roman emperor in a single year. His determination put Rome back on the road to recovery before he was succeeded by his eldest son Titus. This was the first time a son became emperor after his father.

judges at Olympia pay back the huge tip a grateful Nero had given them. Galba survived as long as he did because, with the end of the Julio-Claudian dynasty on Nero's death, there was no obvious choice for the next emperor. Marcus Salvius Otho, another governor from Spain and one of Galba's earliest supporters, used disaffected soldiers stationed in Rome to seize power himself. After a reign of less than a year, Galba's head was in January 69 paraded through the streets, stuck on a spear. The senate had no choice but to acknowledge the fact that Otho was now in control of the capital. Though he made history by being the first Roman emperor to reach office by killing his predecessor, Otho's reign lasted for less than four months. For the arrival in Italy of legions from Germany under the command of Aulus Vitellius, a close friend of Nero, gave Rome its third emperor in quick succession. But Vitellius was not to survive either, for in the eastern Mediterranean the legionaries had already proclaimed Vespasian as emperor.

Vespasian's behaviour

The unprecedented conflict of 69, the year in which Rome had four emperors, Galba, Otho, Vitellius and Vespasian, was a serious setback for the empire. Events revealed that political power now rested with the Roman army. Even though his troops entered Rome without opposition, Vespasian knew his power came from them alone. For that reason he chose to date the start of his reign not from the formal recognition of the senate, but from his acclamation by his men. It was also a reminder to the senators that their role would in future be a lesser one.

The death of Vitellius ended the civil war, but it did not bring peace. There were disturbances in Germany, the Balkans, Africa and Britain, while in Judea Vespasian's son Titus was still struggling to put down a very serious revolt. The last stronghold there, the natural fortress of Masada, held out for several years after the fall of Jerusalem. Between his accession in 69 and his death 10 years later Vespasian dealt with these problems one by one. Provincial taxes were reorganised, frontiers pushed forward at strategic points in Germany and Asia Minor, rebellions put down wherever they occurred, discipline was restored to the army and, to please the populace of

Rome, work began on the Colosseum, a truly gigantic amphitheatre designed to hold 50,000 spectators. This great project, as well as the rebuilding of the urban aqueducts, was part of Vespasian's effort to disassociate himself from the excesses of Nero. The people's palace, the Colosseum, was actually built on Nero's private lake.

Notwithstanding the cost of the Colosseum's construction, Vespasian acted with considerable financial caution, for he had inherited an empire devastated by civil war as well as reckless expenditure. He was on occasion compared with Galba, but people realised that this suggestion of meanness was an unfair comparison. They fully appreciated his commitment to restoring the empire to its former strength, just as his notable relaxation of personal security precautions reminded them of his comparatively humble origins. Vespasian did not reside in Nero's luxurious palace and he left standing, perhaps as a reminder of previous imperial extravagance, a 100-metre high gilded bronze statue with the face of Nero. And Vespasian always made a point of walking through public gardens in Rome like other people. For he never forgot he was only the son of an Italian financier.

Outcomes

Vespasian's critics were exercised most of all by his dynastic plans, as he intended that his two sons, Titus and Domitian, should succeed him. This objective he achieved, for his dynasty, the Flavian, lasted until the assassination of Domitian in 96. It is arguable that, had Titus not died after so short a reign, the Flavians might have lasted longer. Titus successfully managed three disasters – the eruption of Mount Vesuvius, another great fire at Rome, and the plague – so that his death at the age of 50 years in 81 was genuinely mourned. Later it was rumoured that Titus died with one regret: namely, that his younger brother would succeed him. Certainly

Domitian was an embittered man, since he believed that it was Vespasian's wish that he should have ruled jointly with his elder brother.

Why does it matter?

Conflict: causes and effects

On his death bed Vespasian admitted that the moment had come to pass on his authority to his eldest son. Unable to rise, he remarked, 'An emperor should die on his feet'. Vespasian is also supposed to have said, 'Oh! I think I am becoming a god'. But this was just a hostile joke. At 69, the same age at which the hapless Galba had tried to rule the Roman empire, Vespasian could look back on his main achievement with satisfaction, for he had successfully dealt with conflict.

To return an organisation to a healthy, harmonious and productive condition when it has been torn apart by internal conflict requires a particular set of leadership skills, distinct from those needed to keep an already successful business on track, or to initiate new projects or products into established routines. On occasions, there is an understandable tendency for people in leadership roles to walk away from conflict, unlike Vespasian who was prepared to tackle such a difficult task. That at first he was hesitant to assume power, despite the urgings of his eldest son Titus, is an indication of Vespasian's accurate appreciation of the problems he would face in Rome. Nothing short of wholesale reconstruction was required. Dealing with conflict is a complex process, almost always creating a need to challenge existing relationships and confront individuals. But, without intervention, a conflict situation can rapidly escalate and create a highly damaging climate throughout an organisation, something the Roman empire experienced during the fateful year of 69.

It is important for leaders to recognise the ways in which a conflict situation can develop, and be aware of the ways in which they might intervene effectively at different stages. There will always be disagreements between colleagues within an organisation, often arising form different perceptions of a particular situation or challenge; a debate around differing points of view is a healthy and creative part of the decision-making process, and can lead to solutions of much higher quality being identified. As long as the parties involved remain problem-orientated, an agreement based on consensus can often be arrived at. Difficulties really begin when the confrontation moves from the rational to the emotional, when, typically, personal issues and antagonisms begin to dominate, motives become harder to identify and the situation becomes increasingly competitive.

In such situations, a shrewd leader will know at what point to intervene in order to bring the argument back to the substantive point. Without leadership intervention the disagreement can quickly move to a more dangerous stage, where one party will question the integrity of the other, and feelings of resentment and a desire for revenge begin to emerge. The people involved may begin to caricature each other, and most worryingly, start to seek coalitions and alliances in other parts of the organisation. If a situation has developed to this point, leaders have to confront the parties involved and bring their feelings out into the open in order to resolve the position before the conflict moves into a final self-destructive phase, in which self-interest at any price becomes the goal and destruction of the opposition becomes more important than actually gaining anything concrete for one's side. Internal conflict of this severity, intensely difficult to resolve without carnage of some sort or other, characterised the state of the Roman empire at the moment Vespasian was persuaded by his eldest son to assume power. That he was able to resolve it was testimony to leadership skills of a very high order.

The leadership role

As organisations become more complex, so they fragment and divide, with individual loyalties often becoming associated with a particular department or team, rather than with the business as a whole. In *Managing the Dream*, Warren Bennis describes the underlying power of such bonds when he writes of:

tribal patterns and symbolic codes which often work to exclude others (secrets and jargon, for example) and on occasions to exploit differences for inward (and always fragile) harmony.

An important part of the leadership role is to maintain a sense of corporate purpose and direction, to hold people together. The emperor Vespasian, for example, was able to build on the fundamental wish of the Roman people to see the empire restored to its previous unified state after a period of destructive civil war, an aspiration which provided a shared underlying purpose. This formed the basis of a consensus across Roman society which allowed him to restore internal discipline and order and, very significantly, to put the finances of the state onto a firmer footing. There are clear echoes here of the actions taken by CEOs appointed to turn around failing corporations, or of 'superheads' and 'hit-teams' brought in to turn around failing schools or hospitals. Faced with such challenges leaders will often start the reconstruction process, as Vespasian did, by going back to the basics of the organisation, reminding people of its strengths and capabilities. As with Vespasian, in crisis situations there can be no toleration of continued subversion, and opponents to the new regime have to be rooted out early on.

The concern with preventing internal conflict from escalating to the point where it can jeopardise the smooth working of an organisation should not detract from the fact that, on occasions, conflict can still have positive results. A desire to seek consensus at any cost can lead to mediocre decisions and even stagnation. This is a view certainly reflected, for example, in the research of analysts who have examined in detail the workings of large Japanese companies, within which the search for consensus has traditionally been a key working principle. An example of the alternative view is shown in an article by Ronald A. Heifetz and Donald Laurie entitled 'The work of leadership', in which they state: 'A leader helps expose conflict, viewing it as the engine of creativity and learning', or in the words of Jan Carlzon, the highly respected head of Scandinavian Airways, who writes that:

One of the most interesting missions of leadership is getting people on the executive team to listen to and learn from one another. Held in debate, people can learn their way to collective solutions when they understand one another's assumptions. The work of the leader is to get conflict out into the open and use it as a source of creativity.

Underperformance

In 1999 the British Industrial Society (subsequently rebranded as the Work Foundation) undertook a major survey designed to identify the most sought after and valued leadership competencies, both in the eyes of a substantial sample group of leaders, and among those who worked for them. The results showed that the consistent weaknesses among those identified as the poorest leaders stemmed from their failure to respond to their followers as individuals, ignoring their feelings, stress, development and contributions; in effect, 'treating them as human doings, not human beings', in the words of the report. Less predictable were the characteristics identified as the most significant in top-performing leaders, with the highest rated competence being the ability to deal effectively with breaches to standards of behaviour. On the face of it, the significance accorded to this skill area might appear to recall aspects of the old 'command and control' style of leadership and to run counter to the prevailing emphasis on leaders' communication and support skills, in their capacity to provide vision and operate in ethical and fair ways. But, as the report describes it, not only do people value these 'modern' management skills, they also respect leaders who set tough performance standards, monitor them and can achieve business results. In this context underperformance is not acceptable. The report says that:

By identifying the number one competency of the most successful leaders as 'dealing with breaches to standards of behaviour' essentially observers are saying that leaders should be decisive in tackling poor performance and behaviour. Followers obviously do not have difficulty equating supportive leadership behaviours with decisive action to maintain standards.

The findings from this survey are significant in that they emphasise the considerable impact that a leader who fails to maintain consistent performance standards across the organisation can have on staff morale and the conflict that can be generated as a result. Loyal and top-performing staff can quickly become demoralised if the behaviour of underperforming or disloyal colleagues is not confronted and challenged decisively in the way that Vespasian understood.

Just how different Vespasian's management style was from his immediate predecessors can be seen in the historian Tacitus' description of the four emperors of 69. Whereas Galba 'was old and failing', so ineffectual in fact that his courtiers found 'wrongdoing both safer and more lucrative', his murderer Otho, the second emperor, did at least try to curb the growing disorder but with equal lack of success, while Vitellius, the emperor before Vespasian, 'displayed a revolting and insatiable appetite for sumptuous banquets, where all was chaos and drunkenness'. For Vitellius' pursuit of pleasure meant that 'however important the news, he dismissed it with a brief hearing, being unequal to the more serious responsibilities of his position'. In contrast, Vespasian was 'satisfied with whatever rations were available and dressed much the same as a private soldier'. His rugged man-of-the-people style, which was carefully captured in his portraits, derived from his background as much as his character. Vespasian was a most unusual emperor: he came not from one of the great families of the Roman aristocracy, but from the Italian 'middle class'. And, as a financier's son, he grasped the connection between fiscal security and political stability.

What does it mean for you?

Work presents us all with a never-ending procession of conflicts. Sometimes they appear as the most innocent events, and depending on how we approach them, they either get resolved quickly or they brew into major problems.

Let's take, as a case study, a simple issue that could happen in any organisation around the world.

> The organisation has decided to upgrade its systems to new enterprise-wide software. Considerable resources have been devoted to the design, and a team of internal consultants from around the world have been trained to work alongside external consultants in order to manage the implementation.
>
> When the team arrive in a country, they spend six months getting everyone ready. This means identifying 'super-users' who, once trained, are used to localise the software, cleanse the data, and finally train the other users.
>
> It is essential during this six-month period that the consultants are situated close to the business, and you

have been given the job of finding suitable accommodation. You have, along with your team, reviewed the situation and reached the conclusion that you will have to move a department out of the main building and into a Portakabin temporary office situated in the car park. Your decision is to move the purchasing department out, and so free up the west wing of the sixth floor of the head office.

You can well imagine that this is a conflict just waiting to happen. The decision has already been agreed by the CEO, and it is now your job to tackle the formidable purchasing team.

What do you do?

Generally speaking people do not like change, and giving away their personal 'turf' is not going to be an easy change to sell, no matter how temporary it may be.

So what will you do?

Your first step in preparing to manage a conflict is exactly that: PREPARE. Too often we go into conflict situations without having done beforehand the necessary thinking. It is important for you to define what it is you are about to handle:

- What is the decision that you have made?

- Why did you make it?

- How will the people affected react to the decision?

- What sort of relationship do you have with the key players?

- How will you preserve your relationships?

- Is there any room for variation on your decision?

- What's the timing?

- Who holds the power?

Let's start with how you may personally react during a conflict: Does your temper rise, do you become aggressive, or are you cool as a cucumber? Are you inclined to give in just to preserve the peace? Or do you give in on small issues in order to save your strength for the really big problems?

Figure 16.1 shows a really useful chart that identifies the styles you could apply to a conflict.

It is always important to know yourself. If you don't, it will be impossible to identify from the matrix which style

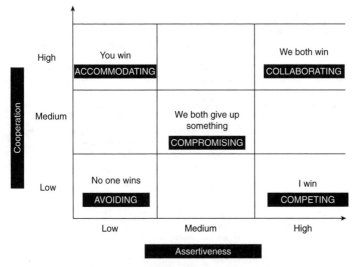

Figure 16.1 Styles that could be applied in a conflict

you tend to use most frequently. Think carefully about this fundamental question. When you are served a bad meal in a restaurant do you complain? Or do you say nothing and never return to that restaurant again?

Try to understand your own limitations and find ways to overcome your natural resistance to using certain styles, because each of these styles could be a valid strategy to be used in any conflict. See Figure 16.2.

Styles	Objective	Strategies	Possible outcomes	Uses
Competing (Win–Lose)	Going all out to win your objective at another's expense	• Withholding information • Ignoring others • Giving orders • Forcing, coercing • Delaying, disrupting • Exploiting weakness	• Relationships deteriorate	• Time is a concern • High stakes • You have the power • No concern about relationships
Accommodating (Lose–Win)	Preserve a relationship – keep everyone happy	• Smoothing differences • Minimising conflict • Giving in • Highly cooperative • Unassertive	• Needs not met • Differences not resolved • Best solution is not reached	• Want to preserve relationship • Other party has the power • Issue not important to you
Avoiding (Lose–Lose)	Sweep conflict under the rug. Pretend conflict does not exist	• Withdrawal • Avoidance • Non-involvement	• Problems unsolved • Differences not addressed	• Timing wrong • Issue not critical • Doesn't have enough information
Compromising (Partial win)	Settling for 'half a loaf'	Bargaining Negotiating	You get some but not all	• Different self-interests that do not conflict • Too costly to fight
Collaborating (Win–Win)	Maintaining the relationship and achieving the task are of equal importance	• Sharing objectives • Clarifying roles/responsibility/authority • Sharing information • Using appropriate influencing styles • Gaining commitment • Using supportive behaviours • Being reliable and trustworthy	• Both parties feel they have gained • Best solution is reached	• Time pressure not great • Interested in long term • Issue important to both parties

Figure 16.2 Understanding conflict styles

Having prepared yourself, and reached an understanding about your personal ability to manage conflict, you then need to have devised a process for conflict resolution.

We recommend the C U D S A method as your framework for conflict resolution. It has five steps. They are as follows:

C	confront the conflict
U	understand each other's position
D	define the problem(s)
S	search for and evaluate alternative solutions
A	agree upon and implement the best solution(s)

STEP ONE – confront the conflict by bringing it into the open

- Assert your experience or point of view.

- Get acknowledgement of existence of problem from the other party.

- Empathise.

STEP TWO – understand each other's position

- Give time for positions to be stated.

- Listen actively.

- Understand cultural issues.

- Focus on issues and not people.

- Preserve your relationships.

STEP THREE – define the problem(s)

- Ask questions/probe/paraphrase.

- Don't keep restating own position or perspective.

- Collaborate.

- Focus on issues.

- Find common ground.

Confront	• To let the purchasing department know as soon as possible in your conversation that you intend moving them into temporary accommodation, and why. 'We have got to locate the consultants close to the business for a period of six months, and as your offices are the least used due to your travelling away from head office we have decided to move you into temporary offices'.
Understand	• Provide quality time to listen to the views and *feelings* of everyone connected. 'I meet external people – what will they think!' 'Why us, why not finance?' 'Why did you pick us?' 'As a team most of you are travelling every week, with very few of you permanently in the office.' • Listen actively and with considerable empathy.
Define the problems	Contact with external people/disruption of the move/status issues.
Search and then solve	• Provide a permanent meeting room in the head office building for meeting up with suppliers. For the purchasing department, facilitate more working from home.
Agree and then act	• It will be communicated to the business that purchasing has agreed to move and that conference room A was now dedicated to purchasing and not available for anyone else. All external contacts would be routed through reception to room A. • The move will take place, with the assistance of facilities management, and only after all surplus documentation had been removed to archives. This will give the opportunity for the department to streamline prior to the move, which should improve its future effectiveness. • It is agreed that the company would make a contribution towards providing broadband access, and provide the wireless modems to facilitate home working.

Figure 16.3   An effective course of action

STEP FOUR – search for and evaluate alternative solutions

- Deal with one problem at a time.

- Most manageable first.

- Generate ideas – options first.

- Evaluate all possible options later.

- Which solution(s) will meet both parties' needs.

STEP FIVE – agree upon and implement best solution(s)

- Clear and specific (like contracts).

- Sometimes put agreements in writing.

- Both parties should own agreements.

Going back to the case study, an effective course of action would be as shown in Figure 16.3.

In every conflict there is always a way of getting buy-in. It always takes time, but it really is worth the effort.

17

Empowerment: Diocletian's Imperial Reforms

What happened?

The leader

In AD 284 Gaius Aurelius Valerius Diocletianus was proclaimed as emperor by his troops, the sole arbiter of imperial power in the late Roman empire. He came to the throne after a period of anarchy, which was made worse by foreign invasions. Whereas his predecessors followed a policy of defence and consolidation, Diocletian (pronounced 'Dee-o-clee-shone') saw deeper into the problems of Roman society and sought radical remedies for it.

The historical setting

In 235 a period of prolonged peace in the Mediterranean world had come to an end, when the legions stationed on the Rhine frontier declared as emperor their own senior officer Maximinus, a man of local origin. With Maximinus' brief reign began a half-century of extreme internal instability and repeated foreign incursions. Over 20 emperors tried to salvage the empire before Diocletian started to restore order. The balance between foreign pressure and Roman resistance had changed, and the initiative now often lay with Rome's enemies. The demands of defence reinforced the military character of imperial power, with the result that emperors were created by the army and deposed by the army. To compensate for their lack of legitimacy, these military emperors developed an elaborate court ceremonial, often borrowed from a resurgent Persia. The imperial court thus became the sole centre of power and policy making.

At the same time as foreign pressure on the empire's frontiers demanded attention, the old balance between city and countryside was breaking down. The effects of plague and the drift to the cities reduced the manpower available for agriculture, the basis of the economy. The patronage of military officers and the growth of large estates with a self-sufficient economy also reduced the income of cities, which found themselves increasingly unable to manage their affairs. Even though fear of foreign invasion did much to strengthen the sense of Roman solidarity, this solidarity tended to show itself in the support of would-be emperors who promised regional security. The period of uncertainty ended with the accession of Diocletian, who hailed from modern Montenegro.

Diocletian's behaviour

The first problem he faced was the usual one of invasion along all the frontiers, complicated by a great rebellion of the peasantry in what is present-day France and a rebellious commander in Britain. Having dealt with these essentially military difficulties, Diocletian sought to tackle the serious problems of succession and legitimacy. Henceforce the imperial government was to rely on a collegiate exercise of authority by two senior emperors and two junior ones. He selected as his senior colleague Maximian in 286, and seven years later Galerius and Constantius became their respective juniors. It was

The Roman emperors Diocletian and Maximian, joint rulers who were assisted by two deputies. Despite the show of co-operation, the empire still remained under the strain of personal ambition This sculpture now decorates the outside walls of San Marco in Venice.

understood that the juniors would automatically move up to the top positions on the death or abdication of their senior respective emperors. Adoption and marriage ties were intended to strengthen the bonds between the four imperial families. There was no territorial division of the empire: all four rulers had authority everywhere. By this new arrangement Diocletian hoped to avoid the civil wars which had dogged the Roman empire for over half a century.

The next problem Diocletian tried to solve by further delegation was the remoteness of imperial decision making from the mass of the population. His solution was to reduce the size and increase the number of the provinces, to group provinces in dioceses (a term that still survives today in ecclesiastical organisations), and to appoint several prefects, senior commanders each responsible for a large part of the empire. In most of the provinces, which were ungarrisoned, the governors had solely civil duties, such as justice and finance. Where there were garrisons in frontier provinces, governors handled military affairs and justice, but not finance. Besides bringing imperial government closer to the Roman people, this administrative reform was also intended to reduce the possibility of military uprisings.

Diocletian seems to have been much concerned that the correct Roman law should prevail throughout the empire; hence the new emphasis he placed on justice. Above all at local level governors were charged with the maintenance of law and order, while collecting taxes, often in kind, supplying recruits for the army and labour for public works. As these duties were now delegated to the smallest provincial units ever created by imperial decree, Diocletian hoped that there would be a chance of maximising the empire's resources. The army had long been in the habit of levying its requirements in kind on the local population, and this practice was developed into a regular system of taxation. A papyrus from Egypt offers an insight into the new degree of regulation. A woman who could not supply two animals for transport duty because one of them was sick had to write a formal report outlining the circumstances and asking to be excused.

Diocletian's reforms made the Roman empire more tightly administered and more homogeneous than before. Nonconforming groups were less tolerable in such a highly structured society and religious communities that refused to acknowledge the divine authority of the throne were persecuted. 'Our laws protect nothing that is not holy', ran an imperial edict, 'and thus Roman majesty has attained so great an extent by favour of the divine powers'. In 302 a general assault on the early Christian church commenced. It proved to be the most severe trial that its followers ever suffered.

Outcomes

Satisfied that he had set the empire on the right course, Diocletian abdicated and obliged Maximian to abdicate with him. Constantius and Galerius replaced them as senior emperors, choosing Severus and Maximinus as their juniors. Even though the transfer of power appeared to have been carried out smoothly, with the retirement of the senior emperors there began a period of political crisis and fragmentation which lasted nearly 20 years. After Diocletian's death in 305, there was no one with stature enough to insist on the continuation of a collegiate system of government. Two years later the situation was so confused that Maximian emerged from a retirement which he had not wanted and established himself as a separate ruler.

Diocletian had overlooked the extent to which the new arrangements he had made for sharing imperial power were dependent on the strength of his own personality. They broke down at their first test. Yet his administrative reforms, which were a parallel of this delegation of authority, survived the turmoil and formed the basis of the final period of the Roman empire.

Why does it matter?

The rationale for delegation

In his thorough overhaul of the system of taxation and army recruitment, his attempt to control inflation, and his radical provincial and military reorganisation, Diocletian showed an enthusiasm for far-reaching reform. And he adopted a similar approach to the problem of imperial rule. But the determined effort he directed at securing stability by means of a collegiate exercise of authority failed. Its neat logic simply overlooked political reality. After his death in 305 it foundered on the rocks of individual rivalry and ambition, and within 20 years Constantine had emerged as sole emperor, the winner of yet another civil war.

Diocletian's imperial failure aside, the idea of a manager delegating an element of his or her duties to other people is a fundamental and familiar part of business practice. It was perhaps undervalued as a management technique in the highly competitive organisational cultures of the 1980s when delegating significant responsibilities to subordinates was sometimes seen as a sign of individual weakness, but in the 1990s, as organisational structures became flatter and hierarchies disappeared, delegation began to be seen as an essential management tool. Not that all managers are of course happy and confident about delegating as a technique; for some delegation is still a last resort, a cause of anxiety both to the manager and the subordinate asked to take on increased responsibility. But the effectiveness of delegation has increasingly been linked to the successful implementation of a systematic and thorough approach to the whole business of coaching, although it is true that not all managers make good coaches.

Empowerment

Management thinkers and writers have moved on from a concern with the apparently simple act of delegation to a focus on the concept of 'empowering'. Empowerment as a management approach implies much more than delegation. Empowerment can be thought of as the creation of an organisational culture in which responsibility and accountability for the job rest with the individual undertaking it. As such, it is a central issue within contemporary thinking about leadership.

Empowerment is about:

- allowing staff to get on with the job and take responsibility for meeting the expectations of customers;

- encouraging and equipping those closest to the customers to take the decisions which they feel are right;

- removing unnecessary bureaucracy and control;

- supporting and developing staff so that they are able to put into practice their ideas for improving the way things are done.

Among the key management writers exploring the benefits of empowerment to organisations is Rosabeth Moss Kanter. In her work she examines the ways in which empowerment can make organisations more flexible and responsive and concludes that:

by empowering others, a leader does not decrease his power, instead he may increase it – especially if the whole organisation performs better.

In a similar vein Professor Henry Mintzberg points up the individual benefits of empowerment to a manager in a foreword he wrote for *The Drama of Leadership* by Patricia Pitcher. Tellingly he holds:

A leader has to be . . . either a brilliant visionary or truly creative strategist in which case he can do what he likes and get away with it or a true empowerer, who can bring out the best in others.

Empowerment in practice

Not surprisingly, there has been considerable interest in seeking to identify organisations which have implemented and benefited from a strategy of empowering their staff. One of the names which regularly figures in such research is the Brazilian company SEMCO. When Ricardo Semler took over the failing business from his father, he initially adopted a traditional and very tough leadership style, sacking 60% of the company's top management on his first day in charge! A period of serious ill health arising from his workaholic approach subsequently prompted a radical rethink of the way he wanted the organisation to function.

Semler then went about creating one of the most empowered organisations of our time. Although managers set their own salaries, they are appraised by the workers in their departments; there are no secretaries or personal assistants. Shopfloor workers make the sort of decisions which managers in 99% of businesses would see as the core of their role, including setting productivity targets, work schedules and the distribution of the profit-sharing scheme. In his own account of his work at SEMCO, in *Maverick*, Semler writes:

At SEMCO we treat them (the employees) as adults. We trust them. We don't make our employees ask permission to go to the bathroom, or have security guards search them as they leave for the day. We get out of their way and let them do their jobs.

By traditional measures this company has been a great success, even within the turmoil which sometimes characterises the Brazilian economy. SEMCO has taken the concept of 'industrial democracy' to a level which is reminiscent of successful cooperative organisations and social enterprises, while maintaining at its core some familiar features of a traditional 'free enterprise' business. Although Ricardo Semler himself acknowledges in his introduction to the 1999 edition of *Maverick* that continued success is not certain, he remains committed to his beliefs when he insists:

Should we do badly in five or ten years' time, nothing will alter our faith in freedom and democracy as guarantors of sustainability.

One of the most radical of Diocletian's innovations, the creation of a leadership team of two senior and two junior emperors, has a parallel in SEMCO where the chief executive's role rotates between five people. There are instances of similar thinking in more traditional businesses too. Within Philips NV in Holland, for instance, the organisational structure is built on joint responsibility being shared by two managers, one representing the 'commercial' end of the business and the other the 'technical'. Formally, both hold equal responsibility for geographical areas of operation or for product groups.

The limits of empowerment

Not all organisations that have sought to implement a 'whole business' approach to empowerment have been so successful of course. Examples would include the secondary school that aimed to operate without any promoted posts or managers except the headteacher, with all responsibilities, and salaries, shared equally and decisions taken collectively. The failure of this particular experiment highlights the highly political nature of empowerment as an approach. All organisations have to confront fundamental questions about where power should reside and who is able to take final decisions. These are precisely the sort of issues that Diocletian addressed in reworking the administration of the Roman empire.

Decentralisation runs hand in hand with empowerment and many large companies have tried to break themselves up into many smaller firms with the specific aim of empowering the workers on the front line. The Taiwanese computer company ACER, for example, took the decision at a critical point in its growth to split itself into 21 subdivisions, each floated separately on the stock market. A common issue arising from such moves towards decentralisation is the difficulty of devolving power to subsidiaries, remote from the centre, while maintaining their loyalty to the parent business and ensuring sufficient consistency of policy and practice. It should be noted how Diocletian's strategy appears to have been designed to increase homogeneity across the empire, in part through the clear identification and application of a common legal framework.

Clearly, if not handled effectively the process of empowerment can produce problems. These include the following:

- Resentment can develop among managers who feel their role and status is being diminished.

- Workers can feel anxious about what they are being expected to do or resentful that they are being asked to take on extra responsibilities without the accompanying benefits.

- In some circumstances individual staff can innovate beyond the normal sphere of control of their jobs and take decisions beyond their competence.

Over-empowerment

This last risk brings to mind the notorious case of Nick Leeson, a highly successful derivatives trader in the Singapore office of Britain's oldest merchant bank, Barings. In 1995 he brought about its collapse by gambling on the Tokyo futures market. Reading his own account of the disaster, one is struck on the one hand by his lack of experience and training in the field and, on the other, by the lack of control over his activities by his superiors. If his gambles had paid off, Barings would conceivably now be in the management texts as an example of successful empowerment in practice. Now the business no longer exists. As John Micklethwait and Adrian Wooldridge summarised the case in their book, *The Witch Doctors*:

The Baring family lost its bank because the management over-empowered one individual, Nick Leeson.

The process of empowerment raises central issues about the relationship between the organisation and its workers, particularly the degree of trust that exists between leaders and led. As Robert Shapiro of Monsanto commented,

If an institution wants to be adaptive, it has to let go of some control and trust that people will work on the right things in the right way.

For empowerment to be effective and sustainable it has to become embedded in an organisation's culture, and not, as in the case of Diocletian, dependent on the force of one strong leader's commitment or enthusiasm. This will probably remain the hardest nut to crack.

What does it mean for you?

The development of a climate in which managers can feel confident in delegating real responsibility to their staff does not happen overnight. The extent to which an individual manager feels unworried about delegating tasks to subordinates will depend on the way they perceive their own role and their familiarity with the working practices and traditions of an organisation or team. In these two case studies two managers from very different organisations describe their experiences. What actions do you feel they should take?

Case study 1

Vina Tomschenko was appointed earlier this year to the post of deputy headteacher of a large secondary school, moving from a similar role in a much smaller school. The main focus of her role is on the curriculum of the school and she has responsibility for managing the work of the 12 heads of department, each of whom manages a subject and the staff that teach it. She was appointed because the governors of the school were impressed with her dynamism and felt she could provide the drive to improve on the school's examination results which are generally acceptable, but have not improved significantly over the previous three or four years, in contrast to neighbouring schools. Six weeks into her new post Vina is facing some problems.

'One of the main issues I'm facing is my relationship with the department heads – they don't seem to see themselves as managers at all. The older ones, particularly the head of maths and the head of science, have a lot of influence on the behaviour of the younger ones and the attitude seems to be that they are experts in their subject and that is enough. Not that they are all bad – I get the feeling some of the people who have been appointed from outside the school in the last two or three years are as frustrated as I am, but they are afraid of putting their heads above the parapet. Things came to a head the other day when a parent complained that one maths teacher wasn't setting any homework. I asked the head of department to investigate and phone the parent, and he told me in no uncertain terms that this was not part of his job! In fact all complaints and problems seem to land on my desk – teachers asking for new sets of books, parents complaining, kids thrown out of classrooms – the lot!

'When I was appointed, the headteacher told me that he believed in empowering the staff – "Let the people closest to the chalk face make the decisions" was how he put it. I liked that idea because I had come from a very traditional and hierarchical school and I had always wanted to work in an environment where people are trusted, know what they have to do but can find their own ways of doing it best. Unfortunately I haven't had much opportunity to speak to the headteacher in any depth since then – he always seems to be dashing off to meetings somewhere. I tried to explain some of the difficulties I was experiencing but he just advised me that I needed to keep them on board and to try another route.

'There do not seem to be any consistent systems in the school – each department seems to run its own affairs without much reference to the others and the performance management scheme, for example, doesn't seem to actually operate in practice at all.

'I thought the heads of department would be used to a devolved way of working, but alarm bells started to sound when I decided to devolve the budgets for books, materials and staff training to them. I thought they would be enthusiastic but in fact there was huge resistance from most of them, or at least the most outspoken ones. The head of science actually said she would need to be taken off a substantial part of her teaching if she was expected to take on these additional responsibilities. I am getting very angry with one or two of them now, but I don't imagine that blowing my top is going to help.'

Case study 2

Ted Jackson could not believe his luck when he was told that he was to become the new CEO of Cactus Crisps. Markus Brennan the current CEO was moving off to a key job in the HQ looking after the European beverage division.

Markus was a tough act to follow, and tough being the operative word. Over the last five years he had taken Cactus from a loss-making business to one of the best performers in the category, and in the process he had made few friends. It was very clear to him that he had to attack the cost base, bring down the variable costs, and write off surplus stocks. He got rid of virtually all of the original board of directors, together with their high-powered BMWs, and had surrounded himself with a team of young bloods who jumped at the chance to leapfrog the deadwood into positions of power. Or so they thought, but the reality of the situation was that Markus made all the key decisions, and generally treated those around him pretty badly.

No one could deny that Markus had the ability to get results, however much he was only a short-term wunderkind. His abrasive manner and his refusal to share power resulted in the free spirits among the directors disappearing fairly quickly. So it was not surprising that Bill Trent, the canny main board CEO decided to 'promote' Markus to an HQ job, where he could keep a tight hold on his reins. Bill had called Ted to his office a month ago and told him the good news. He was very complimentary about Markus, outlining the great work that he had done. He then went on to say that the business now needed a new style of leader, someone who could move Cactus Crisps to the next stage of its development. The cost base was in good shape and the product quality excellent: now it needed to grow the top line. This was going to need considerable insight, creativity, courage and a real team spirit. The bright young things of the organisation needed to be energised and empowered. At this point he cautioned that this would not be easy. Markus had been the main decision-maker for so long that many of the senior managers had become nothing more than yes men, and seldom put forward an opinion. It was Bill's guess that they would struggle to work in a more empowering environment.

Ted had always had a good relationship with Bill, who had brought him into the organisation two years ago in order to run the West Country Hotels chain. This was nowhere near as big as Cactus Crisps, but it too had had its problems. The previous general manager had been rather too fond of the single malt whisky collection and, as a result, after a fireside chat with Bill he had gone off to discover himself in Tuscany. Ted had joined three months later and set about rebuilding the business. After Ted had a stint in America he had always been passionate about customer service and, although very demanding of his direct reports, he had a way of getting people on board with changes. Within six months the business was thriving, and all the employees appeared to be a lot happier in their jobs.

His excitement for the new job rather rapidly evaporated after his first meeting with the Cactus Crisps board. Bill had left Ted to get on with it, and wanted him to take charge and get the show moving. Ted had wanted to start the team thinking about new possibilities, and had taken time out to praise them all for the remarkable profit improvement they had achieved. Somehow this didn't seem to work, and after they overcame their silence, the floodgates suddenly opened. However, it wasn't a deluge of great ideas that hit Ted, as it turned into a huge whinge session. Everyone on the team was offloading all their problems onto him. The meeting ended rather too late, and Ted felt disappointment with the way the meeting had turned out.

This was proving to be much more of a challenge than Ted had anticipated.

18

Recognising Achievement: The Triumph of Belisarius

What happened?

The leader

Belisarius (pronounced 'Belly-sari-us') was the most famous general who served the eastern Roman emperor Justinian. After the collapse of Roman authority in the western provinces of the empire, Germanic kingdoms arose there instead. During the fifth century AD the Franks, the Alamans and the Burgundians shared out between themselves what is now France, the Anglo-Saxons occupied Britain, the Ostrogoths took over Italy and their cousins the Visigoths Spain, while the Vandals dominated the northern coast of Africa. It was Belisarius' destiny to lead the counter-attack, which Justinian launched in 533, to recover the old western provinces strung around the Mediterranean Sea.

The historical background

Justinian ruled the eastern Mediterranean from Constantinople, present-day Istanbul. The city had been chosen as an imperial capital in 330 by the emperor Constantine. As a result of his conversion to Christianity, Constantine wanted a New Rome untainted by pagan associations. Initially, he seems to have thought in terms of any eastern seat of government rather than a rival to the city of Rome itself, but the move eastwards was precipitated by more than religious sentiment. The empire's centre of gravity had already shifted to the Greek-speaking eastern provinces, where its economic and cultural centre had long been. And the defences built for Constantinople by Constantine's successors were so strong that they resisted all sieges and assaults till 1204, when the Fourth Crusade realised its capture was so much easier than pursuing a war against the Saracens.

Yet Justinian was not without danger himself in Constantinople. In 532, the year before he ordered the western offensive, the emperor came close to an enforced abdication. Justinian's reign was marked by tensions in a number of cities, but the disturbance in the capital put all other urban riots in the shade. The trouble began with a confrontation between the Greens and Justinian in the Hippodrome, the great arena for chariot racing. The damp wintry weather had put everyone's nerves on edge, so that protest about the arbitrary action of a certain official included an insult directed at the emperor. The Greens and the Blues, the two chief colours of the racing teams, then had a slanging match, since Justinian habitually supported the Blues. During the next few days there were incidents in the streets and both Green and Blue supporters were arrested. Several were condemned to death, but on the day appointed for their execution the gallows broke and the crowd rushed two of them to a church for asylum. When the city prefect refused to accept that their miraculous escape from hanging should be regarded as a reprieve, a riot broke out in the Hippodrome and, forgetting their rivalry, the Greens and the Blues for the first time united against the imperial government.

The eastern Roman emperor Justinian alongside Maximian, archbishop of Ravenna. This mosaic was made in 547, shortly after Belisarius' reconquest of Italy from the Goths.

A genuine sense of injustice seems to have inspired this unusual alliance of rioters, which included women as well as men, even though women never attended chariot races. Continued refusal to pardon the two asylum seekers led to an attack on the prefect's headquarters. Once these were alight, the rioters fired other public buildings, the flames spreading closer to the imperial palace. Although Justinian made concessions, the Greens and the Blues remained united and, sensing their power, they decided to acclaim another emperor, which suited Justinian's political enemies. Word of a loss of nerve in the imperial palace may have emboldened the rioters, since Justinian was preparing to flee in a fast galley anchored nearby. At this moment of crisis his wife Empress Theodora spoke out strongly against flight. 'There is no nobler shroud', she said, 'than the imperial purple'.

Belisarius' behaviour

Stunned by her intervention, the court fell silent, until two of Justinian's generals, Belisarius and Mundus, began discussing the military option. Fortunately for the besieged emperor, these two commanders had just arrived in the capital with their battle-hardened troops, whose loyalty was not in doubt, unlike the city's regular garrison. The moment for action had come, no matter the casualties. Secretly Belisarius and Mundus left the palace, and by separate routes brought their troops to the gates of the Hippodrome, where the rioters were celebrating the accession of a new emperor. Imperial agents had already been infiltrated into the event so as to stir up trouble. Shouts of 'Long live Justinian' restarted fighting between the Greens and the Blues, when the troops of Belisarius and Mundus burst through the gates and fell on the crowd. Outside, the eunuch guard was stationed, ready to cut down any fugitives who escaped. A massacre ensued and 30,000 people died.

Afterwards a grateful Justinian made Belisarius commander-in-chief. Quickly the grateful general defeated the Vandals and re-annexed Africa. He also sent back to Constantinople the vast treasure accumulated by the Vandal kings from the sack of Rome in 455 and subsequent raids on cities in the western Mediterranean. Justinian was impressed enough to grant Belisarius on his return to the capital a triumph, the only one celebrated by a non-member of the imperial house since the reign of the first

Roman emperor Augustus, half a millennium earlier. In 535 the now celebrated general began the destruction of the Ostrogothic kingdom in Italy. Once again his success in the field led to the transfer of another royal treasure to Constantinople. Later campaigns only enhanced Belisarius' fame, much to the anxiety of Justinian.

From Justinian's point of view, the services of his most famous general were a mixed blessing. His resolute action during the riot, his victories over the Vandals, Ostrogoths and other enemies were achievements for which his emperor could only be thankful. Yet the possibility that Belisarius harboured imperial ambitions of his own always worried Justinian, despite the fact that in Italy the general had already turned down the offer of a Gothic throne. For this reason Justinian never allowed Belisarius a second ride in the triumphal chariot, the ultimate accolade for the successful general.

Outcomes

The scale of the riot that Belisarius helped to put down in Constantinople took contemporaries by surprise, and in seeking to account for it they blamed the usual culprits – conspiring nobles, the senseless mob, demonic activity. Later its devastation was viewed as an opportunity that Justinian grasped to embellish the capital, not least of which was the remodelled cathedral church of the Holy Wisdom. But there is no question that the presence of Belisarius and Mundus alone saved Justinian's throne. The former had been recalled from Syria, the key to the defence of the eastern Mediterranean, after a poor campaign against the Persians. The latter, a Germanic leader who had incorporated his followers in the imperial army, was on a visit from his command in the Balkans. So Justinian survived, and through the efforts of Belisarius reconquered several provinces in the western Mediterranean.

Why does it matter?

Recognition and reputation

Recognition of achievement inevitably has a political context. Belisarius' rivals were ever ready to inform Justinian that his commander-in-chief was plotting treason. Such a report was made by his fellow officers at the end of the African campaign, but on Belisarius' recall to Constantinople the emperor was still willing to award the conquering general a triumph. Belisarius was permitted to ride through the streets of the capital in a procession that proudly displayed the amazing Vandal spoils.

It is easy for a leader to underestimate the effect that a thank you or a word of praise can have on the morale of a member of staff. However, the way in which excellent individual performance is acknowledged and rewarded by management inevitably has a political dimension as it impacts on the subtle power relationships within the organisation. These subtleties need to be considered by managers, but being aware of the complexities of such situations, and the potentially undesirable effects that can stem from the singling out of an individual member of staff for praise or reward, should not moderate the spontaneity which can characterise the most memorable gestures of appreciation. Even though the emperor Justinian was already becoming anxious about the loyalty of his foremost general, he was prepared to acknowledge Belisarius' great achievement by granting him a triumph. An immediate and enthusiastic response by a leader to an outstanding piece of work can, therefore, mean more to the individual than a valuable gift presented at a carefully stage-managed awards event. For Belisarius, the triumph may have served to confirm his loyalty, since the Goths in Italy were later unable to tempt him with the offer of a throne. A modern parallel is provided by the story of a

CEO of a large corporation who was so excited by a piece of work completed by an employee that he was desperate to reward him on the spur of the moment and, finding nothing on his desk but some fruit he had brought in for lunch, presented the individual concerned with a banana. Since then, the company has held an annual 'golden banana' award event to highlight outstanding contributions to the business.

There are clearly echoes of this approach in the numerous and varied awards events and celebrations which are so prominent a part of corporate culture in some businesses. So, what purpose is served by celebrating individual achievement in such a public way? In *The Leadership Challenge*, James Kouzes and Barry Posner argue strongly that recognising achievement is a key skill for leadership; in fact they make this one of their 10 leadership commitments – 'recognise contributions by showing appreciation for individual excellence'. For them, to leave the recognition as a private affair is to miss a huge opportunity to demonstrate to the whole organisation what can be achieved, and to encourage others to aim for similarly outstanding results. It is also true that a leader's own position can be strengthened through association with exceptional individuals. For Kouzes and Posner, it is part of a leader's role to stimulate an environment where it is natural to take pride in the achievement of others. They argue that:

As the leader your job is to create a culture of celebration, but you don't have to be the one to do all the organising and cheering ... You can facilitate everyone's participation in coming together to celebrate spontaneously and quickly.

An effective leader can use a variety of techniques to recognise achievement; the importance of a word of thanks is obvious, but finding the time to listen to colleagues' accounts of a project or initiative and to give appropriate feedback can also be highly motivating and can help foster positive expectations as well. Being creative about the form of the awards themselves can have similar impact: personalised prizes, for instance, which mean something particular to the individual, show that a leader has invested some time and thought in the process, as does a hand-written note or card of thanks or a well-written piece in the organisation's internal newsletter.

The spirit of community

In many cases, leaders who are keen to recognise exceptional achievements are motivated by broader reasons than simply wishing to acknowledge a job well done. The employees who are singled out for special treatment serve an important purpose for the organisation as a whole in that they represent a positive and replicable image of the potential of the business, of its values and successes. In allowing such a powerful and public recognition of Belisarius, for example, Justinian was showing his people what his empire could collectively achieve if his own vision of reconquest were translated into action, a particularly vital point to make after the urban crisis his rule had just faced.

Private rewards may do little to set an example for the organisation's staff, but the inevitable political dimension to a high-profile celebration of achievement, focused on an individual star or a few exceptional members of staff, has its attendant risks. Jack Welch, former CEO of General Electric, strongly advocates 'stroking' and rewarding star players in a business but draws attention to the dangers. He says:

A star's ego can be a dangerous thing. I've seen talented young people promoted too quickly and their ambitions spin out of control. I've seen terrific financial analysts, engineers, and network executives get told one too many times that they are irreplaceable, and they start swaggering around to the point that their teams resent them.

As with Belisarius, other staff whose efforts have not been singled out for recognition in the same way can become resentful and this resentment can, in turn, translate into a whispering campaign against the award winner. Often it is implied that they have aspirations which threaten the leader's own position or status.

In other cases, the perception that management may have of a high-achieving employee may not be shared by all their colleagues. In one organisation, for instance, this 'counter-culture blast' has become expressed in an annual vote for the person they consider to have shown the most ingratiating, toadying and self-seeking attitude to management over the previous year: this person is then awarded the 'Nipper' prize – Nipper being the name of the obsequious little dog staring obediently up at his master's voice in the old HMV corporate image! There are also significant cultural differences in the likely responses of employees to a public awards event. In another organisation, an 'employee of the year' dinner that had become a popular part of corporate culture in the Los Angeles headquarters of a corporation, failed to readily translate in the same format to its Liverpool office!

The ideal celebration event needs to communicate the message that everyone has value and can contribute to business success. Perhaps recognition systems which reward teams rather than individuals may prove to be more effective in the end.

Appraisal, pay and rewards

If recognising achievement is genuinely motivational, then perhaps this should be a central component in an organisation's performance management system. Such systems have, in general, become much smarter and subtler in recent years, with a clearer appreciation of the principles of human motivation lying behind their design. Nevertheless, there remains a significant difference of interpretation regarding the extent to which, within a performance management scheme, individual perform-ance should be linked to pay and rewards. Although it is generally acknowledged that linking base pay increases to individual appraisal does not always produce the desired improvements in outcomes, there are still author-ities who think a clear linkage should be maintained between pay and performance. In *Winning*, Jack Welch, for example, draws on his years of experience as a CEO to make the point that:

Of course, people want to be recognised for great performance. Plaques and public fanfare have their place. But without money, they can lose a lot of their impact. Even the Nobel and Pulitzer prizes come with cash awards.

In contrast to Jack Welch, respected management writer and researcher Alfie Kahn wrote in an article entitled 'Why incentive plans cannot work',

Do rewards work? The answer depends on what we mean by 'work'. Research suggests that by and large, rewards succeed at securing one thing only: temporary compliance. When it comes to producing lasting changes in attitudes and behaviour, however, rewards, like punishments, are strikingly ineffective. Once the rewards run out, people revert to their old behaviours.

Reciprocity

Organisations where the recognition of achievement and success appears to be a natural and harmonious part of the culture are often noticeable for a characteristic that can be termed 'reciprocity'. That is to say that there is a widespread belief that success depends on a genuine and mutual respect for everyone's contribution, both the leaders and the led; thus a principle of give and take runs through the work of the organisation and leads to achievement being seen as an expression of collective, corporate effort. There are leadership theories that consciously have something like this notion of reciprocity at their base, one of the most influential being 'servant leadership'.

Servant leadership as a distinct approach was originally inspired by Christian principles and pioneered in the United States in the 1970s by Robert Greenleaf. The underlying belief in servant leadership is that the best leadership comes from a desire to serve others and that people throughout an organisation have the opportunity both to serve and lead in different ways, and to meet different challenges. There are now 10 'Greenleaf Centres' worldwide, offering training and support to individuals and businesses adopting servant leadership principles. Among the large organisations that have adopted characteristics of servant leadership in the United States are Starbucks and the highly successful South West Airlines. In the United Kingdom, its best-known corporate advocate is the retailer ASDA, now part of the Wal-Mart empire. In practice within ASDA, the principles of servant leadership are manifested in greatly increased levels of consultation with staff and an unusual keenness among managers to get involved in the day-to-day realities of problems in the stores. Staff are encouraged to contribute to the process of strategic decision making through devices such as 'colleague circles', and within the store they are given control of a budget which can be spent on activities or resources to make their working lives easier. As one ASDA employee put it, 'People work best when they feel good about themselves'. For the proponents of servant leadership, it is intrinsic, shared satisfaction in the job that is held to be the key motivator. It is believed to influence long-term behaviour much more effectively than periodic rewards given by management.

In imperial Constantinople a servant leadership approach would not have been readily understood, despite its Christian ethos. But the loyalty of Belisarius might have been strengthened by greater consistency on the part of Justinian, whose fears of him caused the general much unnecessary dismay. Perhaps the emperor forgot what happened at the climax of the triumph. In the Hippodrome, Belisarius and the captive Vandal king Gelimer had prostrated themselves before Justinian and Theodora. But Gelimer may have then got it right. When he saw the cheering crowds and the splendid imperial box, he quietly repeated over and over again the verse from Ecclesiastes: 'Vanity of vanities, all is vanity'.

What does it mean for you?

Get any group of employees brainstorming about ways of improving motivation in the organisation and you will inevitably find 'recognition' close to the top of the list, probably alongside communication.

Recognition is in fact one of the most simple and cost-effective motivation tools available to leaders, and yet it happens to be seldom used effectively.

To appreciate the power of a well thought-out and executed scheme, let's look at a case study.

The South Hills Hospital

Angie Duncan had thought long and hard before she joined the South Hills Hospital, coming out of a well-funded business in the telcoms industry and joining a run-down NHS hospital as quality improvement advisor. She knew being closer to her parents had probably swung the deal, although the main reason was the enormous challenge that her new job presented and the support she knew she would get from Ted Humphreys, the newly appointed CEO.

She had spent her first six months just getting management onside with the change programme she had put together. After endless edits and discussion, negotiations and temper tantrums, she had got the buy-in of all concerned. Her first task was to train the management in the WHY, WHAT and HOW of the project, and then cascade the learning right across the hospital. It had been a stroke of genius when she chose to involve members of the management team as her co-trainers. Apart from being very cost effective, it had also sent out a message to everyone that the management itself was really serious about improving the quality of the hospital.

Twelve months on you could see and feel change. A visit to the wards was a pleasure now, with motivated nurses and doctors feeling that they were able to get problems resolved. Even the look of the wards was different, with clear signs, fun noticeboards, and updated and rapidly improving performance charts.

It was at the July management meeting that Angie proposed the introduction of an annual recognition ceremony. It met with a fair amount of resistance: 'It will be too expensive'; 'It will create unwanted competition'; 'It will be another drain on people's time'. Finally Ted stepped in and nominated a team of progressive thinkers to come up with a workable scheme. This took three months to agree, before it was communicated to the workforce as a whole.

It was 12 months later that the first quality improvement awards ceremony took place. A committee had carefully sifted through all the entries, checking to see how well they met the agreed award criteria. There were teams chosen from each department in the hospital, so that each team would present their departmental achievements. It was then that Ted dictated a few additional conditions. He said: 'I want the teams to be given presentation skills training, and I want them to be free to invite members of their family to the event. I want their families to be proud of their achievements and I want them to be able to do justice to their projects when they present them and this means PCs, photographs and videos'.

A lot of rehearsing took place, mainly after work, until finally the day of the awards ceremony arrived. The nearby town hall had been decorated, and professional audio-visual equipment brought in for the day. A number of local and county dignitaries were also invited to join the teams and their families. One by one the teams came up, overcame their nerves, and enthusiastically presented their quality improvement projects. Each member of the team received a rather grand finalist medallion, inscribed 2005 Awards. The medallions were presented by the local mayor, and teams were photographed by a local press photographer. Finally, a team of porters, who had simplified the waste disposal system, was declared the first winner. The award was a large floating trophy, together with the 'Best of 2005' medallions, plus a weekend at a first-rate, local hotel for each team member and their partner.

The management team concluded at its next meeting that the event had been a resounding success, and that it would now become an annual occasion.

Learning from the case study

A well-conceived and effectively executed recognition scheme can be a very motivating experience. There are a number of guidelines you should follow, however. Always:

- Get the full buy-in of management.

- Spend time defining the details of the recognition scheme, because once it is implemented it will be difficult to amend.

- Look for cost-effective ways of saying thank you.

- Communicate the recognition scheme to all levels of your organisation in a clear and concise manner.

- Ensure you have representatives/champions in each of the departments.

- Ensure the award criteria are fair, clear and open to scrutiny.

- Pick the best in each department and communicate why you have made your choice.

- Involve partners and family, as feeling proud about where you work is a very powerful motivator indeed.

- Communicate through internal and external media.

- Allow the winners to bask in their glory for a short time, but then define the next year's criteria and start the momentum building again.

19

Winning as a Leader

The 18 leaders from the ancient world featured in this book faced staggering challenges and created extraordinary opportunities. Some were driven to respond to crises deriving from external threats, others from changing internal conditions. Their actions stemmed from the force of their own will and their determination to alter the status quo, by improving either their role and status, or that of their state. One thing they had in common was the sheer scale of their ambition. The futures that they envisaged meant bringing about radical change. Some were successful in their projects, others definitely not. But they intuitively understood that they were playing for the highest stakes imaginable. However determined, powerful or shrewd they might be, however loyal and ingenious their followers, and however large or small the resources available to them, the complexity and unpredictability of their very different situations meant that the decisions they took could never guarantee a successful outcome, they were always essentially gambles. If we are quite honest, this remains true of real leadership today.

The business sections of libraries and the management shelves of bookshops are full of accounts of outstanding leaders from the contemporary world or from history:

from politics, the military, exploration, sport and even from business. The popularity of such books speaks for a desire to tease out the determinants of successful leadership, and to draw lessons from these exceptional models of leadership in action, which can then be applied to our own situations. So what are the common threads that can be discerned in the variety of ancient stories recounted in this book? What can we as individuals take forward from them in order to improve our own effectiveness and the success of our organisations? How can we use them to train and develop the current and potential leaders in our teams, departments and businesses? It is these fundamental questions that this chapter seeks to address, no matter that unambiguous and universally applicable answers are always so hard to come by. That individual readers will have responded differently to the ancient leaders presented in the body of this book only serves to remind us that the gamble of leadership is a highly personal business. The best we can ever hope to do is to shift the odds more in our favour.

Leadership in context

The Alexander who was known and respected as a fellow warrior by his Macedonian soldiers was a very different character from the Alexander who was revered as the Great King by his Persian subjects. His attempt to present two such different images of himself at the same time, in order to suit the expectations of these very different audiences, created what were ultimately irresolvable tensions in his relationships with both of them. Nevertheless, his actions provide a fascinating example of a leader being acutely aware of the context in which he was operating, and of seeking to control his behaviour so as to construct an effective public persona. As with any relationship, leaders have to understand and manage their own behaviour and approach so as to suit the cultural setting within which they are working.

It is convenient to categorise the societies that provide the backdrop to the historical accounts in this book as being part of some homogeneous entity conveniently called 'the Ancient World'. In reality, of course, this term masks an extraordinary diversity of cultures. The divine rule of a pharaoh, for instance, inevitably created very different relationships between leader and led than from those forged within the democratic societies of the Greek city-states many years later; as a comparison of, say, the histories of Ramesses II and Epaminondas, the Theban general, readily illustrates. Ancient leaders often had to manage major changes in their behaviour to be effective empire-builders in geographical areas distant from their home states, and the ability to adopt differing methods of working to suit varied conditions in this way is still a key indicator of an effective leader in the business world of today. Some people seem to be naturally attuned and sensitive to the complexities of the context in which they are operating. For others, the absence of this skill, however, can be a major impediment to their success.

The position facing a manager taking up a senior post in an organisation from the outside illustrates the problem very well. It is so tempting to seek to apply the same tried and tested techniques and strategies that proved successful in a previous post; the approaches which had so impressed the selection panel at interview, rather than think afresh about solving problems in the new business. Unfortunately, tactics which may have worked well in one organisation often fail to produce the same results in a different setting, even if, on the face of it, the organisations seem very similar in function and structure. It takes time and attention to absorb the subtleties of an organisation's culture and, in particular, to appreciate the factors that make the staff behave in the ways they do.

Some leaders may try to adopt the style of a Sulla, aiming to impose a new way of working on a reluctant organisation through force of personality or sheer terror. For most of us, though, any long-term impact on a new organisation requires an initial period of analysis and reflection. Even if your intention is to pursue radical change in the way the business works, you really do need time to identify the weak points in its structure, to find reliable allies, and to highlight the likely points of resistance. Even leaders who have stayed with an organisation for a long time and shaped its ways of working, need to adapt their approaches to suit different circumstances and to get the best from a team, which inevitably has a constantly evolving profile. The significance of this facility in a leader is well illustrated in the advice that Liu Bang was given by his court chamberlain Lu Jia, who pointedly told the new emperor that, even though he had won the empire on horseback, there was no way he could rule it that way.

So what characterises a leader who has this sensitivity to context and is able to respond so flexibly? Such people seem to have particularly acute 'antennae'; they sense the direction an organisation is taking, foresee difficulties and appreciate how team members are really feeling. Frequently, they seem aware of the concerns of key individuals and take action to address underlying problems before they become major crises. The increasing ethnic and cultural diversity of organisations, and the globalisation of business activity, have now placed a premium on the skills involved in what has become termed 'managing diversity'. Yet successful leadership has always been about managing the extraordinary diversity of individuals within an organisation, with their different talents, concerns, objectives, attitudes and aspirations. As one CEO put it, 'What else is there to manage but diversity?'

Whether this critical sensitivity to context is a skill that can be learned, or it is an inherent feature of a leader's personality, is a challenging question indeed. In practical terms, a good leader will tend to have effective and reliable networks of contacts across the organisation, often including staff whose status and role may not immediately seem to provide a ready or reliable source of valuable intelligence. Such networking skills can be developed, but what should be emphasised is that all leaders need to cultivate and refine the underpinning skill set of 'active listening', and not take notice of just the good news that we all crave to hear.

Leadership and self-belief

A consistent characteristic of the historical figures in this book is that their actions stemmed from immense self-belief, an absolute conviction that they really could achieve what they had set out to achieve, with their vision hardened, and their purpose strengthened, by the challenges and tests that beset them during times of crisis. Without such a single-minded sense of purpose, Hannibal could never have sustained his campaign against Rome for so many years abroad, nor could the ruler Wuling have convinced his people of the need for such a radical change of direction as the one upon which he had decided. There are, of course, grave dangers to a leader who assumes that his or her individual vision is so cogent, its logic so irresistible, that ultimately everyone is bound to share in it and endorse its pursuit. Such an attitude assumes that contradictory views are, at best, misplaced and, at worst, malicious, and that they consequently present no real threat to the chosen course of action. It was this sort of massive misjudgement that led to Cicero's final failure to bring the power-brokers in Rome in line with his own policies. Similarly, the moment when Alexander's persuasiveness in India finally proved no match for his soldiers' refusal to pursue his imperial dreams farther to the east, marks a point at which a fundamental overestimate of the power of his own vision nearly caused the collapse of all his endeavours.

As people always watch their leaders and are ever alert to inconsistencies in their actions, they are quick to spot gaps between rhetoric and behaviour. The Egyptian army at Kadesh might have completely disintegrated had Ramesses' courageous action at the point of crisis not matched, and exceeded, what they had been brought up to expect from a leader. If a leader's vision and strategy for an organisation is not genuinely heartfelt, then even if it is aggressively publicised and promoted, it is likely that employees will quickly see through it. This is not to say that leaders cannot change their minds over a direction they had previously set. An honest reappraisal of a decision does not necessarily undermine their authority or credibility. It is rather an opportunity to show that they are as capable of making mistakes. Putting them right can actually add to a leader's standing. For it is much better to admit personal responsibility when things go wrong than to blatantly apportion blame to others. Team members are willing to be forgiving, providing mistakes do not occur too often! Maybe it is unrealistic to imagine that we can all emulate the extraordinary integrity shown by Pericles in Athens, but honesty does go a long way.

The self-belief that marks out the most successful of our ancient leaders seems to flow from a deep understanding of their own strengths and weaknesses, from a totally realistic knowledge of themselves. Leadership has to be a learning experience, and the most effective leaders not only draw lessons from setbacks and failures, as well as triumphs, but they exhibit a readiness to seek feedback from others, however uncomfortable an experience this might prove to be. The most notable illustration of this is probably the fascinating account of Li Shimin and his counsellor Wei Zheng, and their complex, difficult, but ultimately rewarding relationship, which provides valuable lessons that we can apply today. For most leaders, the type of 'tough learning' that lies at the heart of this account probably produces greater impact on individual performance than any number of formal training courses. Hardly surprising then are the parallels within the typography of current leadership development activities. The use of coaches to illuminate the direction best suited to an individual leader's style and personality, involvement in 'action learning sets' to share experiences, 360-degree appraisal schemes, all these development strategies have their proponents and their success stories.

Leadership and transformation

The underlying vision that drives the changes which a leader wishes to make may be powerful, clear and appealing, but it can only be turned into reality through the commitment, enthusiasm and effort of subordinates. True motivation can never rely on sophisticated performance management measures, nor afford to depend on the availability of extrinsic rewards. It can only come from binding a leader's people around a common purpose. It is they, after all, who will ultimately translate the vision into plans and outcomes. In bringing this about, the role of a leader is to show confidence and trust in the abilities of staff to develop their own routes to the desired goals, and to support and develop them in the performance of these roles.

In recent years there has been considerable emphasis placed on the notion of 'inspirational leadership', including direct support from government for the idea that this can make a real contribution to improving competitiveness in the United Kingdom. All this has tended to place a premium on such personality traits as drive, energy and charisma as being characteristic of a really effective leader. As has already been noted, people observe their leaders closely and it is important that those at the top of an organisation act as a role model for the behaviour they hope to engender throughout their businesses. We rightly expect our leaders to be distinctive, but this does not mean that every leader has to be the 'high-octane', charismatic, driven performer that sometimes typifies the public perception of leadership. Not all leaders can perform in the ways that Alexander, Thutmose or Hannibal did. In this connection, there are certainly lessons to be drawn from the personal histories within this book. In its own way, for example, the mildness and humanity of Liu Bang provided an entirely viable model of leadership, which his people could respect and identify with after a long period of conflict and uncertainty.

One thing that does appear to be a common requirement of effective leadership, however, is the ability of leaders to show what they are like and what they believe in, with a degree of honesty and humility in their working relationships. Managing the relationship between leaders and their key teams is, in itself, a challenging task. To understand a team's skills, hopes and anxieties is a critical part of building this relationship. Certainly, for some of our ancient leaders, the fact that they themselves came from relatively humble origins helped them to develop an empathetic relationship with their people. Hence, Vespasian's policy of 'getting back to basics' in the early Roman empire came from a desire for stability and financial probity after a period of domestic turmoil which he had shared with his people. Similarly Liu Bang's lowly beginnings gave him a real understanding of the needs and wishes of the Chinese people at the start of his reign.

The ability to enthuse and motivate staff inevitably lies at the heart of transformational leadership in the business setting. To bring about change in a company, leaders are dependent on the willingness of their people to deploy their skills and knowledge with enthusiasm and energy. In achieving this level of engagement, it is critical that employees are given opportunities to develop their own levels of awareness and competence, in the best interests of the organisation. Leaders have a key role, not just in facilitating the training and development of team members by resourcing external training activities, but by actively involving themselves directly in coaching, mentoring, appraisal and other supportive techniques. This also highlights the need for effective leaders to get involved in job and team design, to ensure that team members not only develop a holistic appreciation of the business, but also have the chance to explore their own potential by being exposed to a variety of challenges at work.

Underlying the ancient successes in this book is an impressive illustration of the ways in which individual leaders chose to develop the people around them. For both the emperors Wu Di in China and Candragupta in India, developing a cadre of able administrators was an essential element in the change processes they led. But it is the obvious imperative to develop and train talented people to make an organisation function effectively that creates the same underlying tension for leaders today as it did for leaders then. This revolves around the question of how far leadership can, and should, be distributed around the organisation without jeopardising the central role of the chief executive or other senior post-holders. For leaders to take their people with them means developing them as supporters and, perhaps ultimately, as successors!

A contemporary parallel is shown in the attention now paid to 'talent pool management'. Typically, the process begins with the use of development centres to identify those with the potential to enter the talent pool. Once the talent pool has been formed, an individual development plan is devised for each person that will ensure that over a two-year period they:

- receive the right job experience so that they understand the depth and scope of the business;

- undergo training to improve their functional, management and leadership competencies;

- work with a mentor who can coach, encourage and guide them through their development;

- are supported in their own initiatives and encouraged to take risks with their assignments.

In organisational terms it is equally important to avoid demotivating people that failed to enter the talent pool. It is also important to ensure that the potential future leaders are given the key leadership jobs whenever they are ready for the challenge. This may mean removing people who are blocking promotions, either through sideways moves or quitting the organisation.

Leadership and structure

The idea of 'transformational leadership' has, quite rightly, highlighted the critical need for an effective leader to develop and deploy 'people skills' of a very high order. Yet increasing attention is being directed to a parallel set of skills, too. These are related to the need to develop structures and processes which maximise the impact of the human and physical resources available, perhaps best encapsulated in the notion of a leader acting as an 'organisational architect'. This thinking acknowledges the critical value of a leader's 'structural' sense; that is to say, the ways in which they can design, direct and coordinate the organisational framework of the business, integrating disparate activities, gathering and deploying resources to maximum effect.

Leaders have always needed to be determined in securing the funding necessary to enable a development to take place, and to be creative in their use of what frequently seem to be very limited resources. It was something both Themistocles and Zhu Geliang demonstrated in a high degree: both possessed the invaluable capacity of deploying the physical resources available to them in surprising and innovative ways. Other ancient figures revealed a similar creativity in the broader concern by designing and implementing organisational structures which facilitated the change they were aiming for, and enabled their followers to function efficiently into the future. One of the most radical of these 'organisational architects' was the Roman emperor Diocletian, whose plans for reshaping the imperial administration were far-reaching and audacious. The danger for a leader focusing too single-mindedly on structure as the means of improving effectiveness lies in a temptation to become fixated with internal issues, at the expense of renewing the vision for the business in a competitive and rapidly changing external environment. For some organisations, fads such as 'business processes engineering' have had precisely this detrimental effect. The initial motivation for a radical overhaul of internal systems will probably have been sprung from an entirely healthy determination to improve competitiveness and strengthen the place of the organisation in the marketplace, but delving into the complexities of the remodelling of systems and structures can easily become something of an end in itself.

Despite all these risks, effective leaders do need to accept responsibility for creating the governing ideas which must underpin an organisation's working. In this context, it is important that they are genuinely 'systems thinkers', particularly in relation to the social structures which exist within the business. The notion of an efficient and loyal imperial civil service, such as those created by Liu Bang and Wu Di in China, and mirrored in the British dominion in India much later, may not reflect a style of organisational working much in favour now. But a similar level of concern with organisational structures is necessary to create and maintain the sort of integrated, empowered and team-based businesses that many leaders aim to develop today.

Developing leaders

There is hard evidence that investment in leadership development over time translates into improved organisational results. Sales go up, costs come down and the profit increases. The reputation of the organisation improves, higher calibre people join and there is a virtuous circle of enhancement. Inspired leaders bring out the best in their people, but also face up to tough decisions which may well include removing people who do not fit well with new organisational goals.

If the purpose of a leadership development programme is genuinely to change the fundamentals of an organisation, then starting at the top is essential. If this does not happen, the programme will never succeed in bringing about lasting change in the organisation. Too many leadership development programmes start with the CEO and HR director deciding to 'improve leadership', a decision which inevitably translates into a focus on training the middle managers. If the outlook and behaviour of the top people remain the same, then no matter what the middle managers learn, it will never be fully realised in practice.

The key steps to follow for a leader who wants to transform the way he or she leads their people are these. Notice their order:

- Investigate the current style of leadership and identify the strengths and areas that need to change.

- Agree on the new approach to leadership based not only on what is relevant to the organisation but also on changing trends in the external environment.

- Establish the competencies and behaviours that will reinforce the new approach.

- Find a highly reputable training/academic organisation and develop a training course that includes:

  - a review of current leadership in the organisation and trends in the outside world;

  - an evaluation of personal strengths and areas needing development by using a 360-degree tool that is fully aligned to the new behaviours being sought;

  - an individual review of business and personal life – what is going right and what is going wrong;

  - an inspiring personal and business vision for the future;

  - an understanding of the strategic changes that will have to be made and plan the actions;

  - personal support and coaching throughout as such soul searching and review can be very emotional;

  - a follow-up 9–12 months later.

- Start the training with the top team, and cascade downwards.

- Provide access to coaching throughout as senior managers once they have bought in to the need to change their behaviours need access to safe support and guidance to continue to improve.

- Build the new behaviours into the performance management system, and make sure they are rewarded and through promotion and career development are recognised.

- Support the newly inspired leaders with materials and facilitation to help them take what they have learnt and share it with their own teams.

- Work with senior managers to agree on and role model the behaviours that will make the biggest difference to the organisation.

- Change the training programme to be competency based.

- Recruit the right competencies into the organisation.

Winning bets

As can be seen from the discussion above, there are certain key issues that always exercise those who become leaders, whether by choice or circumstance. Among the clear determinants of successful leadership are a facility for understanding and motivating people, a sensitivity to changing contextual conditions, an appreciation of one's own strengths and weaknesses, a sense of purpose and a capacity to use resources and systems creatively. It should be remembered, however, that leadership provides no 'sure-things' to back in the race for success, and what ultimately turns an individual into an outstanding leader remains tantalisingly elusive. Even in victory, those moments when a leadership gamble appears to have paid off, there are bound to be new challenges.

Thrust upon the Roman general Belisarius was the need to act swiftly and decisively in a Constantinople running riot. His reward for saving the CEO, the emperor Justinian, was leadership of the emperor's western campaigns, but further success in Africa and Italy only caused Belisarius difficulties at the imperial court. The general became an object of envy and fear, something which can still complicate the working lives of successful business leaders today.

Perhaps the only identifiable common feature among the ancient leaders we have examined is that they demonstrated a highly distinctive personal style of leadership, intrinsically suited to their personality and appropriate to the direction they set for themselves. Certainly we can learn from studying them, but perhaps the real trick is to apply the lessons in ways which suit our own way of leading. Know yourself, then use this essential insight to guide your leadership gamble effectively. It will certainly give you a better chance of finding your winning formula.

Suggestions for Further Reading

Because the literature of leadership is so enormous, the suggestions made for further reading here should be regarded as no more than a series of signposts which are intended to assist the reader in pursuing areas of particular interest. Firstly, there are highlighted additional sources of information relating to each of the ancient rulers introduced in this book. And, secondly, routes are provided into the whole body of published work on leadership as a distinct management discipline. In neither can the suggestions be exhaustive: what they do try to facilitate, however, is further study in the hope of bringing into sharper focus some of the perennial problems which face senior managers.

The ancient leaders

Courage: the daring of Ramesses II at Kadesh

At Kadesh in 1274 BC, the Egyptians seem to hold off the Hittite chariotry long enough for reinforcements to arrive thanks to the personal daring of the young pharaoh.

Kadesh and other great chariot battles are discussed in: Arthur Cotterell, *Chariot. The Astounding Rise and Fall of the Worlds First War Machine* (London, 2004). For a general picture of the long reign of Ramesses there is Nicolas Grimal's *A History of Egypt*, translated by Ian Shaw (Oxford, 1992).

Risk-taking: Thutmose III's handling of his forces

The two books already suggested for Ramesses can be consulted, along with Eric H. Cline's *The Battles of Armageddon. Megiddo and the Jezreel Valley from the Bronze Age to the Nuclear Age* (Ann Arbor, 2000).

Motivation: the military revolution of Wuling

This transformation of ancient Chinese warfare is still a matter of debate among ancient historians. For a perspective on the development of cavalry there is Nicola Di Cosmo's *Ancient China and its Enemies. The Rise of Nomadic Power in East Asian History* (Cambridge, 2002).

Vision: the commoner emperor Liu Bang

Recently the Han dynasty has begun to receive more thorough attention in the West for the good reason that it has been realised just how important the dynasty that Liu Bang founded was in shaping ancient China. Chinese people today still refer to themselves as *hanren*, men of Han, in order to distinguish themselves from other peoples. A view of Liu Bang's contribution to this ancient sense of cultural continuity can be found in: Arthur Cotterell, *China. A History* (London, 1990).

Developing people: Han Wu Di's approach

For a perspective on Wu Di's contribution to the Chinese empire there is the book already suggested for Liu Bang. A byproduct of Wu Di's concern to find and develop talented officials was the imperial examination system, the gateway to influence and wealth in ancient China. Its downside, a preoccupation with results, is charted in Ichisada Miyazaki's *China's Examination Hell: The Civil Service Examinations of Imperial China*, translated by C. Schrokauer (London, 1981).

Focusing on results: the strategy of Themistocles

There are plenty of books on the Persian wars and the part Themistocles played in securing Greek freedom. Especially recommended are: A.R. Burn, *Persia and the Greeks: The Defence of the West, c 546–478* (London, 1962), and R.J. Lenardon, *The Saga of Themistocles* (London, 1978).

Integrity: the supremacy of Pericles

Many books have been written on fifth-century Athens and Pericles' political career. Professor Donald Kagan is the doyen of Athenian studies, and recommended are the first two volumes of his monumental history of the conflict between Sparta and Athens: *The Outbreak of the Peloponnesian War* (Ithaca, 1969) and *The Archidamian War* (Ithaca, 1974). Also of interest is his later work entitled *Pericles and the Birth of Athenian Democracy* (New York, 1990). Another approach to the institutional context of Pericles' prolonged leadership can be found in: C.G. Starr, *The Birth of Athenian Democracy. The Assembly in the Fifth Century BC* (Oxford, 1990).

Taking decisive action: the critical decisions of Epaminondas

Two books trace the decline of Sparta and the rise of Thebes in the early fourth century BC. The inability of the Spartans to adjust to the changed political circumstances of Greece then is the subject of C.D. Hamilton's *Agesilaus and the Failure of Spartan Hegemony* (Ithaca, 1991), while the leadership of Epaminondas and Pelopidas is fully explored in: J. Buckler, *The Theban Hegemony, 371–362 BC* (Cambridge, Mass, 1980).

Influencing people: Alexander's multi-ethnic kingdom

Alexander's exploits have received extensive treatment, but the books of Nicholas Hammond are by far the best and most reliable. Recommended are his *The Genius of Alexander the Great* (London, 1997), and *Alexander the Great: King, Commander and Statesman* (London, 1980).

Leaving a legacy: the abdication of Candragupta

Two books by Romila Thapar are recommended for the Mauryan dynasty. The first, *Early India. From the Origins to AD 1300* (London, 2002) places Candragupta's achievement in the context of ancient India, while the second, *Asoka and the Decline of the Mauryas* (Oxford, 1961) deals with the problems Candragupta's Buddhist grandson faced. Towards the end of his long reign, Ashoka began to lose control over the government of this first Indian empire, coming unduly under the influence of his queens. Officials became aggressive with the result that unrest brought about a division of Mauryan territory after his death in 232 BC.

Representing the business: Hannibal's invasion of Italy

Three books place Hannibal's amazing military exploits in perspective. They are: Serge Lancel, *Hannibal*, translated by A. Nevik (Oxford, 1998), Dexter Hoyos, *Hannibal's Dynasty. Power and Politics in the Western Mediterranean, 246–183 BC* (London, 2003) and Nigel Bagnall, *The Punic Wars* (London, 1990).

Creativity: the resourcefulness of Zhu Geliang

To the Chinese the period of the Three Kingdoms, from AD 221 to 265, has always appeared romantic and legendary. The fullest expression of this attitude is Luo Guanzhong, *The Romance of the Three Kingdoms*, written in the fourteenth century. A good read in even an undistinguished translation, this novel follows the ups and downs of fortune endured by kings, ministers and generals during the complicated three-cornered contest.

Learning: Li Shimin and Wei Zheng

For a view of Li Shimin's reign there is C.P. Fitzgerald's biography of the emperor entitled *Son of Heaven* (Cambridge, 1933). But the interaction between ruler and minister receives detailed treatment in: H.J. Wechsler, *Mirror to the Son of Heaven* (New Haven, 1974). So great was the impact of Wei Zheng on imperial policy that his tremendous reputation, especially as the ideal minister admired by Confucian scholars, was already being developed during his own lifetime. A grateful Li Shimin, for one, used to compare him with the greatest ministers of China's past.

Change: Sulla's constitutional reforms

An ambiguous figure ever since he marched his troops on Rome, Lucius Cornelius Sulla has, not surprisingly, always had a bad press. It is probably due to his notorious impatience at opposition. In *Sulla. The Last Republican* (London, 2005), Arthur Keaveney explores the context in which the dictator tried to forcibly reform Rome as well as the personal traits that informed his often drastic actions. A useful insight into Sulla's Rome is available in *The Cambridge Companion to the Roman Republic*, edited by H.I. Flower (Cambridge, 2004).

Networking: Cicero's efforts to find allies

Cicero is the subject of many studies, not least because his own extensive writings form a valuable record of events during the final years of the Roman republic. Worth reading for background are: Ronald Syme, *The Roman Revolution* (Oxford, 1939) and P.A. Brunt, *Social Conflicts in the Roman Republic* (London, 1971). Good biographies are available in: A. Everitt, *Cicero. A Turbulent Life* (London, 2001) and E. Rawson, *Cicero. A Portrait* (London, 1975).

Dealing with conflict: the policies of Vespasian

There are several books available on members of the Flavian dynasty. Barbara Levick's *Vespasian* (London, 1999) offers a thorough survey of its founder's reign, while

The Emperor Titus (London, 1984) and *The Emperor Domitian* (London, 1992) by B.W. Jones examines the actions of his sons. For an insight into the city of Rome itself there is *Rome the Cosmopolis*, edited by C. Edwards and G. Woolf (Oxford, 2003). This book actually begins with the Colosseum, that site of so many deaths, human and animal, since the great arena can stand as a symbol of the all-consuming nature of Roman imperialism.

Delegation and empowerment: Diocletian's imperial reforms

The problems which Diocletian struggled to overcome have long fascinated historians of Rome. A recent publication, however, offers a longer perspective on its troubled imperial administration: it is Christopher Kelly, *Ruling the Later Roman Empire* (London, 2004).

Recognising achievement: the triumph of Belisarius

Recommended for the stirring life and times of this distinguished general are: J.A.S. Evans, *The Age of Justinian* (London, 1996) and J. Moorhead, *Justinian* (London, 1994).

Leadership studies today

The body of literature on leadership itself is very extensive, and it is continually growing. Though the suggestions for further reading given here build on the references found within the book, they should only be seen as useful pointers. For it is not intended to provide a comprehensive bibliography, but rather a personal selection of writers and texts which the authors have found particularly provocative, illuminating and, just as importantly, accessible. To relate particular sources to the specific topics addressed chapter by chapter would inevitably lead to fruitless repetition. Instead, this section approaches the literature of leadership under five categories of publication. Firstly, in 'The thinkers themselves', we identify some of the most significant core texts, while the second part, 'Short cuts and summaries', provides a route towards the numerous books which aim to provide a synopsis of such thinking, perhaps for those readers who are too busy to read the sometimes lengthy analyses themselves. The third part, 'Essays', highlights some particularly useful collections and the fourth, 'Handbooks', introduces the books which seek to help leaders and managers reflect on, and improve, their own performance. In the last part, 'Stories', the focus moves to some of the more impressive autobiographies and biographies, both of individual leaders and their organisations, which actually illustrate leadership in practice.

The thinkers themselves

As management has become a respectable focus for academic study and research, so leadership as a distinct topic has emerged as an increasingly significant part of the resulting literature. Typically, these works are produced by academics who combine a career in teaching or research in prestigious business schools with consultancy work for large organisations or institutions, thus drawing lessons from their analysis of business practice in order to develop theoretical models of leadership.

Warren Bennis was one of the first academics to address leadership as a distinct and crucial set of skills, rather than as one element within a more generalised study of management which characterised much of the literature of the 1980s. Probably the most widely read of his numerous books remains *Leaders: The Strategies for Taking Charge* (Harper & Row, 1985), which he co-authored with Bert Nanus, while *Managing the Dream* (Perseus Publishing, 2000) provides a very effective summary of the way Bennis' views have developed over the years.

Another significant pioneering student of leadership, and a tireless advocate of leadership training over some 50 books and articles, is John Adair, the world's first professor of leadership studies. A good pathway into his thinking is provided by *How to Grow Leaders* (Kogan Page, 2005).

To distinguish among the many significant management 'gurus' of the last 20 years, those whose work makes a specially telling contribution to thinking about leadership is an almost impossible task. But we would particularly recommend the range of books produced by Rosabeth Moss Kanter. Her background as a sociologist provides an interesting perspective on change and the role of leadership, with *The Change Masters* (Routledge, 1983) giving a typically acute and provocative analysis of the topic. You cannot proceed far into the literature of management without encountering the work of Tom Peters and, although following the course of his changing conclusions on what constitutes an effective organisation can often prove frustrating, it is essential to read *In Search of Excellence*, which he co-authored with Robert Waterman (Warner, 1982), and *A Passion for Excellence*, co-authored with Nancy Austin (Collins, 1985), for their acute observations on the impact of leaders on businesses.

The work of John Kotter is referred to within the text, and especially powerful books are *Leading Change* (Harvard Business School Press, 1996) and *John P. Kotter on What Leaders Really Do* (Harvard Business Review

Books, 1999). The work of another Harvard Business School thinker, Richard Pascale, is a similarly influential source and both *The Art of Japanese Management* (Penguin Books, 1986), co-authored with Anthony G. Athos, and *Managing on the Edge* (Simon and Schuster, 1990), are well worth reading.

The concept of emotional intelligence has proved an especially potent model for examining individual competence and capacity in recent years. With *Primal Leadership – Learning to Lead with Emotional Intelligence* (Harvard Business School Press, 2002), published in the UK with the title, *The New Leaders*, Daniel Goleman, with co-authors Richard Boyatzis and Annie McKee, applies this concept very effectively to the discipline of leadership.

In concluding what is no more than a scurry through some of the 'big names' writing on leadership it is worth mentioning the work of one of the most accessible and stimulating contemporary authors, Charles Handy, whose books on organisational development incorporate valuable insights into leadership. Particularly recommended are *Inside Organisations* (Penguin Business, 1985), *The Empty Raincoat: Making Sense of the Future* (Random House, 1995), and *The New Alchemists* (Hutchinson, 2004).

Short-cuts and summaries

The complexity, variety (and sometimes inscrutability) of books on leadership have spurned a genre of publication whose purpose is to steer the reader through the jungle of writers and theories in a safe and satisfactory way. Such books offer either a 'quick-fix' solution for those seeking to bluff their way through a discussion on leadership or, more usefully, they seek to discern trends and themes emerging from the apparently endless analysis.

Several books aim to summarise the key ideas of management gurus in a form that is easy to absorb. In this vein we would suggest *The Guru Guide* by Joseph Boyett and Jimmie Boyett (John Wiley & Sons, Ltd, 1995), as well as the successor volume by the same authors, *The Guru Guide to Entrepreneurship* (John Wiley & Sons, Ltd, 2001). A notably sound and comprehensive survey of thinkers who have changed the management world is provided by Stuart Crainer's *Key Management Ideas* (Financial Times Management, 1998), as well as *The Ultimate Business Library: The Greatest Books that made Management* (Copstone Publishing, 2002). Another good summary of the development of leadership theory can be found in *Leadership* by Philip Sadler (Kogan Page, 1998). Successfully adopting a more thematic approach to the subject is *The New Leaders* by Paul Taffinder (Kogan Page, 1998).

Essays

For those who enjoy exploring the developing views of the most significant thinkers and researchers there is no better source than the Harvard Business Review series. Particularly relevant would be *The Harvard Business Review on Leadership* (Harvard Business School Press, 1990) and *The Harvard Business Review on What Makes a Leader* (Harvard Business School Press, 1998). *The Harvard Business Review on Entrepreneurship* (Harvard Business School Press, 1985) also provides some stimulating approaches to that particular specialism.

Writers on Leadership, edited by John van Maurik (Penguin, 2001), uses a good selection of essays to introduce key themes in leadership. For those wanting a more overtly academic approach to the subject we, however, recommend *Leadership*, edited by Keith Grint (Oxford University Press, 1997). It is part of the excellent Oxford Management Readers series.

Handbooks

Many books promise to motivate and inspire individuals to become more skilled and self-aware leaders in their own roles at work. One of the best is the top-selling *The Leadership Challenge* by James M. Kouzes and Barry Z. Posner (Jossey-Bass, 2002), since it manages to combine a lively narrative with sensible guidance. A thorough and thoughtful alternative, with strong source material, is provided by *A Manager's Guide to Leadership* by Mike Pedler, John Burgoyne and Tom Boydell (McGraw-Hill, 2004), while *The Leadership Manual* by Hilarie Owen, Vicky Hodgson and Nigel Gazzard (Pearson, 2004) covers similar ground in a less intensive manner.

There is, of course, a range of overtly motivational books on leadership. They can tend to be gimmicky and light-weight, but one with rather more substance is *The Naked Leader* by David Taylor (Capstone Publishing, 2002).

Stories

A look at the management shelves in a large bookshop will quickly reveal the current crop of contemporary and historical leaders being examined for the secrets of their success. Figures from the military, from politics and from sport will feature strongly, and there will naturally be accounts of high-profile business leaders, and of their organisations as well.

To make any selection is difficult but we would strongly recommend *Maverick* by Ricardo Semler (Random House, 1993, second edition 1999) as an honest account of the extraordinary business that is SEMCO, and *The Road Ahead* by Bill Gates (Longman, 1999), which provides some fascinating insights into the developing vision of Microsoft. One of the most readable and thought-provoking of the CEO-turned business pundit's revelations must be those of Jack Welch, formerly of General Electric. His distinct brand of abrasive commonsense finds impressive expression in *Winning* (Harper-Collins, 2005). For those interested in learning more about the working practices of successful businesses, one of the most relevant is probably Jeffrey Liker's detailed account of Toyota in *The Toyota Way* (McGraw-Hill, 2004).

Index

Index compiled by Terry Halliday